Speculative Medievalisms: Discography

SPECULATIVE MEDIEVALISMS

DISCOGRAPHY

Edited by

The Petropunk Collective

punctum books ✱ brooklyn, ny

SPECULATIVE MEDIEVALISMS: DISCOGRAPHY
© The Petropunk Collective [Eileen Joy, Anna
Kłosowska, Nicola Masciandaro, Michael O'Rourke],
2013.

First published in 2013 by
punctum books
Brooklyn, New York
http://punctumbooks.com

ISBN-13: 978-0615749532
ISBN-10: 0615749534

Library of Congress Cataloging Data is available from the
Library of Congress.

Cover Image: detail from Voynich Manuscript (15th/16th
c., unknown provenance), folio 86v; General Collection,
Beinecke Rare Book and Manuscript Library, Yale
University.

Facing-page drawing by Heather Masciandaro.

for Anaximander

 PREFATORY NOTE

We do not step beyond anything, but are more like moles tunneling through wind, water, and ideas no less than through speech-acts, texts, anxiety, wonder, and dirt.
—Graham Harman, "On Vicarious Causation"

This book, or 'discography,' comprises the proceedings of two laboratory-ateliers on 'Speculative Medievalisms'—a sort of mashup, or collision, or 'drive-by' flirtation between pre-modern studies and Speculative Realism (SR)—that took place at King's College London (14 January 2011) and The Graduate Center, City University of New York (16 September 2011). The philosophy (if we can call it that) and thinking behind the two events is included as a 'Précis' in this volume, and here we mainly want to thank those who helped us to stage the symposia: the BABEL Working Group, Clare Lees, James Paz, the Centre for Late Antique & Medieval Studies (King's College London), Glenn Burger, Steven Kruger, The Graduate Center, CUNY, the Doctoral Program in English (CUNY), and the Medieval Studies Certificate Program (CUNY). We also wish to thank our presenters for the creativity, liveliness, and provocations of their remarks and for their generosity in allowing us to share those in this volume.

For those wishing to contact or geo-locate the Petropunk Collective, they are in the attic. Please be careful on the ladder.

The Petropunk Collective
Cincinnati, Ohio | Brooklyn, New York | Dublin, Ireland

TABLE OF CONTENTS

London.01.14.2011

Speculative Medievalisms
A Précis

So the medieval studies I am thrown into is a gravely
levitating scholarly being, the lovely becoming light of
weight in all senses: metaphoric, literal, and above all
in the truest most palpable sense of the phenomenal
poetic zones of indistinction between the two. This
means, in tune with the Heraclitan oneness of the way
up and the way down, not flight from but the very
lightening of *gravitas* itself, the finding or falling into
levitas through the triple gravities of the discipline: the
weight of the medieval (texts, past), the weight of each
other (society, institutions), and the weight of ourselves (body, present). Towards this end I offer no
precepts or to-do list, only an indication of the wisdom
and necessity of doing so, of practicing our highest
pleasures, in unknowing of the division between poetry
as knowledge and philosophy as joy, in opposition to
the separation between thought and life that best expresses "the omnipresence of the economy," and in
harmony with the volitional imperative of Nietzsche's
"new gravity: the eternal recurrence of the same": "Do
you want this again and innumerable times again?"
This Middle Ages? This medievalist?

—Nicola Masciandaro[1]

Speculative Medievalisms is a collaborative and interdiscipli-
nary research project focusing on the theorization and
practical development of the speculative dimensions of medieval studies. The term "speculative" is intended to resonate
with the full range of its medieval and modern meanings.
First, *speculative* echoes the broad array of specifically medieval senses of *speculatio* as the essentially reflective and
imaginative operations of the intellect. According to this con-

---

[1] Nicola Masciandaro, "Grave Levitation: Being Scholarly," *The
Whim* [weblog], May 10, 2009: http://thewhim.blogspot.com/2009/
05/grave-levitation-being-scholarly.html.

ception, the world, books, and mind itself were all conceived as *specula* (mirrors) through which the hermeneutic gaze could gain access to what lies beyond them. As Giorgio Agamben explains, "To know is to bend over a mirror where the world is reflected, to descry images reflected from sphere to sphere: the medieval man was always before a mirror, both when he looked around himself and when he surrendered to his own imagination."[2] This sense of speculative, which also gestures toward the humanistic principle of identity between world-knowledge and self-knowledge, becomes crucial for the development and institution of medieval studies as a discipline oriented to the past as both mirror and inscrutable site of origin. Like Narcissus, who at the fount falls in love with himself as another, modern Western culture gazes at the Middle Ages as a self-image that impossibly blurs the distinction between identity and alterity. The speculative principle is accordingly written into the title of the medieval studies journal, *Speculum*, published by the Medieval Academy since 1926. *Speculum*'s first editor E. K. Rand explained the aim of the journal via this principle in the inaugural issue as follows:

> *Speculum*, this mirror to which we find it appropriate to give a Latin name, suggests the multitudinous mirrors in which people of the Middle Ages liked to gaze at themselves and other folk—mirrors of history and doctrine and morals, mirrors of princes and lovers and fools. We intend no conscious follies, but we recognize satire, humor and the joy of life as part of our aim. Art and beauty and poetry are a portion of our medieval heritage. Our contribution to the knowledge of those times must be scholarly, first of all, but scholarship must be arrayed, so far as possible, in a pleasing form.[3]

---

[2] Giorgio Agamben, *Stanzas: Word and Phantasm in Western Culture*, trans. Ronald L. Martinez (Minneapolis: University of Minnesota Press, 1993), 81.

[3] Quoted in Gabrielle M. Spiegel, *The Past as Text: The Theory and*

While *Speculum*'s contribution to our understanding of the medieval past continues to be essential and formidable, its editors' and contributors' fulfillment of these ambivalently secondary yet underscored aims (satire, humor, joy, art, beauty, poetry, pleasure) remains questionable.

* * *

Are we enjoying ourselves? This is a primary question for the BABEL Working Group,[4] a collective and desiring-assemblage of scholars (primarily medievalists and early modernists, but also including scholars working in a broad variety of disciplines in later historical periods), who are especially interested in matters of embodiment and affect and the questions that currently pace and fret around the historically vexed terms: *human*, *humanity*, *humanism*, and the *humanities*. As an important corollary to this interest, BABEL is also deeply concerned with explorations of the nonhuman and the post/human, and with the possibilities of developing affective, cross-temporal (and intra-temporal), and playful-creative relations between different sorts of bodies, human and otherwise, animate and supposedly inanimate. To the question of pleasure and whether or not our historical scholarship could ever be "arrayed, so far as possible, in a pleasing form," BABEL has been laboring to answer, theoretically and practically, with a definitive *yes*.[5] The question of course is not merely one

---

Practice of Medieval Historiography (Baltimore: Johns Hopkins University Press, 1997), 57.

[4] See the BABEL Working Group, http://www.babelworkinggroup.org.

[5] For example, BABEL organized the following conference panels on the subject of pleasure and scholarship/thinking: "Are We Enjoying Ourselves? The Place of Pleasure in Medieval Scholarship," 44th International Congress on Medieval Studies, May 6-10, 2009, Western Michigan University, and "Knowing and Unknowing Pleasures," 35th Annual Southeastern Medieval Association Meeting, October 15-17, 2009, Vanderbilt University. Some of the questions these pan-

of satisfaction, of simply being pleased with our research and teaching, nor of pleasuring ourselves through some sort of narcissistic scholarly practice. More crucially the question concerns the very how, why, and wherefore of scholarly practice and the realization of its individual (personal) and social value. Put succinctly: "the problem of knowledge is a problem of possession, and every problem of possession is a problem of enjoyment."[6] It is here that the importance of speculation, as a constituent pleasure of intellectual work coinciding with the poetic vector of thought—the necessity of its ability to take creative leaps—becomes especially urgent. The speculative constitutes the dimension where discourse remains pleasura-

---

els sought to address: What is useless pleasure, what is essential pleasure, what might be dangerous pleasure, and who or what decides? Is there class in pleasure—or, as Roland Barthes might say, "Einstein on one side, Paris-Match on the other"? What are the ethical conditions of pleasure? Are there fascist specters that haunt the ethics/aesthetics borderlands, or more optimistically, do we see "coexisting multiplicities" where pleasure is, as Deleuze has written, "between everyone," like a "little boat used by others." Further, is the question of pleasure best approached tangentially as the question of intensity? What are the temporalities and localities of pleasure—especially when we think of pleasure, as Daniel Remein has written, as that "small weak thing that empties closed economies so they can be emptied and emptied again, not by being there but constantly passing through"? What relationships, constellations, or astronomical charts can be drawn between medieval definitions, practices, regulations of pleasure, and contemporary philosophy, for instance as articulated in the speculative realism of Graham Harman and in his definition of allure? Finally, what is the part of pleasure in medieval scholarship more particularly: as we locate ourselves, as Julie Orlemanski has argued, between "enjoying the past, judging it, curating it, and reviving it," what parameters of pleasure do we declare or silently draw? How do specific ways of thinking about pleasure shape our present and future scholarly community, the nature and modalities of our collaborations, and our care for premodern texts and artifacts?

[6] Giorgio Agamben, *Stanzas: Word and Phantasm in Western Culture*, trans. Roland L. Martinez (Minneapolis: University of Minnesota Press, 1993), xvii.

bly and daringly open, both with regard to the nature of its object and with regard to its real, enworlded end, its ultimate *for-itself*.[7] To Aranye Fradenburg's question, then—"Do we really mean to take shelter from our *jouissance* in the order of utility, to become 'a branch of the service of goods,' in the mistaken hope that the 'human sciences' will be rewarded for doing so?"[8]—we answer, definitively, *no*, we do *not*.

This is to ask for new forms of literary and aesthetic criticism that would attend to the ways in which, as Iain Chambers has written, artworks reveal "not so much a distinctive 'message' as a sense that is ultimately a non-sense, a refusal to cohere that opens on to that void which resists rationalization," and therefore a

> rationalist pleasure is not confirmed. Rather a border, an intimation of the sublime, the shiver of the world, an encounter with the angelic and the extraordinary, is declared. We are taken beyond ourselves into the eroticism of time and the subsequent sense of loss that proclaims an identity.[9]

This is to also ask for an historical scholarship where we would write, as the poet Joan Retallack has urged, not to "deliver space-time in a series of shiny freeze-frames, each with

---

[7] Compare with: "every inquiry in the human sciences . . . should entail an archaeological vigilance. In other words, it must retrace its own trajectory back to the point where something remains obscure and unthematized. Only a thought that does not conceal its own unsaid—but constantly takes it up and elaborates it—may eventually lay claim to originality" (Giorgio Agamben, *The Signature of All Things: On Method*, trans. Luca D'Isanto with Kevin Attell [New York: Zone Books, 2009], 8).

[8] L.O. Aranye Fradenburg, "Group Time, Catastrophe, Periodicity," in *Time and the Literary*, eds. Karen Newman, Jay Clayton, and Marianne Hirsch (New York: Routledge, 2002), 233 [211–33].

[9] Iain Chambers, *Culture After Humanism: History, Culture, Subjectivity* (London: Routledge, 2001), 4.

its built-in strategy of persuasion," but to "stay warm and active and realistically messy," to "disrupt the fatal momentum" of linear histories.[10] BABEL is therefore also invested in the work of what Carolyn Dinshaw has called a "postdisenchanted temporal perspective" and what Elizabeth Freeman has termed "erotohistoriography," which names the practice of tracing "how queer relations complexly exceed the present." Against pain and loss," erotohistoriography "posit[s] the value of surprise, of pleasurable interruptions and momentary fulfillments from elsewhere, other times."[11]

Because we are scholars who work primarily with objects of the premodern past, we understand that we are often looking backward, but always with the awareness, as Sara Ahmed has written, that "looking back is what keeps open the possibility of going astray" and "where we can respond with joy to what goes astray."[12] Following the work of medievalist Cary Howie, we are devoted to the development of an erotics of scholarship as the practice of an intensification of certain materialities (of texts, bodies, affects, spaces) "in their very mystery and withdrawal," which is also an ardent tracing of acts of *traherence* in which nothing really "gets free of what it ostensibly emerges from."[13]

In exploring the dimensions and borders where historiography, poetics, affect, intensification, and *leaping* might meet, the Speculative Medievalisms project is informed by the contemporary post-continental philosophical development known as Speculative Realism (SR).[14] Speculative Realism is less a

---

[10] Joan Retallack, *The Poethical Wager* (Berkeley: University of California Press, 2003), 5.

[11] Carolyn Dinshaw quoted in Elizabeth Freeman, ed., "Theorizing Queer Temporalities: A Roundtable Discussion," *GLQ* 13.2/3 (2007): 185 [177–195]; Elizabeth Freeman, "Time Binds, or, Erotohistoriography," *Social Text* 23.3/4 (Winter 2005): 59 [57–68].

[12] Sara Ahmed, *Queer Phenomenology: Orientations, Objects, Others* (Durham: Duke University Press, 2006), p. 178.

[13] Cary Howie, *Claustrophilia: The Erotics of Enclosure* (New York: Palgrave Macmillan, 2007), 7–8, 112.

[14] See Mark Fisher, "Speculative Realism," *frieze* [weblog], May 11,

school of thought than a confluence of diverse intellectual investments in the scientific capacity of philosophical discourse to know and describe subject-independent realities and in the necessity of speculation as the means of such knowledge. In dialogue with both the hard sciences and the humanities, speculative realist philosophers seek, from divergent topical trajectories, to restore and enliven the epistemic potentiality and empirical *poiesis* of thinking—the power through which, for example, Anaximander was able to 'perceive' without direct evidence that the Earth is not affixed to anything but surrounded on all sides by space.[15] Speculation in these terms must be distinguished from practical guesswork or conjecture, and even more strongly from the kind of discourse that stays within the supposedly transparent definability of terms and facts. Speculation is, instead, the rigorous exploration of the potentialities of the perceivable, the very foundation and condition of experience and experiment, and thus a practice that must directly engage the risk of 'conscious follies' that the journal *Speculum* has historically precluded from itself.

Even more daringly, perhaps, Speculative Realism, and what is sometimes called Object Oriented Philosophy (OOO),[16] have both displaced (human) language's privileged

---

2009: http://blog.frieze.com/speculative_realism/; Robin Mackay, ed., *Speculative Realism*, special issue of *Collapse* II (March 2007); "Speculative Realism," *Wikipedia.org*: http://en.wikipedia.org/wiki/Speculative_realism; and the essays collected in *The Speculative Turn: Continental Materialism and Realism*, eds. Levi Bryant, Nick Srnicek, and Graham Harman (Melbourne: re.press, 2011).

[15] See Carlo Rovelli, "Anaximander's Legacy," *Collapse* V (2009): 50–71.

[16] See Ian Bogost, *Alien Phenomenoogy, or What It's Like to Be a Thing* (Minneapolis: University of Minnesota Press, 2012) and "What Is Object-Oriented Ontology?" *Ian Bogost: Videogame Theory, Criticism, Design* [weblog], December 8, 2009: http://www.bogost.com/blog/what_is_objectoriented_ontolog.shtml; Levi Bryant, *The Democracy of Objects* (Ann Arbor: Open Humanities Press, 2011); Graham Harman, *Prince of Networks: Bruno Latour and Metaphysics*

status, in Michael Witmore's words, "as the mediator between mind and whatever reality exists," and therefore "things in the world are granted full mediating power: their interactions with each other are as real as our interaction with them and with other humans." Nevertheless, although reality may always be "unfolding with or without a human observer or mediator," it can still be "gestured at or alluded to with metaphors or other forms of linguistic indirection."[17] Here is where Julian Yates has been speculating on the

> speculative turn that a post-human literary history might take, following the passage of things themselves through human discourse, charting the networks or associations that form as things travel from hand to hand, in and out of texts, between and among different spheres of reference, describing a kind of Brownian motion of persons and things, each remaking the other as they are put to use, reanimating aesthetics as a contact zone in which the presence of things is understood to manifest via the installed thoughts and feelings of their human screens.[18]

What the Speculative Medievalisms project desires, then, is fruitful dialogue and creative, mutual cross-contamination between medieval ideas of *speculatio*, the cultural-historical position of the medieval as site of humanistic speculation, and the speculative realists' "opening up" of "weird worlds" heretofore believed impenetrable by philosophy—as Graham Harman has written, "the specific psychic reality of earth-

---

(Melbourne: re.press, 2009) and *The Quadruple Object* (Winchester: Zero Books, 2011); and "Object-Oriented Ontology," *Wikipedia.org*: http://en.wikipedia.org/wiki/Object-oriented _ontology.

[17] Michael Witmore, "We Have Never Not Been Inhuman," *postmedieval: a journal of medieval cultural studies* 1.1/2 (Spring/Summer 2010): 212 [208–214].

[18] Julian Yates, "It's (for) You; or, The Tele-t/r/opical Post-Human," *postmedieval: a journal of medieval cultural studies* 1.1/2 (Spring/ Summer 2010): 228 [223–234].

worms, dust, armies, chalk, and stone."[19] The BABEL Working Group is especially keen to serve as a launch site of this dialogue because of its broad investment in co-affective (even co-poetic) forms of scholarship, that is, shared intellectual work that takes seriously the medley of personal and political desires that inform research and structure its academic and para-academic communities.[20] Speculative realist work, as the term would suggest, is broadly characterized by the self-contradictory intensity of a desire for thought that can think beyond itself. Yet it pursues this desire in thoroughly rationalist terms. At the same time, speculative realist work is gaining appeal and influence outside of the specifically philosophical academic community, among artists and literary scholars. This is due primarily to the palpable (albeit under-acknowledged) ethical, aesthetic, and even sensuous lineaments of speculative realist writings, which have the heroic-quixotic charm of works that, as the editors of *The Speculative Turn* put it, "depart from the text-centered hermeneutic models of the past and engage in daring speculations about the nature of reality itself."

From the perspective of the kind of present-minded medieval studies represented by the BABEL-affiliated journal *postmedieval: a journal of medieval cultural studies* (and also punctum books), the wonderful (and ironic) thing about Speculative Realism's humanistic allure, its attraction to persons who are not so concerned about constructing definitive arguments about the nature of reality, is that speculating about the nature of reality with "the text-centered hermeneutic models of the past" is not a bad description of what "we medievalists" do. In short, there is between medieval studies and speculative realism something like the space of a compelling, magnetized shared blindness that might be realized as

---

[19] Harman, *Prince of Networks*, 213.

[20] On this subject see the collection of "Manifestos-*cum*-Love Letters" penned by Eileen A. Joy on BABEL's website, dating from May 2007 through October 2012: http://blogs.cofc.edu/babelworkinggroup/category/who-we-are/manifestos-cum-love-letters/.

love at first sight. The gap concerns the age-old problem of the boundary between poetry and philosophy, meaning and truth—in short, the reality of the image in the mirror of thought. A speculative medievalism might proceed from the insight that the desire for a thought that can think beyond itself is precisely the problematic explored in medieval theories of love (whence Andreas Capellanus's famous definition of love as *immoderata cogitatio*, immoderate contemplation). In other words, speculation might be a mode of love, which then might also be imagined as comprising forms of intellectual work with medieval texts and objects that would work to (re)awaken the discipline of philosophy to the reality of love (*philia*).

London.01.14.2011

Toy Stories
Vita Nuda Then and Now?

Kathleen Biddick

In his important study *Bíos: Biopolitics and Philosophy*, Roberto Esposito asks the following question: "How can modern man (sic) tear himself from the *theological matrix*?"[1] This morning I want to show how such a question discloses the unthought medievalisms of contemporary theory and accounts for the traumatic reinscription of the flesh as incarnational and eschatological among contemporary theorists.[2] How can the flesh of history and a history of the flesh rethink such aporia of contemporary theory? My brief comments this morning are a Morse-Code version of a long chapter devoted to the medievalisms of biopolitics taken from my forthcoming book, *Entangled Sovereignty: Studies in Premodern Political*

---

[1] Roberto Esposito, *Bíos: Biopolitics and Philosophy*, trans. Timothy Campbell (Minneapolis: University of Minnesota Press, 2008), 55.

[2] The question of the medieval as the unconscious of contemporary theory grows more pressing: see, Bruce Holsinger, *The Premodern Condition: Medievalism and the Making of Theory* (Chicago: University of Chicago Press, 2005) and Andrew Cole and D. Vance Smith, eds., *The Legitimacy of the Middle Ages: On the Unwritten History of Theory* (Durham: Duke University Press, 2010) and my review in *The Medieval Review*, 10.09.12: http://hdl.handle.net/ 2022/9063.

Theology. Eileen Joy and Anna Kłosowska's response is this volume is based on that book chapter.

My book traces the medievalisms of biopolitics as they appear in the work of Michel Foucault, Giorgio Agamben, and Roberto Esposito.[3] It claims that without an understanding of the intertwining of medievalism and biopolitics, it is not possible to think what Esposito calls an *affirmative biopolitics* of the flesh. For me, the notion of an affirmative biopolitics of the flesh poses the following question: what would a postjuridical justice, arrived at through serious play, look

---

[3] Kathleen Biddick, *Entangled Sovereignty: Studies in Premodern Political Theology* (under consideration with the Insurrections series, Columbia University Press); Michael Hardt and Antonio Negri, *Multitude* (New York: Penguin, 2004); Giorgio Agamben, "Gigantomachy Concerning a Void," in *State of Exception*, trans. Kevin Attell (Chicago: University of Chicago Press, 2005), 64; Michel Foucault, *Society Must Be Defended: Lectures at the College de France 1975-76*, ed. Mauro Bertani and Alessandro Fontana, trans. David Macey (New York: Picador, 2003), 254–59; Giorgio Agamben, *The Time that Remains: A Commentary on the Letter to the Romans*, trans. Patricia Dailey (Stanford: Stanford University Press, 2005). Agamben brackets off the medieval (see Agamben, *The Time That Remains*, 74, 98, 107 and Esposito, *Bíos,* 11). For an important study of medieval *immunitas* that challenges Esposito's normalizing understanding of immunity and exemption, see Barbara H. Rosenwein, *Negotiating Space: Power, Restraint and Privileges of Immunity in Early Medieval Europe* (Ithaca: Cornell University Press, 1999). For an attempt to deal with the traumatic medieval kernel that Agamben brackets off, see Kathleen Biddick, *The Typological Imaginary: Circumcision, Technology, History* (Philadelphia: University of Pennsylvania Press, 2003) and "Dead Neighbor Archives: Jews, Muslims, and the Enemy's Two Bodies," in *Political Theology and Early Modernity*, eds. Julia Reinhard Lupton and Graham Hammill, with a postscript by Etienne Balibar (Chicago: University of Chicago Press, 2012), 124–42. For the vitality of considering temporality as a cross-disciplinary concern, see Michael Uebel, "Opening Time: Psychoanalysis and Medieval Culture," in *Cultural Studies of the Modern Middle Ages*, eds. Eileen A. Joy, Myra J. Seaman, Kimberley K. Bell, and Mary K. Ramsey (New York: Palgrave, 2007), 269–74.

like?[4] I am exploring this question by playing with the law in order to arrive at a biohistory of the flesh.

My stakes in this exploration are the following: the flesh is an historical as much as it is a theoretical issue. Thinking about the flesh brings us to the limits of periodization, the limits of representation, and the limits between the sovereign exception and the rule.[5] I seek to think the "unhistorical" twining of flesh and sovereign across the normalized divides of medieval and modern in an effort to reconceive biopolitics of the flesh as a traumatic scene that expands and sediments as it maintains a deadly kernel, a medieval suture of liturgical flesh to law.

My long paper explores the implications of suturing Eucharistic flesh to the law, a new suture fabricated by Lanfranc of Canterbury (c. 1005-1089 AD) in the course of the theological debates over the Real Presence of the Eucharist waged in the latter part of the eleventh century. What interests me from the point of view of a biohistory of the flesh is how Lanfranc's treatise goes beyond the well-worn stock litany of theological polemic—Berengar as adversary of the Catholic Church, sacrilegious violator of oaths, heretic—to pioneer an accusation of *treason* (*jurare perfidiam*).[6] Berengar, in Lanfranc's opinion,

---

[4] Catherine Mills, "Playing with the Law: Agamben and Derrida on Postjuridical Justice," *South Atlantic Quarterly* 107 (2008): 24 [15–36].

[5] Kathleen Davis points to the traumatic medievalisms of sovereignty. My book is trying to engage them. For insight into this uncanny persistence of sovereignty in these purported acts of deconstruction, see her *Periodization and Sovereignty: How Ideas of Feudalism and Secularization Govern the Politics of Time* (Philadelphia: University of Pennsylvania Press, 2008). For my review of Davis's book, see *The Medieval Review* 09.04.06: http://hdl.handle.net/2022 /6531.

[6] Lanfranc, *De Corpore et sanguine Domini adversus Berangarium Turonensem* (c. 1063), in J.-P. Migne, ed., *Patrologia Latina*, 221 vols. (Paris, 1844-1864), 150:407−42. This text is translated in *Lanfranc of Canterbury: On the Body and Blood of the Lord and Guitmund of Aversa, On the Truth of the Body and Blood of Christ in the Eucharist*, trans. Mark G. Vaillancourt, in *The Fathers of the Church: Medieval*

not only challenges theological orthodoxy; he also traitorously undoes the universalism of the Catholic Church, a universalism constituted by the flesh of Christ.[7] To think against this flesh is to commit treason, because, according to Lanfranc's vision, the flesh of Christ is constitutively both sacramental and sovereign. The flesh of Lanfranc's Eucharist is a theological and sovereign problematic. In the gap in between the visible and the invisible, in which Berengar had meditated pro-provocatively on the unhistorical nature of Christ's flesh, Lanfranc instead sutured sovereign law to that flesh and in so doing paradoxically immunized the universal flesh of Christ as a body politic.

As royal judge in post-Conquest England, Lanfranc deepened this suture of flesh to law to produce liturgical flesh as bare life. When Lanfranc took up his appointment as Archbishop of Canterbury (1079) and came to serve as royal judge to William the Conqueror and his son, he mapped the suture of flesh and law that he had materialized in earlier Eucharistic disputes onto royal justice. Take, for example, his intervention in the exemplary trial (1088) of William de Saint-Calais, Bishop of Durham, accused of treason for his alleged role in a rebellion against the young royal successor of the Conqueror, William Rufus.[8] As Durham stood on the threshold of the royal court, where the litigation would proceed amidst the assembled lay and ecclesiastical barons, he asked Lanfranc, who presided as royal judge, for permission to enter the hall

---

Continuation, Vol. 10 (Washington, DC: Catholic University of America Press, 2010), 40.

[7] For a recent consideration on Lanfranc on universalism (his resurrection of Augustinian themes), see Patrick Healy, "A Supposed Letter of Archbishop Lanfranc: Concepts of the Universal Church in the Investiture Contest," *English Historical Review* 121 (2006): 1385-1407.

[8] R.C. Van Caenegem, *English Lawsuits from William I to Richard I,* Vol. 1 (London: Selden Society, 1990), #134, 90–106 (hereafter called *Durham*); Alain Boureau, "Conflicting Norms: Liturgical Procedure and the Separation of Divine Law from Human Law (England, Eleventh Century)," *The Medieval History Journal* 3 (2000): 17–40.

vested (*revestitus*) in his episcopal robes (distinguishing liturgical vestments and regalia of mitre, crozier, ring) according
to his order (*secundum ordinem suum*). He wished, Durham
said, to plead his case robed before those who were themselves
robed (*revestitus anti revestitos*).[9] Lanfranc famously replied:
"We can certainly discuss the king's and your business dressed
as we are; clothes do not hinder truth" [*Bene possumus hoc
modo vestiti de regalibus tuisque negotiis disceptare, vestes en-
im non impediunt veritatem*].[10]

Were Durham and Lanfranc (himself an archbishop fully
vested with distinguishing liturgical garments and regalia) just
cattily arguing over fashion accessories on the way to the treason trial, or were there critical epistemologies of flesh, liturgy,
and sovereignty at stake in their conflict? To answer this question it is important to understand, at least schematically, the
liturgy of episcopal ordination in which vestments and regalia
became the constitutive integuments of consecrated episcopal
flesh.[11] In the course of the ordination ceremony, the bishop-

---

[9] *Durham*, 95.

[10] *Durham*, 96.

[11] Major clerical orders were distinguished by vestiary accessories.
For a detailed historical analysis of such liturgical vestments around
the time of the Conquest and the Durham case, see Sarah Larratt
Keeffer, "A Matter of Style: Clerical Vestments In the Anglo-Saxon
Church," *Medieval Clothing and Textiles*, eds. Robin Netherton and
Gale R. Owen-Crocker (Rochester: Boydell Press, 2007), 13–40. The
bishop's mitre was just being introduced at this time. See Raghnall Ó
Floinn, "Bishops, liturgy and reform: some archaeological and art
historical evidence," in *Ireland and Europe in the Twelfth Century:
Reform and Renewal*, eds. Damian Bracken and Dagmar Ó Riain-
Raedel (Dublin: Four Courts Press, 2006), 218–38. See also Joseph
Braun, *Die Liturgische Gewandung Im Occident und Orient: Nach
Ursprung und Entwicklung, Verwendung und Symbolik* (Freiburg:
Herdersche Verlagshandlung, 1907); Eric Palazzo, *L'Eveque et son
image: l'illustration du Pontifical au Moyen Age* (Turnhout: Brepols,
1999), and the essays collected in *The Bishop: Power and Piety at the
First Millennium*, ed. Sean Gilsdorf (Münster: Lit Verlag, 2004). A
useful glossary of liturgical vestments may be found in Janet Mayo, *A
History of Ecclesiastical Dress* (New York: Holmes & Meier, 1984). I

elect donned piece after piece (a kind of counter-striptease) of the vestiary insignia of his office.[12] At his consecration Mass, he first appeared in his underclothes, so to speak, the white linen garments that underlay the distinguishing outer vestments of consecrated priests. As the liturgy of consecration unfolded, he was presented with his episcopal sandals, dalmatic (wide-sleeved ornate over-garment), chasuble (another ornate outer garment for celebration of the Eucharist) and gloves. After the singing of the Kyrie Eleison, the hands and the head of the bishop were anointed with holy chrism. He was then invested with yet another layer of insignia: the episcopal ring, crozier (pastoral staff) and mitre (a newish episcopal accessory that proliferated at the time of Lanfranc). Then and only then, anointed and fully integumented, was the new bishop to be enthroned. The anointing with holy oil and the performative donning of liturgical vestments rendered the flesh of the bishop episcopal. Episcopal flesh and sovereign flesh were also closely bound, since only a consecrated bishop could transform the flesh of a royal heir into kingly flesh through anointing.

Durham's request and Lanfranc's answer thus enacted a deeply conflicting epistemology of the flesh. Durham was insisting that there was no split or suture between his episcopal and baronial flesh (he held the important Castle of Durham as baron of the king). Nor was Durham juridically naïve. Con-

---

am grateful to Maureen C. Miller for discussing these points with me and sharing a draft chapter from her now published book, *Clerical Clothing in Medieval Europe 800-1200* (Ithaca: Cornell University Press, 2011).

[12] In addition to the references in footnote 4, see the ordinals, or liturgical instructions for episcopal ordination, in the following text: Cyrille Vogel with Reinhard Elze and Michel Andrieu, *Le Pontifical Romano-Germanique du Dixième Siècle*, Vol. 1 (Città del Vaticano: Biblioteca apostolica vaticana, 1963). I am condensing my liturgical schema based on the variations of these instructions for episcopal ordination; also, Sharon L. McMillan, *Episcopal Ordination and Ecclesial Consensus* (Collegeville: Liturgical Press, 2005).

vinced that the king had succeeded in silencing all witnesses, Durham also came to the trial equipped with yet another prop, his annotated copy of the legal textbook of the day, the *Collectio Lanfranci*, composed by none other than Lanfranc.[13] Lanfranc refused the request and, thus, as judge, he ruled for a sovereign gap between episcopal and baronial flesh. Just as he had sutured the flesh of Christ to the law of sovereignty to accuse Berengar as both heretic *and* traitor in the Eucharistic controversy, so in the Durham treason trial he split liturgical and sovereign investment and in so doing he produced Durham as a baronial traitor against the royal sovereign and concomitantly reduced Durham's episcopal flesh to a state of liturgical nudity, a liturgical bare life. The case exemplifies, I argue, how liturgical bare life needs to be understood as the biopolitical kernel at the heart of sovereign legal innovations of the eleventh and twelfth centuries. Such an understanding precludes any simple periodization of political theology and sovereignty and, perhaps more importantly in reference to Esposito, any linear periodization of sovereignty and biopolitics, or flesh and immunity. This suturing performed by Lanfranc also set the framework for yet another radical, juridical innovation of the 1130's to be found in the *Leges Edwardi*, which invented the juridical category of the "Jew" subject to the sovereign and his decision to call the state of exception.[14]

At this juncture let me recap briefly. The medieval genealogy of the biopolitics of flesh that I have sketched out in the long paper puts into question the conventional narrative of

---

[13] For an introduction to context and bibliography of Lanfranc's legal composition, see Herbert Edward John Cowdrey, *Lanfranc: Scholar, Monk, and Archbishop* (Oxford: Oxford University Press, 2003), 138–43. Durham's annotated copy of the *Collectio Lanfranci* can be consulted: Cambridge, Peterhouse MS 74.

[14] A full account of these clerical circles, their interventions into fiction and the law, and their fabrication of the category of the Jew as state of exception is given in Kathleen Biddick, "Arthur's Two Bodies and the Bare Life of the Archive," in *Cultural Diversity in the British Middle Ages: Archipelago, Island, England*, ed. Jeffrey Jerome Cohen (New York: Palgrave Macmillan, 2008), 117–34.

Western sovereignty. My account radically inverts the accepted metanarrative of political theology and sovereignty to be found in *The King's Two Bodies*—the magisterial work by Ernst Kantorowicz whose paradigm Michel Foucault subsequently promoted in *Discipline and Punish*.[15] Kantorowicz proposed a linear, secularizing narrative of political theology in which liturgical flesh gives way to a secularized body politic. My account of the suture of sacramental flesh to sovereign law thus raises two interrelated questions pertinent to Kantorowicz and to contemporary theoretical discussions of flesh and biopolitics. First, how is it that Kantorowicz, steeped as he was in medieval law and theology, foreclosed a history of suture of the law with liturgical flesh, a suture that produces both the traitor and liturgical bare life, or, *homo sacer*, as Giorgio Agamben would nominate it? And, secondly, if we switch back along the track I have introduced so far, what then are the challenges of thinking how medieval biopolitics might "transcrypt" into affirmative biopolitics today?[16]

The second part of my book chapter, which I shall briefly summarize here, turns to a reading of Kantorowicz through

---

[15] Ernst H. Kantorowicz, *The King's Two Bodies: A Study in Medieval Political Theology*, 2nd edn. with an introduction by William Chester Jordan (Princeton: Princeton University Press, 1997). The pagination of the text in the first and second edition is the same. The literature on Kantorowicz is copious also and I cite here an insightful starting point: Alain Boureau, *Kantorowicz: Stories of a Historian*, trans. Stephen G. Nichols and Gabrielle M. Spiegel (Baltimore: Johns Hopkins University Press, 2001). Michel Foucault praises the recently translated study of Kantorowicz at the opening of *Discipline and Punish*.

[16] Bracha Ettinger, *The Matrixial Borderspace* (Minneapolis: University of Minnesota Press, 2006), speaks of the concept of transcryptum: "Our posttraumatic era becomes, by virtue of this art, transtraumatic. The forgotten trauma becomes transitive; its traces wander and are shared affectively . . . . Cross-cryption is a transcription that becomes possible when co-affective tracing transgresses the boundaries of the individual Psyche. In transpassing the boundaries between I and non-I, it dangerously transgresses the boundaries between the death-drive and the life-drive" (167). Her work has inspired my critique of Esposito.

the untold story of this medieval suture, a suture Kantorowicz traumatically foreclosed. When on April 20, 1933, he, as professor of medieval history at the University of Frankfurt, under the pressure of recently instituted Nazi race laws, wrote to the Minister für Wissenschaft to resign his university post, he poignantly defended his record of decorated military service in World War I and invoked the strong national sympathies he expressed in his popular book on Emperor Frederick II.[17] He went on to assert that because of his Jewish ancestry (*Herkunft*), he was being treated like a traitor (*Landesverräter*). At this moment, Kantorowicz decisively (if unwittingly) distilled what Agamben has called the undecidability of Western sovereignty. In essence, Kantorowicz was pointing out that he was being treated as both homo sacer (as a Jew) and also as a traitor. Agamben has argued that the murder of *homo sacer* and the treasonous murder of the sovereign are structurally undecidable. Treason against the sovereign (that is, killing the sovereign, *crimen laesae maiestatis*) is never a "just" act of homicide, because it is always more than homicide: "it does not matter from our perspective, that the killing of *homo sacer* can be considered as less than homicide, and the killing of the sovereign as more than homicide; what is essential is that in neither case does the killing of a man constitute an offense of homicide."[18] In my critical reading of Kantorowicz I examine how such undecidability haunted one of the great treason cases of the twelfth century, the trial of Thomas Becket, which took place in the aftermath of the disputes of the Constitutions of Clarendon in January 1164.[19] At Clarendon, King

---

[17] The full text of the letter is printed in *Dokumente zur Geschichte der Frankfurter Juden (1933-1945)*, Kommission zur Erforschung der Geschichte der Frankfurter Juden (Frankfurt, 1963), 99–100.

[18] Giorgio Agamben, *Homo Sacer: Sovereign Power and Bare Life*, trans. Daniel Heller-Roazen (Stanford: Stanford University Press, 1998), 104.

[19] For an account of this trial, see Raoul Charles Van Caenegem, *English Lawsuits from William I to Richard I*, Vol. 2 (London: Selden Society, 1991), case #421, 433–57, hereafter called *Becket*; see also Anne J. Duggan, "Roman, Canon and Common Law in Twelfth-

Henry II, who bullied his Archbishop of Canterbury and other clerical barons into consent in January 1164, decisively asserted sovereign right over what is known as bare promises or *nuda pacta* in cases of debt. The bare promise is an oral plight of faith made between two persons regarding the exchange of land or loan of money. An early notion of binding contract, *pactum vestitum*—a clothed or veiled pact—depended on written instruments. Article 15 announced that an oral faith-plight (otherwise known as bare promise) in a debt transaction could *not* be the grounds for sending such disputes over money-lending to the church courts. Thus when it came to debt, both faith promise and documentary writing became the domain of the king's justice. The sovereign, then, is the one who decides on debt, even in disputes over faith-promise or oath, sacral transactions that had traditionally been the province of the bishop's court. It could be said that Article 15 secularized the promise when it came to debt and removed it from the sphere of church law that judged in matters of faith. Article 15 also effectively ended any interventions church courts might make into disputes over debt. Article 15 triangulates liturgy, law, and debt.[20]

Century England: The Council of Northampton (1164) Re-examined," *Bulletin of the Institute of Historical Research* 83 (2010): 379–408.

[20] For Clarendon, see William Stubbs, *Selected Charters and other Illustrations of English Constitutional History from Early Times to the Reign of Edward the First* (Oxford: Clarendon Press, 1870), 167. This argument about the over-riding (overwriting) of what came to be known as the "nudum pactum"—the naked pact made on faith between two legal persons—challenges us to rethink arguments about "memory to written record" as a crisis of sovereignty and faith and not some accretion of governmentality. See Michael Clanchy, *From Memory to Written Record: England 1086-1307* (London: Wiley Blackwell, 1993) and Frederick Pollock and Frederic W. Maitland, *History of English Law before the Time of Edward I*, 2nd edn. (Cambridge: Cambridge University Press, 1911). For the long-term problematic of sovereign and liturgical conflict over debt claims, see Richard H. Helmholz, *Roman Canon Law in Reformation England* (Cambridge: Cambridge University Press, 1990), 25–33.

In the long version of this paper in my forthcoming book *Entangled Sovereignty*, I show how, in a breathtaking spiral, the coterie of Thomas Becket judaize King Henry II and his lay and clerical supports in a stream of polemic and visual imagery, among which visual artifacts I count the Cloisters Cross.[21] What is important for a biohistory of the flesh is to see how these accusations of treason (of Becket and of Kantorowicz) touch each other at the core of the undecidability of medieval Western sovereignty as it was fabricated over the twelfth century through the juridical category of the Jew and then judaized as sovereignty broadened its state of exception to include liturgy itself over the twelfth century.[22] The kernel of sovereignty is thus a biopolitical suture of Eucharistic and Jewish flesh. The Becket case and Kantorowicz's plaint make exactly the point that Agamben has made about the undecidability between *homo sacer* (he who can be killed without taint of homicide, but he who cannot be sacrificed) and the sovereign when it comes to the nature of their death (not quite homicide and always more than homicide).

My argument gets at the unhistorical (not ahistorical) vertigo of flesh and law as it was sutured in Eucharistic disputes and treason trials between the 1060s-1160s. I argue not for some transhistorical essence to the state of exception. Instead, I am pointing to a profound transmedieval trauma that immunized the communal flesh of Christ into a biopolitical entity sutured to sovereignty. Further, around that violent suture emerged another layer of immunization, that of immunizing the so-called universal biopolitical community of Christians from the "Jew," that juridical category fashioned to foreclose

---

[21] Readers will want to consult my forthcoming book for full citations. I will keep them brief here. The cross measures 23 inches high and has an arm span of 14-¼ inches (577 x 362 mm). For an excellent overview and bibliography of scholarly debates about the cross to 2006 see, Elizabeth C. Parker, "Editing the *Cloister's Cross*," *Gesta* 45 (2006): 147–60.

[22] See Biddick, "Arthur's Two Bodies and the Bare Life of the Archive," 117–34.

the suture undertaken by Lanfranc and his fellow theologians and jurists. Such biopoliticization of the Jew, as *homo sacer* (he who could be killed without taint of homicide, but who could not be sacrificed), could paradoxically be used against the sovereign, who was judaized by his opponents, as he attempted to widen the state of exception around the question of promise and faith-pledge made in cases of debt. It is at this traumatic juncture that Esposito and Agamben need to be brought together into close proximity (a proximity against which Esposito anxiously defends in *Bios*). Can speculative medievalisms (such as I have engaged in here) undo the immunization of biopolitics against its transmedieval traumas? An affirmative biopolitics, as espoused by Esposito, needs to embrace its own medieval matrices.

§ Coda

So that's my paper in Morse Code. Before you tap out SOS, let's bring on the toys. What does it mean to open up the medieval toy chest? Let me begin my toy story with a comment made recently by Louis Menand (the Ann T. and Robert M. Bass Professor of English at Harvard University). In his widely circulating book, *The Marketplace of Ideas: Reform and Resistance in the American University*, he wrote: "Why support medievalists in the history department, the English department, the French and German departments, the art history department, none of them probably attracting huge enrollments, when you can hire one supermedievalist and install her in a Medieval Studies program, whose survival can be made to depend in part on the ability to attract outside funding?"[23] His argument has become an administrative commonplace, but it reminds me that the academy is miniaturizing medieval studies and producing it as a chest of disused objects, what Benja-

---

[23] Louis Menand, *Marketplace of Ideas: Reform and Resistance in the American University* (New York: W.W. Norton, 2010), 119.

min would call "mislaid, broken, and repaired."[24] Agamben would imagine the toy as an object that "permits release from a continuous and linear time and the realization of and a return to history."[25]

What strikes me as productive of the Babel Working Group and this meeting on speculative medievalisms is that it implicitly accepts that medieval studies has become a set of discarded objects. Rather than trying to restore them into continuous and linear time, and, rather than become nostalgic about a world of toys we have lost, instead, like the toy characters in the film *Toy Story 3,* medievalists have joined hands on the way to the incinerator. This joining of hands enables the kind of playing with the law that deactivates it and renders it inoperable, and is also the gate to the postjuridical. So, I look forward to future speculative medievalisms as a kind of *Toy Story 4* in which we play with the state of exception, each of us following our own strategy, "to study [the law] and deactivate it, to 'play' with it."[26]

---

[24] Walter Benjamin, "Old Toys," in *Walter Benjamin: Selected Writings, Vol. 2, Part 1, 1927-1930,* trans. Rodney Livingstone, eds. Michael W. Jennings, Howard Eiland, and Gary Smith (Cambridge: Harvard University Press, 1999), 101.

[25] Giorgio Agamben, *Infancy and History: On the Destruction of Experience,* trans. Liz Heron (London: Verso, 2007): 104–5.

[26] Agamben, "Gigantomachy Concerning a Void," in *State of Exception,* 64 [52–64].

Cryptomnesia
Response to Kathleen Biddick

Eileen A. Joy and Anna Kłosowska

§ An Isolated Non-Conscious Cavity

In Kathleen Biddick's longer (as yet unpublished) essay, from which her contribution to this volume is "Morse-Coded," she writes:

> [E]ntrapped by his periodization, Foucault puzzled over a historical aporia: 'How can the power of death, the function of death, be exercised in a political system centered upon biopower?' Nazism, with its untimely unleashing of the 'old sovereign power to take life' concomitant with the most intense forms of biopower . . . presented Foucault with an anguishing temporal paradox.[1]

Given the incoherence between Foucault's narrative of how sovereignty ("the power to take life or let live") was superseded by biopolitics ("to foster life or to disallow it"), and actual

---

[1] Kathleen Biddick, "The Biopower of Medievalisms: Toward a Bio-history of the Flesh" (unpublished chapter), in Kathleen Biddick, *Entangled Sovereignty: Studies in Premodern Political Theology* (under consideration with the Insurrections series, Columbia University Press).

modern history (the merger of biopolitics and sovereignty in Nazism, for example), Foucault acknowledged something that we all struggle against as we use his concepts—the narratives of where and how modernity emerges into sight occlude as much as they explain.

That is why, when Agamben proposed the biopolitical principle through his delineation of *bios* and *zoe* in ancient Greek society, and later, of *homo sacer* and the sovereign exception in the Roman empire,[2] medievalists started tracking the possibilities for modifying Foucault along these lines. But as Biddick has pointed out, the disappointing part of Agamben's account of biopolitics was that—although he "argued for biopower as the kernel of power from the ancient world to the present," he did so by also proposing a temporality (messianic time) informed by typological relations (*littera* to *figura*) that he was at pains to "bracket off" from medieval forms of typology, and therefore, as Biddick has elegantly argued, Agamben's "messianic time becomes haunted by an inexplicable amputation." So, in the end, both Foucault and Agamben immunize biopower from the medieval, whereas for Biddick, what she calls "liturgical bare life" is "the biopolitical kernel at the heart of sovereign legal innovations of the eleventh and twelfth centuries,"[3] and she has plenty of examples to solidify her case.

---

[2] See Giorgio Agamben, *Homo Sacer: Sovereign Power and Bare Life*, trans. Daniel Heller-Roazen (Stanford: Stanford University Press, 1998), *State of Exception*, trans. Kevin Attell (Chicago: Chicago University Press, 2005), and *The Time That Remains: A Commentary on the Letter to the Romans*, trans. Patricia Dailey (Stanford: Stanford University Press, 2005).

[3] Biddick, "The Biopower of Medievalisms." See also Biddick's attempts to engage and grapple with Agamben's "amputation" of the medieval in his account of biopolitics, see Kathleen Biddick, *The Typological Imaginary: Circumcision, Technology, History* (Philadelphia: University of Pennsylvania Press, 2003) and "Dead Neighbor Archives: Jews, Muslims, and the Enemy's Two Bodies," in *Political Theology and Early Modernity*, eds. Graham Hammill and Julia

Let's remind ourselves, too, that this could never be a simple case of simply re-inserting medieval evidence into some sort of linear biohistory, where liturgical flesh eventually "gives way to a secularized body politic";[4] rather, for Biddick, any accounting of a biohistory today, and by extension, biopolitics, will have to shuck linear temporalities in favor of tracing the topographies (which may be more trans-affectively *spatial* than temporal) of what the psychoanalyst and theorist Bracha Ettinger calls "transcryptums": sites where past, forgotten traumas are both archives/crypts and also *transitive*, traveling into the future along the desert trade routes of "transsubjective borderspaces."[5]

To the case study, shared by Biddick, of how the German-Jewish medievalist Ernst Kantorowicz, against his own better knowledge of medieval law and theology, misrecognized the

---

Reinhard Lupton (Chicago: University of Chicago Press, 2012), 124–42.

[4] Kathleen Biddick, "Toy Stories: *Vita Nuda* Then and Now?" (in this volume).

[5] See Bracha Ettinger, *The Matrixial Borderspace*, ed. Brian Massumi (Minneapolis: University of Minnesota Press, 2006), 163–64. Biddick performs a dazzling feat of theoretical innovation in bringing Ettinger's formulations of the transcryptum into contact with contemporary narratives of biohistory and biopower. Ettinger is, we believe, a woefully overlooked thinker in premodern *and* modern psychoanalytic studies. But we should also note that Ettinger's idea of a transcryptum resonates with Aranye Fradenburg's recent argument that, "undead life seems more apt a description of the signifier's mode of existence (as Derrida himself thought) than does simple absence or nonexistence. . . . given how susceptible we are to the signifier's designs, there is more connectedness than we think between living subjects and dead letters. Nature's signifiers vary in their realizations, but something, a shape, insists": L.O. Aranye Fradenburg, "Living Chaucer," *Studies in the Age of Chaucer* 33 (2011) 44 [41–64]. See also Fradenburg's commentary on transitive signifiers, pockets, recesses, and archives in her essay "(Dis)continuity: A History of Dreaming," in *The Post-Historical Middle Ages*, eds. Elizabeth Scala and Sylvia Frederico (New York: Palgrave Macmillan, 2009), 87–115.

"new epistemologies of flesh, time, law and biopolitics emerging among clerical circles . . . in early twelfth-century Anglo-Norman England,"[6] we might apply Ettinger's idea of the crypt as "the buried unthought of knowledge"—"buried alive," moreover, "in an isolated nonconscious cavity"[7]—and we might *also* say, still following Ettinger's psychoanalytic formulations, that the "Event," as it were, of, say, Lanfranc's splitting of liturgical and baronial vestments in the case against the Bishop of Durham for treason in 1088,[8] couldn't be seen or remembered by Kantorowicz as *belonging to Kantorowicz*: Durham's liturgical nudity, his bare life, couldn't be *his* bare life, living as he did in a supposedly post-liturgical time.

Kantorowicz's book, *The King's Two Bodies*,[9] becomes a sort of artwork-transcryptum that both exposes and veils the "transitive effects" of the trauma of the medieval past. It becomes, finally, an act of what Ettinger calls "cryptomnesia."[10] This is especially troubling when we consider Biddick's delineation of the ways in which the fraudulent twelfth-century law codes known as the *Leges Edwardii* created the juridical category of the Jew as a subject solely under the will of the king "whose sovereign right was to protect or to suspend protection." Jews, in other words, in the medieval period, had been made *uniquely* vulnerable to the reduction to bare life, and for

---

[6] Biddick, "The Biopower of Medievalisms."

[7] Ettinger, *The Matrixial Borderspace*, 166.

[8] In her contribution to this volume, "Toy Stories," Biddick shares an account of the 1088 trial of the Bishop of Durham (William de Saint-Calais) for treason, where Archbishop (of Canterbury) Lanfranc, the prosecutor, would not allow the Bishop to wear his episcopal vestments to his trial, thus "splitting" Durham's episcopal and baronial "flesh," and also instituting a "sovereign gap" between these two "bodies" as well—a significant moment in any account of biopower or political theology.

[9] Ernst H. Kantorowicz, *The King's Two Bodies: A Study in Mediaeval Political Theology* (Princeton: Princeton University Press, 1950).

[10] Ettinger, *The Maxtrixial Borderspace*, 170.

Biddick, the double-whammy (or double-bind) of the medieval biopolitical is that its very kernel is a "suture of Eucharistic and Jewish flesh."[11] Nazi biopolitics, then, under the watchful and anxious sight of Kantorowicz-as-medievalist, staged for Kantorowicz a return of the "same" that could never really be *the* same, for, cadging from Ettinger, it carried the "marks of a peril of a disappearance [Kantorowicz's *own* disappearance] in the new appearing."[12]

§ THE PERFORMANCE OF THESE CALCULATIONS

In the spirit of Biddick's own commentary, let's invert our tracks here for a moment and return to Lanfranc, Bishop of Canterbury, and his refutation of Berengar of Tours in the debates over the Real Presence of the Eucharist of the late eleventh century.[13] In our supposedly posthuman age, where human rights debates still linger over issues of the "dignity" and "sanctity" of human persons and where continental (or post-continental) philosophy is also currently investing in "weird realisms" and "guerrilla metaphysics,"[14] it is an episode

---

[11] Biddick, "The Biopower of Medievalisms."

[12] Ettinger, *The Matrixial Borderspace*, 159.

[13] Lanfranc, *De Corpore et Sanguine Domini*, in *Patrologia Latina*, ed. J.-P. Migne, 221 vols. (Paris, 1844-64), 150:407–42 (hereafter cited parenthetically by page number; translations are ours). These Eucharistic debates were highly complex, but in (one sort of) nutshell they hinged on whether or not one believed that the Eucharist contained the real, actual, "true" presence (body, flesh) of Christ (transubstantiation) or rather represented a "spiritual" (immaterial) version of Christ. Sometime in the 1050s, Berengar of Tours, a theologian who led the cathedral school at Chartres, wrote a letter to Archbishop Lanfranc expressing his doubts over the so-called "Real Presence," after which, due to Lanfranc's urging of Pope Leo IX, Berengar was excommunicated.

[14] See, for example, the work of Graham Harman, especially *Circus Philosophicus* (Winchester: Zero Books), *Guerrilla Metaphysics: Phenomenology and the Carpentry of Things* (Chicago: Open Court, 2011), and *Prince of Networks: Bruno Latour and Metaphysics* (Melbourne: re.press, 2009). See also Ian Bogost, *Alien Phenomenology, or*

worth lingering over in relation to rethinking the history of contemporary biopolitics.

In his refutation of Berengar, whom Lanfranc accused of treason, Lanfranc asserted the oneness of the Trinity, using at one point the Greek word *homousion* (411), "same-essence" or "same-being." Lanfranc asserts the materiality of the host, that is, the so-called "Real Presence": for Lanfranc, the ritual of the mass produces not just a material *symbol* of Christ (as Berengar had argued) but the actual body and blood of Christ at a specific moment of the Passion, "both in property of the matter and in truth of the substance" (411). Throughout Lanfranc's refutation of Berengar there emerges, like a powerful underground stream that breaks out onto the surface trajectory of the text, Lanfranc's paranoid obsession with the dual nature of human being: humble and submissive on the surface, but possibly unrepentant at the core. For instance, Lanfranc attributes Berengar's recantation of 1059 not to "love of truth but fear of death" (408), and he imagines Berengar burning his own books "with his body bowed but his heart not humbled" (409). In Lanfranc, biopolitical thinking extends from theology (constubstantiality of the Trinity and of the Host) to social relations (Berengar is condemned not just for his thought but also for teaching those who have "no knowledge to resist him," 409) to rhetoric, as Berengar is accused at the same time of splitting the Host, splintering the indivisible church, and harboring opposition under the outward appearance of submission: a split being proliferating fractures. The distinctions argued over here are ultimately between "Real" presence and "sacramental" presence, but further distinctions are current in the theology of the period; presence could be, for instance, "spiritual" or "intellectual,"

What It's Like to Be a Thing (Minneapolis: University of Minnesota Press, 2012); Levi Bryant, *The Democracy of Objects* (Ann Arbor: Open Humanities Press, 2011), and Levi Bryant, Nick Srnicek, and Graham Harman, eds., *The Speculative Turn: Continental Materialism and Realism* (Melbourne: re.press, 2011).

meaning that something was present only in intelligence or memory.[15]

Berengar's recantation of 1059, cited in Lanfranc's condemnation of him, *De Corpore et Sanguine Domini*, is itself interesting, because it is a text that will be much in use. The key moment is when Berengar was asked to take an oath swearing that, during Communion, there was "tearing or breaking [of] our Lord Christ's body and blood with the hands of the priest and grinding with the teeth of the faithful" (410). We encounter it later both in Gratian's *Decretum* and in Peter Lombard's *Sentences*, as well as in future heresy cases, for instance at the abjuration of Perer Maurandus, a burgher of Toulouse. It becomes an oft-reprised text in polemical writings by Jews and Muslims, because of its vivid phrasing, interpreted as a reference to cannibalism.[16] And of course, the parallel between priests tearing Christ's body into quarters and Brazil's cannibals resurfaces in Protestant polemic in the 1500s.[17]

This thinking on indivisibility and trans-substationation went in a number of different directions. For instance, in a treatise on trans-substantiation written ca. 1070, Lanfranc's student Witmund gives analogies for similar commonplace

---

[15] See Charles Gore, *Dissertations on subjects connected with the incarnation* (London: John Murray, 1907), 261.

[16] John Hinde Mundy traces the fortunes of this oath and notes that when it was "inserted into the *Pontificale* of William Durand the Elder at the end of the thirteenth century it had become a rather anodyne loyalty oath" (John Hinde Mundy, *Studies in the Ecclesiastical and Social History of Toulouse in the Age of the Cathars* [Aldershot: Ashgate, 2006], chap. 4, "The Abjuration of Peter Maurandus," 167 [161–69]).

[17] See George Hoffman's splendid article, "Anatomy of the Mass: Montaigne's Cannibals," *PMLA* 117.2 (2002): 207–21, at 210: "Catholic priests surpass even the most carnivorous of beasts in that they devour 'chunks as large as entire quarters, and of the whole body,' a precise allusion to the Fractio, during which the consecrated bread was torn in four by the priest, along lines stamped in it in the shape of the cross to recall Christ's mutilation."

"translations" and indivisibles: wine and bread become our own flesh and blood as we eat; our voice, the material form of our thoughts, is equally absorbed by all our hearers without being divided between them; and our soul (*anima*) is undivided in all parts of our body.[18]

The "Northern School," centered in Liège, and influenced by Augustine and Plato, developed a less material interpretation, exemplified by Alger of Liège (1050-ca. 1132) who proposed a dual or "ambivalent mode which allowed for two simultaneous eatings—spiritual and carnal."[19] Twelfth-century Paris became the influential center of an interpretive tradition that was closer to Berengar than to Lanfranc. In late twelfth-century Byzantium, theological discussion focused on whether the real body of Christ was corruptible, and it was decided that it was, from the consecration to communion, but as it was digested it became the glorious body and was mixed with the soul, "bestowing upon it [the soul] its own incorruptibility and preserving it for eternal life."[20] In Western intellectual history, the trajectory of the thinking on transubstantiation can be compared to the turn from nominalism ("there is nothing general except names," or in other words: universals are *nuda intellecta*, bare names) to Platonic realism in the twelfth century, with Abelard (1079-1142) as the turning point. Abelard's contribution includes his discussion of abstractions, that is, our ability to draw similarities and paradigms from infinitely vast collectivities of infinitely differentiated individuals.

Can we then, in turn, compare these two alternatives— realist versus dualist understandings of transubstantiation and nominalism versus realism—to shifts in the humanities more

---

[18] Charles Gore, *Dissertations on subjects connected with the incarnation*, 261.

[19] Miri Rubin, *Corpus Christi: The Eucharist in Late Medieval Culture* (Cambridge, Eng.: Cambridge University Press, 1991), 21.

[20] See, among others, Martin Jugié, "Un opuscule inédit de Néophyte le Reclus sur l'incorruptibilité du corps du Christ dans l'Eucharistie," *Revue des études byzantines* 7.1 (1949): 1 [1–11].

recently, from nominalism to "new" materialisms, from the "linguistic turn" to the rise of speculative realism and post- or "guerilla" metaphysics, concerned with new *carnal* phenomenologies of substances and relations from the perspective of non-human-centered modes of access?[21] Compare the debate between Berengar and Lanfranc with this definition of new material culture studies from anthropologist Ewa Domanska:

> [A]n interest in things has its own long tradition, including the history of material culture. However, present-day "thing studies" and the so called "new material culture" reject constructivism, narrativism, and textualism on the grounds that these approaches have "dematerialized" things by comparing the thing to a text, and research to a reading, by perceiving the thing solely as a message or sign. In an attempt to reverse those tendencies, "new material studies" points to the agency of things, accentuating the fact that things not only exist but also act and have performative potential. Thus, in the

---

[21] The term "guerrilla metaphysics" (cited above also) comes from Graham Harman's object-oriented philosophy where it denotes the philosophical attempt to speak of "not the physical but the *metaphysical* way in which objects are joined or pieced together, as well as the internal composition of their individual parts." Further, since "the vacuum-sealed nature of objects makes direct communication impossible, all conjunction or coupling must occur through some outside [vicarious] mediator" (Graham Harman, *Guerrilla Metaphysics*, 2). On new materialisms, see also Karen Barad, *Meeting the Universe Halfway: Quantum Physics and the Entanglement of Matter and Meaning* (Durham: Duke University Press, 2007) and Jane Bennett, *Vibrant Matter: A Political Ecology of Things* (Durham: Duke University Press, 2010). A useful bibliography of this "turn to things" across the disciplines (film, anthropology, literary studies, sociology) can be found in the work of political scientists and sociologists, for instance, in Frank Trentmann, "Materiality in the Future of History: Things, Practices, and Politics," *The Journal of British Studies* 48.2 (2009): 283 [283–307]. "New material culture" in anthropological studies begins with the *Journal of Material Culture* (1996).

> "return to things," it is not the topic that is new, but
> the approaches to things and the forms of studying
> them.[22]

Among the elements that supposedly precipitated the "mate-rial turn" or the "return of the non-human," according to Ewa Domanska, are: the critique of anthropocentrism, the decline of metaphysics, the "crisis of identity" as it relates to things as guarantors of identity and markers of change, and the some-what paranoid awareness that things shape individuals and collectivities in consumer society, rather than being shaped by us or just passively existing.[23]

Returning again to Lanfranc, as Biddick so importantly illustrates, the sophisticated manipulation by Lanfranc of dif-ferent substances and their relations (flesh, clothes, law, litur-gy, speech, heart, mind)—sometimes added together (as with Berengar's heresy hearings), sometimes subtracted (as in the legal case against Durham)—produces a calculus of law and power, similar to the *secular* accounting of royal debt in the medieval Pipe Rolls, that is based on the entitlement to per-form these mathematical operations for others; and *vice versa*, the performance of these calculations establishes and produc-es power. And with these operations, all of the exits from mo-dernity have been locked in advance.

§ THE DEACTIVATION OF THE LAW?

In the end, the question of a possibly *affirmative* biopolitics today is, for Biddick, the question of uncovering the cryptic structures of contemporary law and sovereignty as well as re-tuning the "forks" or "antennae" of various transtraumatic crises of the suture of flesh and law, in the past and today, represented in artifacts: textual and otherwise. At five centu-

---

[22] Ewa Domanska, "The Material Presence of the Past," *History and Theory* 45 (2006), 339 [337–48].

[23] Domanska, "The Material Presence of the Past," 339.

ries' distance, relics, like toys, reclaim, in a positive sense, their shared, originary *thingness*, which is open to what might be called a continual natality of new uses. If a toy is a hybrid of Heidegger's two distinct categories (thing *at*-hand, and a tool or thing *to*-hand), then toying and playing with the law, through the study of the mislaid, discarded, and disused objects of the past, as Biddick imagines here, might open the door to a post-juridical, positive biopolitics.

The more difficult question, of course, as Catherine Mills mentions in her essay on Agamben's thinking on toys and "playing" with the law, is how this might look in *practice*, not just in *theory*.[24] Somewhat frustratingly, Mills does not offer any possible *practical* scenarios, but by way of offering some food for further thought in that direction, here are some *questions*.

First, what if, as Donna Haraway has suggested, Foucault was narrativizing a form of power at its "moment of implosion," when the discourse of biopolitics was giving way to "techno-babble,"[25] or put another way, when power is no longer wholly centralized in a sovereign body of any sort, but rather, becomes dispersed as a dynamic mesh of runaway inter-connections and fluid mobilities in a transnational modernity that "accelerates mobility between unevenly constituted zones of finance, technology, culture, race, geography, and gender," and where individuals, often migrant, fugitive, refugee, and without the "proper names" or "proper papers," are "at risk of being [partitioned], parceled and substituted in such a way as to render the absolute life of the whole body immaterial"?[26]

---

[24] Catherine Mills, "Playing with the Law: Agamben and Derrida on Postjuridical Justice," *South Atlantic Quarterly* 107 (2008): 15–36.

[25] Donna Haraway, *Simians, Cyborgs, and Women: The Reinvention of Nature* (New York: Routledge, 1991), 245n4.

[26] Mrinalini Chakravorty and Leila Neti, "The Human Recycled: Insecurity in the Transnational Moment," *differences: a journal of feminist cultural studies* 20.2-3 (2009): 195, 194–95 [194–223]. Chakravorty and Neti's essay is an important exploration of "expendable or recyclable humanity" in a transnational modernity that

Second, as a way to start thinking about how to move forward strategically through this state of affairs, we are reminded of an anecdote Biddick relates about a papal immunity and protection granted to the monastery at Cluny in 1080, which "was procedurally innovative in that it topographically mapped the territorial space of protection as a sacred circle of land extending out for three kilometers from the center of the monastic precinct." As Biddick writes, "The Cluniacs imagined their sacred ban as the womb of the Virgin (thus, the strategic timeliness of its celebration on the feast day of the Purification of Mary), which uterine flesh God had miraculously immunized from encroachment and invasion."[27] We might say, as we think Biddick implies, that here in the Cluniac ban is one of the "kernels" of modern biopower, and we wonder: is now the time for different conceptions of more horizontal, asymmetrical communities of subjects without identity or subjectivization, based not on ties of proximity but on a sort of territorial unboundedness that would also be collectively invested in projects of rogue contamination and radical non-purity under the sign of the de-activation of the law?

In which case, as Neti and Charavorty argue, now might be the time for radical forms of affection and sociality "in a way that is not wholly reducible to the workings of capital. . . . That is, the possibility of love."[28]

routinely devalues "life." See also Zgymunt Bauman, *Liquid Modernity* (Cambridge, Eng.: Polity, 2000) and Ulrich Beck, *Risk Society: Towards a New Society*, trans. Mark Ritter (London: SAGE, 1992).

[27] Biddick, "The Biopower of Medievalisms."

[28] Chakravorty and Neti, "The Human Recycled," 215.

Divine Darkness

Eugene Thacker

Darkness has more Divinity for me . . .

—Edward Young, *Night Thoughts*

§ DARKNESS AND HORROR

Nearly everyone can relate, I suspect, to the feeling of being "scared of the dark." It is no doubt for this reason that darkness saturates the horror genre, from the earliest examples of gothic novels and graveyard poetry, to the most recent films, comics, and video games. We do not know what it is that dwells in the darkness, only that our not-knowing is a source of fear. Darkness seems to steadily creep forth, submerging everything in an anonymous, pitch blackness. Our fear of the dark seems as ambiguous as darkness itself. This ambiguity is at once horrific, and yet, because of its ambiguity, it also obtains the quality of the mystical. Georges Bataille, writing about religious art, highlights this ambiguity: "What I suddenly saw, and what imprisoned me in anguish—but which at the same time delivered me from it—was the identity of these perfect contraries, divine ecstasy and its opposite, extreme horror."[1]

The concept of darkness evokes this combination of religion and horror; it is the shift from the horror of something *in* the dark, to the horror *of* darkness itself. Put simply, the concept of darkness invites us to think about this basic metaphysical dilemma of a nothing that is a something . . .

§ DARKNESS AND MYSTICISM

From the time when Bataille, as a teenager, entered a Catholic seminary (which he promptly abandoned), to his later experiments with the secret society Acéphale, to his last writings on religious art, one can trace the themes of mysticism, darkness, and negation running through nearly all of Bataille's works. Religion is, for Bataille, the practice whereby the discontinuous, human being seeks out a continuity that can neither be experienced nor known, a continuity that exists before and after the life of the human being, a continuity that has both been lost and yet is never attained.

This inaccessible continuity, neither empirical nor ideal, is what Bataille calls *divinity*, and divinity is, in short, that which is radically unhuman. The divine is, for Bataille, that which stands outside of subject/object relations altogether. The most basic distinctions—between life and death, for instance—are dissolved in the anonymous continuity that is the divine. As Bataille notes, in religious sacrifice "death reveals life in its plentitude and darkens the order of the real."[2] For Bataille, the divine negates the anthropomorphic, sovereign God as much as it does the individuated, human being. The divine is the horizon of the human. The divine is the impossibility of the human.

---

[1] Georges Bataille, *The Tears of Eros*, trans. Peter Connor (San Francisco: City Lights, 1989), 206–7.

[2] Georges Bataille, *Theory of Religion*, trans. Robert Hurley (New York: Zone Books, 1992), 47.

Humanity, defined by its inauguration of the subject/object split, attempts to re-capture its lost continuity through rituals of sacrifice, war, and consumption. The endpoint of such rituals, from a religious standpoint, is the dissolution of subject and object that is the hallmark of divine continuity. But, at the same time, the human being must maintain a minimal distance (and thus discontinuity) in order to possibly experience and comprehend the divine as such. It appears that divine continuity can only have a negative character, can only be intuitable to us as an enigmatic something that recedes into shadows, obscurity, and darkness. The divine is the blind spot of the human:

> But how even for a moment can I dismiss this unknowing [*ignorance*], a feeling of having lost my way in some underground tunnel? To me this world, the planet, the starry sky, are just a grave (I don't know if I'm suffocating here, if I'm crying or becoming some kind of incomprehensible sun). Even war can't light up a darkness [*une nuit*] that is this total.[3]

This dilemma Bataille refers to as *mediation*. In passages such as this, the boundaries of the human become fuzzy and obscure, at once tomb-like and yet planetary and even cosmic.

The darkness that Bataille evokes has a number of precedents in the mystical traditions. Dionysius the Areopagite, for instance, asks how we can know the "ray of divine darkness" (Θειου σκοτους ακτινα). Dionysius presumes a concept of darkness that is neither simply privative nor oppositional, but also distinct from the more familiar mystical tropes of light, illumination, and radiation:

> The fact is that the more we take flight upward, the more our words are confined to the ideas we are capa-

---

[3] Georges Bataille, *Guilty*, trans. Bruce Boone (Los Angeles: Lapis Press, 1986), 12.

ble of forming; so that now as we plunge into that darkness which is beyond intellect, we shall find ourselves not simply running short of words but actually speechless and unknowing.[4]

In spite of the fact that Dionysius brings us to the point of silence, where there is nothing to say, this has obviously not had the effect of silencing mystical discourse. In fact, the opposite is the case.

A thinker like Meister Eckhart will take Dionysius's notion that there is nothing to say quite literally—as in, "nothing" or "darkness" is the only thing that there is to speak of, when one speaks of the divine. In his *Commentary on Exodus*, Eckhart outlines four basic types of mystical darkness. There is, first, darkness as an indicator that one is, in Eckhart's words, "in tribulation." That is, darkness is a symptom of a spiritual crisis that leads one to seek out the divine. We can call this the "darkness of despair." Second, there is darkness as an indicator that one is, as Eckhart says, "with tribulation," or with the divine in tribulation. This is the spiritual duration of one in suffering and prayer. We can call this the "darkness of suffering." Third, there is darkness that creates confusion about what to do, that causes one to be caught, in Eckhart's words, between "prosperity or adversity." Here one is caught between a conditional relation to the divine (based on reward or punishment) and an unconditional relation to the divine (irrespective of an outcome in the world). We can call this the "darkness of the world."

With these first three types of darkness, Eckhart describes the contours and limits of the human. The human arrives at a point of tension, poised between a relation to the world that would preserve the human (via a religious economy of debt, reward, and punishment), and a relation to the world that would negate the boundary between human and not-human.

---

[4] Dionysius the Areopagite, *Pseudo-Dionysius: The Complete Works*, trans. Paul Rorem (Mahwah: Paulist Press, 1987), 139.

This leads to the final type of darkness: "Further and fourth, the 'darkness' can be understood as the immensity and surpassing excellence of the divine light . . . into the surpassing light that beats down and darkens our intellect."[5]

The fourth type of darkness is that moment when one basically gives up, or really, gives oneself up—in Eckhart's words "emptying oneself" so that nothing remains except darkness. For Eckhart, the divine paradoxically makes itself accessible in its inaccessibility, a something that presents itself as absolutely beyond the human, and thus as nothing. As Eckhart notes in one of his sermons, "you cannot do better than to place yourself in this darkness and in unknowing."[6]

This preoccupation with the limit of the human finds one of its most dramatic manifestations in John of the Cross' poem, *The Dark Night of the Soul*. John provides a more streamlined typology, distinguishing between two types of darkness, a "darkness of the senses" and a "darkness of the soul." But we risk a great misunderstanding if we read John as advocating a direct, human experience of the divine. For John, mystical experience does not reaffirm or bolster the human subject; quite the opposite. Mystical experience is "dark" precisely because it is that which cannot be experienced—the *impossibility* of experience. This point is made more clearly when John hints at a third type of darkness that lies beyond the darkness of the senses or the soul:

> . . . the clearer and more obvious divine things are in themselves, the darker and more hidden they are to the soul naturally . . . . Hence when the divine light of contemplation strikes souls not yet entirely illumined, it causes spiritual darkness, for it not only surpasses

---

[5] Meister Eckhart, *Meister Eckhart: Teacher and Preacher*, eds. Elvira Borgstadt and Frank Tobin (Mahwah: Paulist Press, 1986), 117.
[6] Meister Eckhart, *The Complete Mystical Works of Meister Eckhart*, ed. and trans. Maurice O'C. Walshe (New York: Herder & Herder, 2009), 56.

them but also deprives and darkens their act of understanding. This is why St. Dionysius and other mystical theologians call this infused contemplation a ray of darkness . . .[7]

John's evocation of the dark night and the impossibility of its experience brings us back to the work of Bataille. The writings of the darkness mysticism tradition exercised a great influence on Bataille's writings of the 1940s and '50s. These influences can be readily detected in the pages of books like *Inner Experience*:

I read in Denys l'Aréopagite: 'Those who by an inward cessation of all intellectual functioning enter into an intimate union with ineffable light . . . only speak of God by negation' . . . So is it from the moment that it is experience and not presupposition which reveals (to such an extent that, in the eyes of the latter, light is 'a ray of darkness'; he would go so far as to say, in the tradition of Eckhart: 'God is Nothingness'). But positive theology—founded on the revelation of the scriptures—is not in accord with this negative experience . . . . In the same way, I hold the apprehension of God . . . to be an obstacle in the movement which carries us to the more obscure apprehension of *unknowing* [*l'inconnu*]: of a presence which is no longer in any way distinct from an absence.[8]

Bataille's mystical writings are not simply a ventriloquizing of mystical authors, and neither are they about the existentialist crisis of the modern subject; with a thinker like Bataille they run the gamut from the most basic forms of "base material-

[7] John of the Cross, *Selected Writings*, ed. Kiernan Kavanaugh (Mahwah: Paulist Press, 1988), 201.

[8] Georges Bataille, *Inner Experience*, trans. Leslie Anne Boldt (Albany: SUNY, 1988), 4–5.

ism" and inorganic matter, to the planetary and even cosmic cycles of production, accumulation, and expenditure. That is, this kind of darkness mysticism has to be placed in the context of Bataille's own version of political economy. In the same way that divine darkness is in excess of the individuated, human being, so is there a divine darkness that is in excess of the world—at least the world that we as human beings construct for us and fashion in our image. Divine darkness is precisely this negation that cuts across self and world, the human and the non-human—not by virtue of a bountiful, vitalistic, life-force, but by way of a process of emptying and darkening. In an almost Lovecraftian vein, Bataille notes that, "beyond our immediate ends, humanity's activity in fact pursues the useless and infinite fulfillment of the universe."[9] One passage from Bataille's mystical poem "*L'Archangélique*" reads:

> *the excess of darkness*
> *is the flash of a star*
> *the cold of the tomb is a die*[10]

The "I" of the poem immediately dissolves and is "entombed" into a kind of planetary, climatological materialism, just as the anonymous, base materialism of the world courses through and is inseparable from the self. Clearly, this is no hippie love-in. For Bataille, as for Dionysius, Eckhart, and John of the Cross, all the roads of the *via negativa* lead to darkness, an absolute limit to the human capacity to know itself and the world: "I imagine that it is as in vision, which is rendered sharp in darkness [*l'obscurité*] by the dilation of a pupil. Here darkness is not the absence of light (or of sound) but absorp-

---

[9] Georges Bataille, *The Accursed Share, Volume 1*, trans. Robert Hurley (New York: Zone, 1991), 21.
[10] Georges Bataille, *The Collected Poems of Georges Bataille*, trans. Mark Spitzer (Chester Springs: Dufour, 1998), 65. The original passage reads: "l'excès de ténèbres / est l'éclat de l'étoile / le froid de la tombe est un dé."

tion into the outside [*dehors*]."[11]

Now, this "outside" that Bataille evokes is not some ideal other place, much less the experience of a transcendent beyond—that is, this darkness that is "outside" is not "above" or "beyond." It is a limit that is co-extensive with the human, at its limit. And this is why I think Bataille's project is interesting. It does not attempt to pass beyond the human, whether we call it the posthuman or the transhuman. It also does not attempt to undermine the human, be it in terms of objects, actants, or technics. In borrowing from the darkness mysticism tradition, Bataille's texts opt to darken the human, to undo the human by paradoxically revealing the shadows and nothingness at its core, to move not towards a renewed knowledge of the human, but towards something we can only call an unknowing of the human, or really, the *unhuman*. Bataille's mysticism, then, is a mysticism of the limits of the human, and this divine darkness would be something like a mysticism of the unhuman.

§ DIVINE DARKNESS

At this point, I'd like to shift gears a little, from the mode of commentary to that of exegesis, and try to distill some of the salient aspects of the concept of darkness in relation to mysticism. In fact, I would suggest that there are three basic modes of darkness in this mystical tradition: a dialectical darkness, a superlative darkness, and what I've been calling a divine darkness.

The first mode—dialectical darkness—entails a concept of darkness that is inseparable from an opposing term, whatever that term may be. Dialectical darkness is therefore structured around the dyad of dark/light, which finds its avatars in the epistemological dyad of knowledge/ignorance, the metaphysical dyad of presence/absence, and the theological dyad of gift/privation. Dialectical darkness always subsumes darkness

---

[11] Bataille, *Inner Experience*, 17.

within its opposing term, and in this sense, darkness is always subordinate to something that opposes or comes after darkness. With dialectical darkness, the movement is from a negative to an affirmative experience of the divine, from the absence of any experience at all to a fully present experience. However, at the same time, this affirmative experience comes at the cost of a surreptitious negation: a "vision" (*visio*) that is also blindness, an ecstasy (*ecstasis*) or standing outside oneself that displaces the subject, and a rapture (*raptus*) in which the self is snatched away into a liminal otherness. We should note that the recuperative power of dialectical darkness is such that it inhabits all attempts to think a concept of darkness—even those that claim to pass beyond oppositions. Dialectical darkness is at once the ground of, and the obstacle for, any concept of darkness.

This management of boundaries shifts a bit when we move to superlative darkness, the second mode. Superlative darkness is a darkness precisely because it lies beyond the dialectical opposition of dark and light. Paradoxically, superlative darkness surpasses all attempts to directly or affirmatively know the divine. Hence superlative darkness contains a philosophical commitment to superlative transcendence. Superlative darkness makes an anti-empiricist claim, in that it is beyond any experience of light or dark. It also makes an anti-idealist claim, in that it is beyond any conception of light or dark. What results are contradictory, superlative concepts of "light beyond light," the "brilliant darkness," or the "ray of divine darkness." With superlative darkness, there is a movement from an affirmative to a superlative experience of the divine, from a simple affirmation to an affirmation beyond all affirmation. Claiming to move beyond both experience and thought, superlative darkness harbors within itself an anti-humanism (beyond creaturely experience, beyond human thought), leading to a "superlative darkness" or, really, a kataphatic darkness. We should note that with superlative darkness we are brought to a certain limit, not only of language but of thought itself. The motif of darkness comes in here to indicate this limit. And it is a horizon that haunts every concept of darkness, the possibility of thinking the impossible.

This play between the possible and impossible finally brings us to the third mode—what we've been calling divine darkness. Divine darkness questions the metaphysical commitment of superlative darkness, and really this means questioning its fidelity to the principle of sufficient reason. Now, the interesting thing about superlative darkness is that, while it may subscribe to a minimal version of the principle of sufficient reason, it does not presume that we as human beings can have a knowledge of this reason. That everything that exists has a reason for existing may be the case, but whether or not we can know this reason is another matter altogether. Superlative darkness is thus an attenuated variant of the principle of sufficient reason.

Perhaps we should really call this the *principle of sufficient divinity*. The principle of sufficient divinity is composed of two statements: a statement on being, which states that something exists, even though that something may not be known by us (and is therefore "nothing" for us as human beings), and a statement on logic, which states that that something-that-exists is ordered and thus intelligible (though perhaps not intelligible to us as human beings). Superlative darkness still relies on a limit of the human as a guarantee of the transcendent being and logic of the divine, or that which is outside-the-human. The limit of human knowing becomes a kind of backdoor means of knowing human limits, resulting in the sort of conciliatory knowledge one finds in many mystical texts.

Now, a divine darkness would take this and make of it a limit as well. This involves distinguishing two types of limit within darkness mysticism generally speaking. There is, firstly, the limit of human knowing. Darkness is the limit of the human to comprehend that which lies beyond the human—but which, as beyond the human, may still be invested with being, order, and meaning. This in turn leads to a derivative knowing of this unknowing. And here, darkness indicates the conciliatory ability to comprehend the incomprehensibility of what remains, outside the human.

Then there is, secondly, the limit of that which cannot be known by us, the limit of the limit, as it were. With the limit of human knowing, there is still the presupposition of something outside that is simply a limit for us as human beings. The limit of the limit is not a constraint or boundary, but a "darkening" of the principle of sufficient divinity. It suggests that there is nothing outside, and that nothing-outside is absolutely inaccessible. This leads not to a conciliatory knowing of unknowing, which is really a knowing of something that cannot be known. Instead, it is a negative knowing of nothing to know. *There is nothing, and it cannot be known.*

If we were to summarize these points, we could say the following: divine darkness is the conjunction of these two types of limits, the limit of human knowing and the limit of that which cannot be known. This is an *apophatic darkness.* There is nothing to know, and it cannot be known. Divine darkness is therefore the unknowing of nothing.

§ CONCLUSION

In what we've been calling the darkness mysticism tradition, a concept of negation is put forth that is tied in some way to the motif of darkness, though darkness is not always negative in each of these thinkers. This divine darkness, or really, a mysticism of the unhuman, is not in any way an answer, much less a solution, to some of the issues we face today concerning the posthuman or what Bataille once called "the congested planet." And, perhaps, its greatest lesson is the one repeatedly stated by Eckhart—that this darkness, in its unknowing, is not separate from us, but really within us as well. It is not a darkness "out there" in the great beyond, but an "outside" (to use Bataille's term) that is co-extensive with the human at its absolute limit. It runs the gamut from the lowest to the highest, from the self to the planet, from the human to the unhuman.[12] It is a sentiment echoed by Bataille when he speaks about darkness as a form of impossibility:

> I enter into a dead end. There all possibilities are exhausted; the 'possible' slips away and the impossible prevails. To face the impossible—exorbitant, indubitable—when nothing is possible any longer is in my eyes to have an experience of the divine . . . .[13]

---

[12] The concept of "planetary darkness" is explored in Nicola Masciandaro's chapbook *Abjection of the Spheres: Augustine and Boethius* (Brooklyn: Contrapasso Editions, 2012).

[13] Bataille, *Inner Experience*, 33.

Per Speculum in Aenigmate
Response to Eugene Thacker

Nicola Masciandaro

Introductory comments: I will address divine darkness by focusing on the distinction between thought and experience, a
distinction which parallels the distinctions between *that* and
what, and between soul (or life) and body. I am interested
here in darkness as an occluded relation or blind spot between
thought and experience. At the same time I would like to
ground the concept of divine darkness in the traditional aim
or purpose of mystical contemplation, which is to become
God, to achieve union with God. This is a desire which is legible, but also refused in Bataille's work, in which we see a kind
of reification of the limit of experience and with it, necessarily,
a mystification of mysticism. An important figure for my response is the figure of the cephalophore, the head-bearing
saint. Of course Dionysius the Areopagite, identified as St.
Denis, was a cephalophore. I will try to suggest that the cephalophore should be reinvented by speculative medievalists as a
human ideal proper to congested humanity, the anthropocene, the so-called age of man—the global dead which Eugene
ended with. I should also note that there is an intimate relation between the mirror and beheading. When we look into a
mirror or speculate, we are non-violently beheaded.

 The significance of divine darkness, and darkness in general, is inseparable from the distinction between thought and

experience. In the basic scenario of 'being afraid of the dark' with which Eugene began, this distinction is made clear in the conflict between what we know and what we feel of the dark, a conflict one may try resolve with self-reminders that the fear is irrational or ungrounded in real knowledge, or that the especially frightful movie scene is an illusion or merely film footage. But in the example wherein "the shift from the horror of something *in* the dark to the horror *of* darkness itself" is never completed but always underway in a manner than compounds rather than that displaces the horror, such that the darkness becomes doubly horrible, the magnified synthesis of an unpredictable violent potentiality out of which something might *get* you and an abyssic void into which one might slip and fall, here darkness also reveals its strange power to join thought and experience in ways that they could never connect themselves. That is, in being something *inseparable from the distinction* between thought and experience, darkness is by the same virtue exactly what joins them unforeseeably and supradiscursively, in ways that arrive marked from a place one cannot think or talk one's way towards, a space one can enter only, alonely via a terrifying or tortuous event. This is the singular 'gnosis of the victim,' as discussed by Georg J. Sieg,[1] or, for Bataille, a kind of decapitation: "The human being arrives at the threshold: there he must throw himself headlong [*vivant*] into that which has no foundation and has no head."[2] Beheading was essential for Bataille, who clearly intuited its esoteric significance as real symbol of mystical union, the unlocatability or non-appearance of a real headsman for *Acephale*'s human sacrifice perfectly figuring the Godlessness,

---

[1] George J. Sieg, "Infinite Regress into Self-Referential Horror: The Gnosis of the Victim," *Collapse IV: Concept Horror* (2008): 29–54. Cf. the shower murder in Alfred Hitchcock's *Psycho* (1960), in which dying eye and camera intersect, and Pascal Laugier's *Marytrs* (2008), which reprises Bataille.

[2] Georges Bataille, "The Obelisk," in *Visions of Excess: Selected Writings, 1927-1939*, trans. Allan Stoekl (Minneapolis: University of Minnesota Press, 1985), 222.

though certainly not the undivinity, of his mysticism.[3] According to the pheneomenological principle voiced by
Heidegger and demonstrated in the ancient literal meaning of
symbolon, that a severing is also a joining,[4] beheading elegantly performs the *operation of the dark* as a separation of
thought and experience that opens them to a new relation, an
opening from within into an absolute outside, what Reza Negarestani calls "a line of openness that slashes through the
god, the human, and the earth."[5] That is, our fear of a knife in
the dark discloses the knife of darkness itself as a mirroring
blade cutting through head and body, thought and experience,
only to reveal in a blinding flash their essential unity.[6] Such a
uniting-by-separating of thought and experience is correlative
to John of the Cross's description (via the *verbum absconditum* heard by Eliphaz the Temanite in the Book in the Job) of
the bodily disjointing, similar to the auto-dismembering *dhikr*

---

[3] Note the proximity of heresy, martyrdom, and prophecy. "The
original martyr (witness) is neither a martyr nor not a martyr. . . . It
is the death of one who cannot survive his witnessing and the
witnessing of one who cannot not die. . . . In a strange and
unspeakable way, the martyric meaning of John's beheading
poetically approaches its precise impossibility. It becomes the
performance of exactly what it can never be, the necessarily
decapitative murder of the theological traitor, the killing of one who
says *I am God*" (Nicola Masciandaro, "*Non potest hoc corpus
decollari*; Beheading and the Impossible," in *Heads Will Roll:
Decapitation in the Medieval and Early Modern Imagination*, eds.
Larissa Tracy and Jeff Massey [Leiden: Brill, 2012], 27).

[4] "Severing also is still a joining and a relating" ("[A]uch das Trennen
ist noch ein Verbinden und Beziehen." Martin Heidegger, "Logik:
Heraklit's Lehre vom Logos," in *Heraklit*, 'Gesamtausgabe,' Bd. 55
[Frankfurt am Main: Vittorio Klostermann, 1970], 337).

[5] Reza Negarestani, *Cyclonopedia: Complicity with Anonymous
Materials* (Melbourne: re press, 2008), 207.

[6] This happens when you are in a dark space and become hyper-
aware of your own being, the substantiality of thought, etc. and that
is what is really terrifying: not having something to distractively
identify with, occupy yourself.

of some subcontinental Sufis, accompanying mystical ecstasy, in which the soul-body nexus of human nature is strained like a knot being pulled from both ends: "The torment experienced in these rapturous visits is such that no other so disjoins the bones and endangers human nature. . . . Indeed it seems so to the soul in which this happens, that she is being loosed from the flesh and is abandoning the body. . . . The reason for this is that such favors cannot be received wholly in the body . . . Thus the soul must in some fashion abandon the body. As a result the body must suffer and, consequently, the soul in the body because of their unity in one suppositum [i.e. individual substance]."[7] On this point, I feel that Eugene's *unhuman* must be tweaked to *inhuman*, with a prepositional pun on the negation, so as to register that the human passes beyond itself from within, inside an exacerbated realization of its own nature as more and other than whatever it is. So Bataille defines the "THE OBJECT OF ECSTASY" as "THE ABSENCE OF AN OUTSIDE ANSWER. THE INEXPLICABLE PRESENCE OF MAN IS THE ANSWER THE WILL GIVES ITSELF, SUSPENDED IN THE VOID OF UNKNOWABLE NIGHT."[8] In other words, if "the divine is the impossibility of the human" (as per Thacker) it is so only in intimacy with its own generic actuality or *that*. "Not *how* the world is, is the mystical, but *that* it is."[9] The absolute intensification of *that* inversely throws the *what* into darkness (a blackened wonder), or, the maximization of *that* is darkness itself.[10] Note how this

---

[7] John of the Cross, *Collected Works*, trans. Kieran Kavanagh and Otilio Rodriguez (Washington: ICS Publications, 1991), *Spiritual Canticle* 13.4.

[8] George Bataille, *The Bataille Reader*, ed. Fred Botting and Scott Wilson (Oxford: Blackwell, 1997), 45.

[9] Ludwig Wittgenstein, *Tractatus Logico-Philosophicus*, trans. C.K. Ogden (Mineola: Dover Publications, 1998), 6.44.

[10] For Eriugena, this is the divine image, an eclipse of *what* by *that*: "the Divine likeness in the human mind is most clearly discerned when it is only known that it is, and not known what it is . . . what it is is denied in it [*negatur in ea quid esse*], and only that it is is

principle of maximal facticity corresponds to Dionysius's description of dark union with the divinity that is "beyond assertion and denial": "he plunges into the truly mysterious darkness of unknowing" [*in calignem ignorantiae occidit vere mysticam*]. Here, renouncing all that the mind may conceive, wrapped entirely in the intangible and the invisible, he belongs completely to him who is beyond everything. Here, being neither oneself nor someone else, one is supremely united by a completely unknowing inactivity of all knowledge, and knows beyond the mind by knowing nothing."[11] Note that *occidit* also means falls or perishes, or slays, as if the event were also an unnameable, subjectless and objectless, simultaneous slaughter of both self and God.

To conclude, let me pose three questions that are important here: 1) What is the relation between the thought/experience distinction and divine darkness? Why do we need 'divine darkness' in order to understand how our own being structures that distinction? My answer is basically that we are cephalophores who do not know it (yet). The cephalophore is also a great figure for panpsychism, and for life that exists beyond and opens the distinctions through which life is conceived; 2) What is the dialectical work of 'darkness' in contemporary discourses? The intellectual productivity of the concept of darkness, its poetic force, has to do with bringing forth and imagining absolute substances and voids, new vistas and kinds of matter. Darkness is about potentiality ('dark materials'), but also necessarily about leaving potentiality undetermined or unsaid, and about keeping dark the distinction between the concept of darkness and darkness itself. Here there are real points of connection between mysti-

---

affirmed" (John Scotus Eriugena, *Periphyseon (De Divisione Naturae)*, eds. I. P. Sheldon-Williams and Édouard A. Jeauneau, trans. John. J. O'Meara, 4 vols. [Dublin: Dublin Institute for Advanced Studies, 1999-2009], IV.73).

[11] Pseudo-Dionysius, *Mystical Theology*, 100D-1001A, in *The Complete Works*, trans. Colm Luibheid and Paul Rorem (New York: Paulist Press, 1987), 137.

cal discourse, the language of unsaying, and places where we see a conjunction of philosophies of immanence and affects of incommunicability—for example, Agamben's science without object, Laruelle's non-philosophy, and speculative realist investments in the vector of thought as immanent touching of an outside; and 3) What does speculative medievalism have to learn from mysticism? The mystic is a being who weaponizes the correlation, who becomes correlation-as-weapon. The mystic shatters the mirror of speculative reflexivity and wields it as a knife against self and world—a sacrificial tool. But somehow the mystic also shatters the mirror without breaking it, breaks it without violence, which is the work of love.

The Speculative Angel

Anthony Paul Smith

§ LET THE ANGEL COME

"Let the angel come." This is how Guy Lardreau and Christian Jambet preface their heretical, perhaps misguided and certainly maligned, but utterly fascinating fusion of Lacan, Mao, and political theology in their *L'Ange* of 1976. They are more pleading later in the book, writing: "The angel must come."[1] But what does any of this mean? Why, when considering

---

[1] Guy Lardreau and Christian Jambet, *L'Ange. Pour une cynégétique du semblant – Ontologie de la révolution 1* [*The Angel: Towards a Cynegetic of the Semblance – Ontology of Revolution 1*] (Paris: Barnard Grasset, 1976), 36. (All translations are my own unless otherwise noted.) For the event "Speculative Medievalisms: A Laboratory-Atelier 1," each speaker was asked to provide specimen texts that would be circulated prior to the event for the audience and other participants to read. While many of my texts were from the medieval period, and you'll see those figures discussed, there were three important contemporary French texts with which I was engaging heavily that were and continue to be unavailable in English. I translated some short selections from those texts and circulated them with my other specimens. I assume a certain familiarity with those specimens in this piece, treating them as giving me some melody or a little rhythm to riff off of and play with. Since I don't summarize much of what is said in those pieces I've included them here as "intermezzos" breaking up this short essay and providing the underlying themes.

speculative medievalisms, have I chosen to write about angels, those beings that seem the least contemporary and perhaps most reactionary of medieval theory? And why have I chosen to do so largely via a virtually unknown or forgotten text by two Maoists whose work has largely been ruined for us by its placement as one species of the cynical, often racist and imperialistic, neo-liberal and anti-communist New Philosophers? What does this ostensibly political text, one that the authors declare is nothing but a Maoist philosophy (contrary to the idea that they are fellow-travellers with the Sarkozist ex-Maoists like Glucksmann or Bernard-Henri Lévy), have to say about speculation today?[2] And in what way is it grounded in the premodern condition? The answer is, in part, because I want to understand what speculation may have to do with revolt, with struggle, and it is in the figure of the Angel that such questions come together, both historically and within wildly speculative ultra-left French theory. For the Angel is both a negative name for something that is not Worldly and the Angel is a field of battle where one either becomes a domesticated, pacified bureaucrat of the way things are or where one separates and divides what is from what could be.

🖙 FIRST INTERMEZZO[3]

We openly call this discourse, without fearing the misunderstandings, *an angelism.*

Yes, in a sense, what we spoke of is the discourse of desire. But something is wrong here. The problem is one of extension. These terms: desire, discourse, they do not even have logical power [*puissance*]—and so we can escape from the impasse that we've seen. All desire is of the Master, not every discourse. So that you may

---

[2] On their commitment to Maoism, Lardreau writes, "I don't pretend to create anything except a Maoist philosophy" (*L'Ange*, 91).
[3] Selection from Lardreau and Jambet, *L'Ange*, 34–37.

understand me I will introduce here a double dichotomy in a strict parallelism:

Body/Sex,

Discourse/Discourse of the master.

To say that sex is of the Master is a tautology, like
saying that the discourse of the master is from the
Master. But if sex is not the body, then the discourse of
the master is not discourse itself. And since we speak
from the West: reason is not thought.

So, when we say that there is no reason of the slave,
we are not saying that the slave does not think, but that
he thinks, and speaks, outside of reason, not that he
talks nonsense [*déraisonne*], that which is the misuse of
reason proper to the argumentative [*raisonneur*] slave.
Just as saying that there is no good sexuality, then we
are not saying that every body is of the Master. If we do
not hold that disjunction, of thought and reason, body
and sex, then we would discuss the impossibility of rebellion.

To confuse reason and thought, or if one takes it
that the slave is endowed with reason, then one sinks
into the illusion which promises the revolt to the master's normalization; or else that he otherwise lacks it,
and only the master thinks and speaks. The reticence
of the subject is only disrupted by cries, by pantings, by
all the poor expressive devices of the affect, of the animal. Where a new dichotomy is proposed: whether we
hate the animal, see what Sade says about it, or we regard the animal with sympathy, pity, we almost succeed in giving sense to its mumbling—you know, when
you have lived a long time with it—we find that it was
only lacking speech, so we charge ourselves with making it acquire language, and as you know it sometimes
becomes clever, like the crow of Barnaby Rudge; in *Le
Singe d'Or* [*The Golden Ape*, Lardreau's first theoretically focused book] I attempted to show that this voice
was, following Kautsky, that of the Leninists.

But for all that we still hardly dare to imagine a man without a body, that is, to confuse body and sexuality, the same eternalization. But if sexuality is the entirety of the Master, nothing which exists prior to his law, then it goes the way of all *flesh*, but this does not go the way of the *body*. Flesh, sex, this is the mode of the body's being as submitted to sin—to the Master, this is not the eternity of the body. But more than reason is the eternity of thought. Hence our reference to the Angel, and it is obvious from there that we have again taken up the theological distinction of body and flesh. Though we simply add that our Angel, without being heretical, is nonetheless "reckless," since it is not the absolutely spiritual angel (not united to a body) of Saint Thomas and of the modern Church. Although the Angel can no longer commit the sins that involve passions of the flesh, it is granted a body, an ethereal, radiant, spiritual body, as it was accorded by the first Fathers and a large part of the tradition up to Saint Bernard and Peter Lombard.

The Angel is not zero sex, neither is it "n" sexes: in both cases Freud would have a field day bringing us back to two. This is not an asexual being. It is nothing that can be assigned a sex. If the quarrel over the sex of angels could not find a resolution, that was because it is impertinent; we can not say the angel has or does not have a sex. Sex is impertinent as to the Angel.

The Angel must come.

And so that he comes, being invisible, he must have been visible in his works, he must have been announced in history, he must have been there, not two objects of desire, that is where the Fathers lost them, but two desires.

Or rather, a desire, that is to say a sexual desire, and a desire that has nothing to do with sex, not even the desire for God: rebellion.

On the one hand pleasure, *jouissance*, and on the

other not even beatitude. Something still unnamed, that we have called desire under the pressures of language, which we must force into delivering us a name. But the Angel is anonymous, or polynymous. We only say that by way of negative metaphors. That's how pseudo-Dionysius wants to speak about that which is God. Negative theology.

Speaking about the world before the break from which it will be born, we can say nothing except from the negative.

I do not see how else we could hold on to the hope of revolution. We will have to go it alone, to go a long way seeming like we are taking up the passion of the Stylites.

As I have said: we will see where all this takes us.

It remains that today the Angel has no enemy more relentless, more horrible than the semblance. And yet, if as Olympius Nemesianus said, there are a thousand ways to hunt, there is only one cynegetic. And for the cynegetic of the semblance, it is in that hour that Lacan gives us the laws. And him alone.

G.L. December '74

§ WHY MUST THE ANGEL COME?

L'Ange is more than a melodramatic attempt by two young militant intellectuals to come to grips with the failures surrounding the French Maoist movement they were involved in, though it is, of course, that as well. It is self-consciously an ontology, carrying the general title "Ontology of Revolution" that was supposed to span three volumes. Of the other two, on the Soul and the World, only the World appeared, but the general title was dropped there due to the authors' horror at yet another failed revolution, this time the Cambodian one that turned from total cultural revolution to the killing fields. But there still, as in *L'Ange*, the figure of the Angel is the image that designates the possibility of a revolution that is one.

That is, a revolution that doesn't simply move from one master to another master, one that doesn't return to the Master, with a capital M, that nominally lies behind all mastery. It is a live question today, when we seem to be living in an age where every act of rebellion fails to overthrow the Master, whether it be the largest peaceful protest in history failing to end a war or the slide from Boliverianism to concessions to neoliberal austerity.

But I am not going to engage in political posturing here. I don't anywhere in this article say what the people should do. Instead, following Lardreau and Jambet, who say that "the masses don't need the Angel, for they are the Angel,"[4] I am going to question the relationship between the theorist involved in the speculative project (let's call this the subject) and the foreclosed or unattainable Real that is in-person within a revolution without a Master (let's call this the identity of a generic body or a radically immanent identity prior to the subject). For this ultimately is the object of *L'Ange*'s ontology of revolution. This is then a kind of political non-theology that treats the three French texts sampled and played with as themselves heretical mutations of the tradition of medieval angelology and the place of that angelology within political theology. For, as we will see, angels are the speculative organon within creation and so angelology can become speculation about speculation. The goal then is to provide a wandering, almost talmudic, speculation on a thought that speculates autonomously, under no sign of the Master. There is surely a bit of a naivety to the idea and more than a little foolishness, but, as Lardreau says, "we will see where all this takes us."[5]

A short note on the methodology of the paper: I am not tracing any historical influences, though I assume some are there. Instead I will treat the questions of angelology and political theology as ahistorical or transhistorical. Again, following Lardreau and Jambet's thought-experiment, I consider

---

[4] Lardreau and Jambet, *L'Ange*, 79.
[5] Lardreau and Jambet, *L'Ange*, 37.

angelology from a position that rejects any strong ontological status to history, the same regarding the status of angels in nature (whatever that might mean), and posit instead that there are only two discourses—that of the Rebel and that of the Master. I hasten to add that I place discourse under François Laruelle's realist suspension, so I am not absolutizing discourse and language at the cost of the Real, but instead treating discourse from the Real. This seems to me to accord with and radicalize Lardreau and Jambet's use of negative theology as method for an ontology of revolution.

* * *

So, why must the Angel come? Is this not another way of asking what is the Angel for Lardreau and Jambet? Here I will provide only a very truncated summary of Lardreau and Jambet's book. As already said, they carry out a thought experiment of extreme manichean nominalism that reduces every political ontology to a question of discourse—that of the Master or the Rebel. Yet, they see within the discourse of the Master a dialectic of Rebel and Master that the Rebel has entered into, thereby finding himself mastered again. They locate this dialectic in various philosophies of desire, the main target being Lyotard (with little convincingly said about Deleuze and Guattari). The point here is not that desire should not be liberated, but that if the identity of the Rebel is dictated by a discourse of sexuality or the body (i.e. the workers' body, or the body of the slave, or even the body of the woman), then the Rebel is not overthrowing the Master as such, but bringing the rebellion under the logic of an identity still mediated by mastery.[6]

That is why the Angel is "not zero sex, neither is it 'n' sex-

---

[6] Regarding this point, see Benjamin Noys, "The End of the Monarchy of Sex: Sexuality and Contemporary Nihilism", *Theory, Culture, & Society* 25.5 (2008): 104–22.

es," but rather sex is simply "impertinent."[7] The Angel must come because it is a negative name for the true generic quality of the Rebel.

🐟 Second Intermezzo[8]

9. – The Christ-division

9.1 – Who is the angel? The Christ who does not serve as a sponge—that is, the Christ who enlists an absolute dialectic or one that is incessantly dialecticized rather than one relative and figured in the State and ultimately the market (or dissolved) uni(versi)ty to which it submits the situation. [9]

Let's be clear: what is at stake in the present recovery of the hatred of relativism and of its correlate survival is radically *christic* (we would only say "Christian" with caveats [*avec pincettes*] since the regulated corruptions of Christianity, Roman Catholic or Reformed, are obvious). Moreover, do not the Gospels, whether canonical or apocryphal, carry, in black and white, the injunction concerning that hatred which is pure rebellion? Thus, the logion of Luke 12:51: "Do you think I came to bring peace on earth? No, I tell you, but division", which (with Matthew 10:34) echoes (although a bit muffled) the logion of Thomas cited as

---

[7] Lardreau and Jambet, *L'Ange*, 36.

[8] Selection from Gilles Grelet, *Déclarer la gnose. D'une guerre qui revient à la culture* [*Declaring Gnosis: On a War that Returns to Culture*] (Paris: L'Harmattan, 2002), 87–88.

[9] One sees equally that the Angel, on account of incarnationism, could not be of value except as an ornament: the becoming-ornament of the Angel (which is consistent with the disjunction of the Christ and the Angel making the former the "filler" [*mastic*] of rationality in its enterprise of conjunction in all directions) alone sums up the obscurantism of the conjuncture in its occidental determination (cf. Christian Jambet, "Les Valeurs de la Nouvelle Économie," *Revue des Deux Mondes,* February 2001: 55–61).

the general epigram to this book. ["Men think, per-haps, that it is peace which I have come to cast upon the world. They do not know that it is dissension which I have come to cast upon the earth: fire, sword, and war." Gospel of Thomas, Logion 16. - *Trans.*]

What is said must be heard: Christ does not bring resolution to the conflicts that form humanity's mis-fortune, he does not come to absolve the world's con-tradictions in the pacified (spiritualized) unity of the Whole of being where each finds their place (and this is so even though one assuredly can produce a number of gospel [*évangéliques*] passages that could go in this direction), in short he never in any way intended to found the State.

Completely to the contrary, Christ bears forth the demands for the *masterly* [*magistrale*] division be-tween the truth and the semblance (the former is claimed to be the occidental pole, dark or exilic from existence, the latter is the oriental or angelic pole), the imperative of absolute war against the State stretches as a mortified state of the situation. So, *far from allowing the auto-divinization of historical becoming under the aegis of the Incarnation, Christ is the agent of anti-history, the Angel of all the angels: Christos Angelos.*[10]

---

[10] Translator's note: Grelet includes a two-page-long footnote here entitled "The Other Incarnation." The content of the footnote clari-fies somewhat the idea of the *Christos Angelos* in relation to Christ as the "means for overthrowing rule," that is the Kingdom of Caesar, and of "instituting the Kingdom of the Angel where man, in the Light of the Cross which consumes objectification, overcomes chooseification." Christ then is "Angel of all the angels, the Gnostic Christ is the Envoy charged with delivering men from their enslave-ment in this world by liberating within them the knowledge of their origin and the means of getting back to the place from which they have been exiled: *Christos Angelos* frees through the knowledge that gives men the means of rebellion that they are, against all humility, fundamentally driven by."

9.2 – Taken from his angelic edge, therefore, rather than from his marshmallow state,[11] Christ imposes a complete rupture with the uni(versi)tary conception of the world that characterizes occidental thought. What is signified by the "christo-rebellion" is not ideological—or relative to this or that position of mastery, and for Mastery as such—but cultural or absolute: *the unrespectable-Christ is the Angel that delivers the soul from its occidental exile, orienting it towards the Light that has not submitted to the relativist corruption.*

The reason for this literally *absolute* aberration is to be found here, that Christ is the Light, and so John 1:5 says that this light shines in the darkness and that the darkness did not overcome it (in order to be "overcome" [*saisi*], or "understood" as we may also translate it, it was necessary that Christ be capable of a rational reception, of a inscription into the schemas of rationality, in short: that he can be related to something else, set in relation, captured [*saisi*] in a relation). . . . That is why,

9.3 – Theorem: the *Christ, constant reference of the West for two-thousand years, is also, and more still, the principle of the war that comes back to its eternitary [éternitaire] mastery.*

§ Thomas's Angelic Yuppie

The Angel, for Lardreau and Jambet, is the negative name for the matrix of thought and practice that avoids the capture of cultural revolution into ideological revolution. Lardreau and Jambet differentiate two different forms of revolution here: cultural revolution refers to the unmediated overturning of

---

[11] The marshmallow offers the perfect image of relation between the "fundamentally Christian" West and Christ, since we know that the soft and very sweet candy does not, in fact, contain any marsh mallow.

the Rebel/Master dialectic, it is a rebellion against the Master in all forms of mastery and against all oppression; ideological revolution refers to rebellion that is mediated within socio-historical causes, that is, which seeks some form of restitution and that critiques a master in favor of another master, a change from one ruling idea to another.[12] Both are forms of overturning or revolt, but only one recognizes that another world is possible, while the other holds to the truth of the sékommça ("it's like that"), a kind of French version of the British motto of Capitalist realism which says, in the grating voice of the Iron Lady, "there is no alternative." This is, then, a Gnostic Angel, an Angel from another World, which can only be spoken of through the method of negative theology: "Speaking about the world before the break from which it will be born, we can say nothing except from the negative."[13]

But, if Lardreau and Jambet's Angel is the apophatic name for the Rebel-masses beyond the Master's dialectic of Rebel-Master, a Rebel beyond any mediating identity found in sexual difference, desire (as defined by Lacan), or the dualisms of dominant culture, then they must rend the concept back from its domestication at the hands of Aquinas. Aquinas is an example of the invariant intellectual of ideological revolution. Aquinas must be named by Lardreau and Jambet, because it is his angelology, that of the established Worldly Church, the home of a settled Christian ideological revolution, that most obscures their concept of the Angel. For Aquinas takes any body and any form of rebellion, away from the Angel and places him within the ordered economy and governance of God. Though, it should be noted, the competing angelologies of the rebellious Spiritual Franciscans and those sympathetic to them within the Order of Friars Minor proper, who pro-

---

[12] See also Peter Hallward's "Introduction" to Lardreau in Guy Lardreau, "The Problem of Great Politics in the Light of Obviously Deficient Modes of Subjectivation," trans. Peter Hallward, *Angelaki* 8.2 (2003): 85–89.
[13] Lardreau and Jambet, *L'Ange*, 4.

claimed an end to the earthly Church, and that of St. Bonaventure, the Franciscan Minster-General at the time, is probably a better model of the split in revolutions between cultural
and ideological. But in naming Aquinas, Lardreau and Jambet
continue a long tradition in French theory, that of addressing
and struggling against Aquinas' thought, both at the institu-
tional level (though not so much now) and at the transhistorical level. The most famous example of this struggle with
Thomism is to be found in Bataille's work, most notably in the
nom de plume that Bataille wrote *Ma Mère* under: Pierre Angélique. Pierre Angélique is the first-person narrator of the
book, and thus the one who is subject to and perpetuator of a
number of debaucheries, including fucking his mother. The
allusion, cleverly but not obscurely coded, is to the Père Angélique—the Angelic Doctor, Thomas Aquinas.[14] Where
Aquinas domesticates, when he brings Christianity back to an
ideological revolution, a kind of search for the true Master,
Bataille struggles to overturn him, but he does so through his
atheism, locked within the dialectic of theism / atheism. Is not
the true struggle with Aquinas to be waged at the level of
gnostic autonomy against his hierarchical mediation? That is,
again, between cultural and ideological revolution?

However, I want to be clear here: Aquinas participated in
rebellion, of a kind. As a giant of the move from credal, monastic education to dialectic, university education, Aquinas is
part of an overturning of thought, but it is one which strives
to secure the place of the new master, (who is the same as the
old Master). And so Aquinas has to practice ideological cor-
rection of any absolute rebellion, as an intellectual of the
Christian ideological revolution, as differentiated from cultural revolution. This is evident in his angelology in so far as,
with the exception of some slippages, the Angel is first made
incorporeal, a purely spiritual being, and then, when that rad-

---

[14] Bruce W. Holsinger, *The Premodern Condition: Medievalism and
the Making of Theory* (Chicago: University of Chicago Press, 2005),
56.

ical difference threatens the stability of hierarchy and thus God's uniqueness, and so also God's power, when the Angel threatens to be a sign of rebellion, it is then that Aquinas must spend a great deal of time accounting for the Angel under the sign of the Master, the Big Other.

This is the real impetus behind Aquinas' famously detailed and elaborate investigations into angelology. For the Angel must be brought under a relation, and so Aquinas accounts for them along the usual axes of "proportion" and "magnitude", or, in other words, accounted for within a hierarchy of dependence upon a single power and so always within a relation, a *ratio*.[15] The former focus of angelology, like that found in Pseudo-Dionysus, as organon of knowledge about the unknowable, is downplayed in Aquinas. This embedding of the Angel within hierarchy goes beyond his theological metaphysics of creation, to his political theology of how God governs the world and heaven. As Agamben notes, Aquinas spends more space, nearly twice as much by my reckoning, discussing angels within the context of governance than he does within the purview of pure angelology. Angels, for Aquinas, are less mediators of that which is beyond the State and more bureaucrats of that State, accountants within the divine economy.[16] Aquinas' remarks on angels in the *Summa* can be taken as a shift from the cultural to ideological angel, from the Rebel in its purity to the Accountant that characterizes the shift from the 60s and 70s culture of rebellion to the 80s and 90s culture of conformism. By making the Angel purely spiritual and embedding it within the discourse of the Master, or as part of a system of exchange outside of question, Aquinas' Angel is domesticated.

---

[15] St. Thomas Aquinas, *Summa Theologica*, Ia q.53 a.3 ad. 1.

[16] See Giorgio Agamben, *The Kingdom and the Glory: For a Theological Genealogy of Economy and Government*, trans. Lorenzo Chiesa with Matteo Mandarini (Stanford: Stanford University Press, 2011), chap. 6.

§ The Angelic Mirror

This tension between a conception of the Angel that stands as a negative name for a world without the Master, for a new world, and the Angel as a name for the Master can be found in the Angelology of Pseudo-Dionysius. His angelology is the root from which all orthodox angelology would subsequently be developed. One can plainly see from the beginning that the folding of the Angel into a hierarchy of "it's like that," the *sékommça*, runs throughout Pseudo-Dionysius' angelology. The very reason to speculate on the celestial hierarchy of heavenly beings, grouped under the one name Angel, is that this hierarchy should be mirrored in the hierarchy of the church, the ecclesiastical hierarchy. That is, at first glance, Pseudo-Dionysius fuses the two discourses into one, an anti-gnostic move. Some, in the name of claiming a powerful source within the tradition itself, might be tempted to proclaim that Pseudo-Dionysius is fusing the two discourses under a single, unilateral discourse of the rebel, since the ecclesiastical hierarchy is modeled on that of the celestial hierarchy. However, I am not sure that this is actually true, though a creative recasting of Pseudo-Dionyisus could bear it out, but would have to deal with the same kind of circular slippage you get in Aquinas' doctrine of analogy. In the doctrine of analogy what is taken as a sign of the divine, say "goodness," is ultimately only known through what is, where merely is, *sékommça*. And so as regards politics of the divine, Aquinas slips immediately to a defence of monarchy, not on the basis of some argument for monarchy, but simply because it *is* the dominant form of governance during his time.

In the case of Pseudo-Dionysius, the ordering of the heavenly beings into a hierarchy mirrors both the semblance of hierarchy in the Church, ordained from authority, and the discourse of Neo-Platonism (this is why there are three orders of angels and within each of those orders there are three types). That is, the speculation occurs under the guise of established systems, rather than from the discourse of the ultimate rebellion.

But even when Pseudo-Dionysius does sneak earthly powers into this celestial hierarchy, as the rulers of this World (following Paul in Romans 13), this still exists under a general and radical unfettering of the Angel from the World.[17] After all, Pseudo-Dionysius claims, even Jesus, because he was in worldly flesh, submitted to the Angels.[18] This tension suggests that there is something that can be recovered from this foundational angelology for a heretical angelology. It is to be found in the *generic* definition of angels that Pseudo-Dionysius presents in Chapter Five of "The Celestial Hierarchy." There he says that all heavenly beings are called angel in common, that their essence is generic angelicity, because they all share, in lesser and greater ways, in making known "the enlightenment proceeding from the Deity."[19] Ultimately, that is what the Angel is—the one who reveals the Divine, or completely Other, to the World (I hope the gnostic resonances of this thesis can be heard).[20] Angels, as Pseudo-Dionysius says, are mirrors of the Divine, they are specular, but not towards themselves.[21] They point towards the Real and mediate the foreclosed, in Laruelle's terminology; they are clones of the foreclosed, making it known and able to be used as material.

---

[17] On this point see Pseudo-Dionysius, *The Celestial Hierarchy*, in *The Complete Works*, trans. Colm Luibheid (New York: Paulist Press, 1987), 167.

[18] Pseudo-Dionysius, *The Celestial Hierarchy*, 158–59.

[19] Pseudo-Dionysius, *The Celestial Hierarchy*, 159.

[20] Pseudo-Dionysius, *The Celestial Hierarchy*, 157.

[21] Pseudo-Dionysius, *The Divine Names*, in *The Complete Works*, trans. Colm Luibheid (New York: Paulist Press, 1987), 22. Aquinas also holds to this view, cf. *Summa Theologica*, I a q.56 a.2.

🐟 THIRD INTERMEZZO[22]

Those Names naming divinity are all names of Angels, formed with the suffix –el: Anafiel, Seraphiel, Uri-
el, Michael, Gabriel, etc. There are a multitude; many
have gone, as Arabic shows us. The *Absconditum* ceases to be the unnameable, the ineffable, as soon as it can
be named, but the names which name it can only be
the names of its theophanies. And yet these Names are
essentially the names of Angels, that which we already
indicated by saying that every theophany is an angelophany. The supreme divine Name can not be pro-
nounced. But there is Yahoel.

This theophanic level which itself reveals the divine
Names is the one where the Unique-One manifests itself in the plurality of Lords designated by the word
rabb, itself being the Lord of Lords (*Rabb al-Arbâb*).
The word *rabb* designates, in Ibn 'Arabi, the personal
and personalized lord who is tied together with the one
to whom he reveals himself under this name, that one
is, then, the lord (his *marbub* [vessel]), a bond of inter-
dependence so intimate that it returns them united one
to the other. This is what we call the secret of the lordly
condition (*sirr al-rububiyyah* [lordship]), the secret of
the tied bond, not at the level of divinity itself, but at
the level of its theophany, that is of its angelophany
(one might even say "not at the level of YHVH, but at
the level of the Angel of YHVH"). This secret is the secret even of what we could call a fundamental angelology, because, without that angelology, we would only
have a theoretical theology without theophany.

* * *

[22] Selection from Henry Corbin, "Nécessité de l'angélogie," in *Le
Paradoxe du Monothéisme* (Paris: Éditions de l'Herne, 2003), 105–6,
114–15, 119–20.

For now, we see that without angelology everything which has preceded makes understanding the meaning of the proposition that asserts the *tawhid*, monotheism, impossible. When the shi'ite doctors say, "impossible without the Imam, without imamology," we understand better, because we have just seen it, that the two concepts may overlap. That is, angelology or imamology are radically necessary to avoid the double trap of agnosticism (*ta'til*) and anthropomorphism (*tashbih*). They will escape this trap because they give a base to the divine Names and Attributes that is not the pure divine Essence, the *Absconditum*, which can neither support Names nor Attributes (so it is not anthropomorphism), but they still give them a real base (so it is not agnosticism), and by the same token remove all allegorism. It is as well that in certain *hadith* the Imams, speaking in their spiritual capacity of enlightenment, declare, "We are the Names and the Attributes; we are the Face of God, we are the hand of God", etc. All of these affirmations can be composed with the names of the Angels. No allegory; these affirmations are literally true of the theophanic forms in their spiritual reality. And so, the paradox resolves itself: from one side the refusal of the vision denied to Moses (*lantarani*, "you will not see me"), and from the other side the affirmation of the Prophet in the famous *hadith* of the vision: "I have seen my lord under the most beautiful of forms."

* * *

That same theophanic function includes an aspect which gives its highest signification to the term which designates them: *angelos*, messenger. The henad of henads, the God of Gods and all the divinities, being unknowable in itself for earthlings, the entire universe of the Gods beyond our world would remain the world of

the Unrevealed, the world of Silence, if there were not
the Angel. The Angel *is* the hermenaut, the messenger
of light who announces and interprets the divine mys-
teries. Without his mediation, we could not understand anything or say anything. This is an aspect that
we will find ourselves solemnly pronouncing, in the
course of an initiatory dialogue, in Sohravardi, the
leader of the Persian neoplatonists (cf. Chapter VI). It
is also necessary to recall that, already at the exoteric
level of prophetology, the mediation of the Angel is in-
dispensible for the Prophet as he was awakened to his
vocation and his message. The prophet Mani, he too, is
awakened to his prophetic vocation by his Angel, his
"Paraclet."

§ The Reckless Body of the Gnostic Angel

The comparative philosophy of angels and theo- or angelophany we find in Henry Corbin, who Jambet studied under
and whose work on angelology no doubt inspires *L'Ange*, reveals a way that speculation may take the form of a body,
which is radicalized in Gilles Grelet's *theorrism* (or theory-
terrorism) of proletarian gnosis. Again, we will see where this
takes us . . . .

In Corbin's work, he shows that angelology is necessary to
avoid idolatry.[23] To speak of God, without merely falling into
the silence of absolute negative theology, one can speak, without allegory, through the names of the Angels, through the
experience of the Angels. Every theophany is an angelophany
and vice versa. Corollary to this angelophany we find in Shi'ite
Islam, a certain necessity of Imamology. At the same time
Corbin appears to back away from equating the two, speaking
of the Imam's spiritual capacity separate from their fleshly

---

[23] For the most extended example of this argument see Henry
Corbin, "Nécessité de l'angélologie," in *Le Paradoxe du Monothéisme*
(Paris: L'Herne, 2003), 97–210.

capacity, while still making the Angel that being who animates Prophets, those who speak for the unsayable in the political-cultural realm.

Ibn Khaldûn's angelology is also found in his discussion of the Prophets. He separates the souls of people into three categories, and Prophets belong to that category of souls who may leave their own human essence, their humanity, and become angelic in "a flash."[24] An in-depth comparative reading of Ibn Khaldûn and Pseudo-Dionysius would reveal major differences in terms of their respective hierarchical ordering. It may appear as if there isn't a difference, since both have different levels of souls based on a Neo-Platonic schema, but importantly the third kind of soul can change essence in Ibn Khaldûn. Both Aquinas and Pseudo-Dionysius have a charitable hierarchy where the higher support the lower in knowledge and power, but there can be no change in essence or form, because the hierarchy is what it is, a pronouncement that matches Lardreau and Jambet's *sékommça*. It is the truth, at least under the discourse of the Master, and as truth determined by the Master it can only be a semblance.[25]

For all of Corbin's genius, and he is surely a forgotten genius of collage in the 20th Century, he aims towards an angelology subsumed into the general category of theophany. According to Grelet this is a metahistorical discourse focused on knowledge and located in the emerald city, a reference to the good, kindly Master, the Wizard of Oz.[26] He even says that this form of discourse plunges gnosis into the spirtualist soup, which tires Grelet "more than anything."[27] We can see Grelet saying that Ibn Khaldûn's angelology of the Prophets too is suspect, even if there is this chance of breaking the semblance

---

[24] See Ibn Khaldûn, *The Muqaddimah: An Introduction to History*, trans. Franz Rosenthal (Princeton: Princeton University Press, 1970), 77–78.

[25] Lardreau and Jambet, *L'Ange*, 22–24.

[26] See the first chart in Gilles Grelet, *Déclarer la gnose. D'une guerre qui revient à la culture* (Paris: L'Harmattan, 2002), 92.

[27] Grelet, *Déclarer la gnose*, 91.

of reality's fixity, for his is ultimately an angelology of the foundation of human society.

Grelet, instead, unilateralizes the Angel along the lines of absolute rebellion, of an anti-culture. The angel is Christ, the Christ that divides, rather than the Christ that founds the State. The Angel is the body of anti-history, of those who are left outside of history, those who remain despite the Master. In its radical sense, the Angel is the body of messianism, the Other-than-this-World manifested, who abolishes the Law and sets life within the absolute itself.[28] This though is an unknown collective body, a body of the proletariat conceived under the auspices of negative theology, marking an important difference between his work and the ideas in *L'Ange*, with its all too certain recognition of "the People," upon which Grelet's ideas are based.

The lesson (or perhaps rather the axiom that one must either choose to labor under or not) of Grelet's ultra-leftist angelology gives us is that speculation must take place at the level of absolute separation if it hopes to be other than merely ideological. The figure of the Angel is, perhaps beyond allegory or perhaps as folly, the site of struggle between whether the rebellion of thought overturns the Master itself or finds itself yet again fettered within its relation to the Master. What remains unaddressed, even if by necessity, however, is what forms of barbarism (from the perspective of this World) comes when the Angel comes and if we are willing to wager such barbarism for the Messianic World. In other words, can the Gnostic Angel overcome the one single catastrophe named progress, helplessly witnessed by the Angel of History?

---

[28] Grelet, *Déclarer la gnose*, 91.

Lapidary Demons
Response to Anthony Paul Smith

Ben Woodard

Given the problem of localizing the power of speculation in the pre-modern assisted by the impertinent form of the angel, I wish to approach the irruption of workable forms, of the non-ideological message, through *Naturephilosophie*, through somewhat weird (and hopefully medieval) means, with the construction of Lapidary Demons as a diagonal response.

Stone appears as the recapitulation of immanence, of matter seemingly foreclosed and foreclosing, the material of internment and memorial. The stone, the movement of the inorganic, indexes deep time and the failure of the category of the inorganic itself in *Naturephilosophie*, since we find stone participating in the partial dominion of life on matter, in DeLanda's well known narrative of mineralization in *homo sapiens* endoskeletons.[1] Similarly, dwelling or the carving of knowledge on stone redirects the torpid trajectory of its re-shapings, albeit only slightly.

Stone is the one of the first notable occurrences of substance, a recapitulation of nature as naturing, but the first step of a slowed becoming or detectable interruption of meontolo-

---

[1] Manuel DeLanda, *A Thousand Years of Nonlinear History* (New York: Zone Books, 2000), 27.

gy. As Jeffrey Jerome Cohen has shown[2], stone has a liveliness—a particularly medieval liveliness—the coveted gemstone or the philosopher's stone, the latter being the contradiction, the stone that is not a stone, that Albertus Magnus passed on in secret. Stone seems to bear mostly negation and hence gives birth to a Deleuzian demon. Stone is not what it is—it is not the first calcification of immanence. But Deleuze's negativity is always secondary, even if it is chronologically before (the dark precursor), demons become the hiccup of becoming, a concretization, a clump of dead lightning ready to be carved.

Twisting back to the temporal, Reza Negarestani's inorganic demons, the dreams of haunted reliquaries, are the always older, the archives of possible generation and corruption—thousands of dead lineages of actualizations.[3] Actualizations not of a thinkable virtuality but a thoroughly unprethinkable chaos, what Schelling circles in his engagement with evil and mythology.[4]

Schelling is unhappy with negation as mere limitation (for which he takes Leibniz to task) and the Devil and his demons are the most limitless creatures. Being escapes the concept (how are the angel and the demon differently conceptually-excessive, or is there a difference?) for the chance of a being that can be worked on, with, yet the relative non-being of the stone, the bedrock, the ground or unground, harbors a productive difference. While the angelic descends from the full-nowhere of the heavens, the demonic always operates in terrestrial complicity.

In this meontology where the darkness is both constant

---

[2] Jeffrey Jerome Cohen, "Stories of Stone," *postmedieval: a journal of medieval cultural studies* 1.1/2 (2010): 56–63.

[3] See Reza Negarestani, *Cyclonopedia: Complicity with Anonymous Materials* (Melbourne: re.press, 2008).

[4] While Schelling addresses these interrelated issues in numerous texts, I am specifically thinking here of F.W.J. von Schelling, *Philosophical Investigations into the Essence of Human Freedom* (New York: SUNY Press), 30–48.

change (becoming beyond becoming) as well as the unsure difference between the known and the unknown, and being and non-being, the earth is uneasy footing bearing the force of gravity which is its night, where the demonic in man is what's left beneath the ground—the demonic being *caput mortuum*[5] or a materiality that is seemingly inert, but always potentiated even after it seems it has exhausted itself in creation. Most dramatically, Schelling notes that "following the last catastrophe, hell will be the foundation of nature."[6]

Schelling's unofficial meontology leaves us between the dumb muteness of stone and the imperceptible tumult of nature's great engine, but things are even worse, as this problem clones itself in our own thought. While "thatness precedes us," the whatness of our thinking seems to come first, to close off what the thing can do for the sake of grasping whatness.[7]

What, then, is the relationship between the foreclosed Real of François Laruelle[8] and the One with only a name in Schelling, and the speculating theorist? In the Stuttgart Seminars, Schelling discusses the Identity of Real and Ideal, of subjective and objective, and the relation of identity and difference (here as a sedimented yet progressive demonology, as a doubling or unity of opposition[9] that takes on a distinctly Laruellian tone in *The Grounding of Positive Philosophy* and the *Ages of the World*). Reason posits simple being so it can use it for the concept and posits the transcendent in order to make the absolute immanent "as something that exists and is only possible

---

[5] F.W.J. von Schelling, "Stuttgart Seminars," in *Idealism and the Endgame of Theory: Three Essays*, ed. Thomas Pfau (Albany: State University of New York Press, 1994), 237.

[6] Schelling, "Stuttgart Seminars," 242.

[7] F.W.J. von Schelling, *The Grounding of Positive Philosophy* (Albany: State University of New York Press, 2007), 211.

[8] See, for example, François Laruelle, *Philosophies of Difference: A Critical Introduction to Non-Philosophy*, trans. Rocco Gangle (London: Continuum, 2010).

[9] Schelling, "Stuttgart Seminars," 201.

in this way."[10]

Speculating about a speculating autonomous thought (the angel) is, for Schelling, nature trying to catch its own tail through a perilous and twisted stream of actualizations (which Hegel perverts into history by cramming it into the bone of spirit). The angel may very well function as the voice of the formless clamor of the real, but the demonic's teeming productivity may be secondary (maybe demons cannot shed their secondary stature). Demonic productivity is of immanence, of a different generative utility.

The very first art, the carving of stone, is a preliminary occurrence of materiality, the human hand onto the slowed immanence of stone, and also the first means of extilligence (what Jack Cohen and Ian Stewart define as the human capacity for documenting our thinking materially), of writing and monumental speaking.[11] If the angelic is the message from the Real or clones of the foreclosed, demons, monsters made of stone and encased in the inorganic, are the immanent bubbling of rock, of the ground and unground to be. The knowledge of the proliferation of grounds, of the weight of materiality and also its eventual decomposition, or spectral fade, traps the utility of baseness between a gargoyle materialism and gray ecology with the excluded third of myth and place—how place itself is recapitulated in the ideas of a particular place, as in Schelling's "Deities of Samothrace." In the gargoyle, the banal is made particularly monstrous, made monstrously communicative, whereas in gray ecology the banal is made supremely useful, necessarily so.

From his remarks on art, Schelling notes, "Sculpture is the perfected informing of the infinite into the finite"[12] and "the indifference of divine natures" and "a deity into itself" and the

---

[10] Schelling, *The Grounding of Positive Philosophy*, 209.

[11] See Jack Cohen and Ian Stewart, *The Collapse of Chaos: Discovering Simplicity in a Complex World* (New York: Viking Press, 1994).

[12] F.W.J. von Schelling, *The Philosophy of Art,* trans. Douglas Stott, (Minneapolis: University of Minnesota Press, 1989), 192.

first potency of formative arts in general and aesthetics itself.[13]
There is, in his discussion of the formation of myth, an urgency where mythology is made when there is no time for invention.[14] The churning potentiated darkness in Schelling is then
that of many pasts and that of the possibility of past, and of
another past, of myth. Myth as coming to terms with unprethinkable being.[15]

An odd example of these actualizations is in Melville's
Pierre, with the Memnon stone, or terror stone,[16] a large rock-
ing stone grown over with trees and vines, deemed wondrous
by some and a mere stumbling block to others. The stone,
along with so many cloying forms of nature, buries Pierre in
the deep past out of which which philosophy cannot dig itself.
The problem is the impossibility of actual separation alongside the apparent divisions of reflection and freedom—instead
of 'What is X?' shifting to 'How can we know X?' we are buried up to our neck in actualizations. Existence becomes: 'What
is in X that allows and disallows us to ask how can we know x
and operate on it as it operates on us, as it natures through
us?' Progress, like nature, is too intimate a catastrophe.

The Gnostic angel, appearing in its divine stature, part of
yet amputated from God, at first glance may simply re-edify
that separation which we wish to abolish. But the relation of
the observable to the unobservable is close to our own material creation as opposed to our own 'invisible ideation'—we
have the sculpted angel and the miraculous one, or the ad-
vent-angel and the pre-invented.

Rebellion requires an impertinence and not a proliferation
of bodies or identities, nor a negation of them. An imperti-

---

[13] Schelling, *The Philosophy of Art*, 195.
[14] F.W.J. von Schelling, *Historical-Critical Introduction to the
Philosophy of Mythology* (Albany: State University of New York
Press, 2007), 49.
[15] Terry Pinkard, *German Philosophy 1760-1860: The Legacy of
Idealism* (New York: Cambridge University Press, 2002), 329–30.
[16] Herman Melville, *Pierre or The Ambiguities* (New York: Penguin
Books, 1996), 132.

nence against the hierarchical tallying of Aquinas, of divinities and not part of the One divine. Is then the angelic the occasional cause of transcendence where demonology is the method of cloning energetic demons, two manners of the absolute?

The mute side of stonework, which is imparted with the timely necessity of mythology, is the heavenly ascent of architecture. It is being, as ground, extended upwards. Stone, as it is used in religious architecture particularly, functions as a recapitulation of Schelling's proper primordial being.[17] The tension of the primordial and the divine separates thinking from the ground, but this does not mean the only response to the clawing immanence of nature is the hastened dissolution of the architectural. Rather, the architectural, as DeLanda's hardened exoskeleton or mineralization shows, requires an infectious softening. The confluence of divinity and raw nature can be seen in the barbarism of Benjamin's Angel of History's horror show, partially in advance, as the ecological equivalent of the run of history. Architecture merely accelerates the clutter the further it is from the baseness of stone.

* * *

Like Professor Lidenbrock, who took his nephew up the steeple to impart vertigo lessons in *Journey to the Center of the Earth*, the dizzying height of structures mirrors the perilous and productive bowels of the earth itself.

Naturephilosophie functions as Enceladus, as the self-contesting and titanic vulcanism, which the positive philosophy can shroud but not destroy, and we cannot but realize that nature, even in its seeming deadness, is the construct of all that is deemed unnatural. The supernaturalness of the angel is the possibility of fulfilled futurity where the demonological, or as Schelling puts it, a spirit (and not the spiritual) ventriloquizes the apparent deadness of the present, in the inor-

---

[17] Schelling, "Stuttgart Seminars," 199.

ganic or demon-as-stone—an old curse but one that is sculptable.

If both are needed for a rebellious world thought, but not quarantined by thought, a great Outdoors (both voluminous above and clustered below) is found in the medieval taxonomies of being to which Schelling is an odd and futuristic stepping stone.

Abstraction and Value
The Medieval Origins of Financial
Quantification

Nick Srnicek

We live in an era plagued by the debilitating fallout of financial implosion. By now credit default swaps, collateralized debt obligations, options, futures, and other "financial weapons of mass destruction" have all entered into the common lexicon. While the economically speculative nature of finance is abundantly clear, the philosophically speculative nature of finance is less well recognized. Perhaps surprisingly, it is in finance that we find the purest attempt at the quantification of all available material, to an extent conceivably greater than even modern natural science. Empirical and non-empirical, actual and possible, order and chaos—all are available for measurement and calculation within the algorithms of modern financial models.

One of the primary hypotheses of this paper is that when we examine the history of finance what we see is a leading edge of quantification in the world. This quantification program consists of development in three separate areas: measurement, the application of numbers, and calculation.[1] Stand-

---

[1] Measurement need not require numbers, as phrases like "more" and "larger" suggest. Similarly, the application of numbers need not require measurement, as ordinal series demonstrate. Calculation can

ard histories of modern finance have presupposed the first two aspects and focused solely on the development of the third, which occurred almost entirely in the twentieth century.[2] Yet to cognize the worldview that modern finance embodies, one needs to understand the development of the first two aspects as well. It is in the late medieval era, with the first inklings of the quantification program that will become modern science, where we can discern the origins of financial quantification. This period is significant because it is the first time where finance and quantification start to resonate together and develop along a parallel path. Financial products like options and futures had existed in some form prior to the thirteenth and fourteenth centuries, but it was the emergence of quantification in the late medieval period that would definitively change the nature of finance.

In part, the aim is to situate the current economic crisis in a wider historical perspective. This is a step undertaken by Marxist analyses as well, which view the process of financialization as a cyclical phenomenon repeating over long centuries.[3] The historical take here, however, aims to set financialization within a properly philosophical viewpoint that sees it as the culmination of a project bordering on a *mathesis universalis*. Finance, it is argued, is of interest to philosophy independently of its recent devastating effects. To fully understand this shift resulting from the linkage between finance and quantification, it is necessary first to return to the pre-quantitative era of the late medieval period.

---

exist without measurement (as the entire pre-scientific history of quantification shows), but it arguably requires the use of numbers as a precondition.

[2] Peter L. Bernstein, *Capital Ideas: The Improbable Origins of Modern Wall Street* (Hoboken: John Wiley & Sons, 2005).

[3] The classic reference here is Giovanni Arrighi, *The Long Twentieth Century: Money, Power, and the Origins of Our Times* (London: Verso Books, 2009).

§ MEDIEVAL STATE OF QUANTIFICATION

For medieval Europeans, everyday existence was an almost entirely qualitative world—space could be demarcated according to qualities like cold and warm for North and South; time was considered qualitatively different between periods;[4] and even recipes spoke vaguely of "medium-sized portions" and "a bit more."[5] Quantification was not unheard of, but it largely resided in loose theoretical quantification, rather than rigorous empirical measurements. There were declarations that numbers were crucial to understanding the order of being, but as late as the thirteenth century, physics had few measurements and few calculations, there were no quantified procedures, and no rigorously quantified concepts available.[6] The thirteenth and fourteenth centuries saw a proliferation of work done on the quantifying of physics concepts, yet this mathematical schema was derived from intuition and abstract reasoning, rather than from measurement of empirical reality.[7] This was the emergence of a theoretical quantification, but without a corresponding quantification of reality and measurement.

Yet by the sixteenth century, a revolution in thought had occurred and a quantified vision of the world had become standard for the educated classes. Various explanations of this shift have been given, though they tend to presuppose a smooth shift from the Aristotelian qualitative view of the world to the mathematical stratification of reality. Two explanations in particular are common within the literature.

---

[4] This conception of time also helped explain how people could live to be hundreds of years old in the Bible.

[5] Alfred Crosby, *The Measure of Reality: Quantification and Western Society, 1250-1600* (Cambridge: Cambridge University Press, 1997), 27–40.

[6] Alistair Cameron Crombie, "Quantification in Medieval Physics," in *Change in Medieval Society*, ed. Sylvia Thrupp (Toronto: University of Toronto Press, 1988), 190.

[7] Crombie, "Quantification in Medieval Physics," 201.

First, there are those who see it as a matter of developing the means of cognition. The traditional Roman numerals in use were unwieldy for large numbers and anything more than basic arithmetic.[8] At the time, calculation was sometimes done through an elaborate and inefficient system of counting using finger gestures.[9] The arrival of Hindu-Arabic numerals, first through the universities and eventually through the merchant classes, made it much simpler to perform mathematical calculations.[10] Similarly, the spread of the abacus and counting board made long calculations possible for the first time. Yet these technical shifts in the means of cognition leave aside the conceptual shift required for thinking of the world itself in quantitative terms.

A second explanation focuses on the practical pressures for increased quantification. In particular, the need in the emerging commercial society for some way of calculating profit and keeping track of inventory. In this more Marxist explanation, economic needs dictated the construction of new methods of calculation, and new measuring instruments. The textbooks of arithmetic and emerging algebra in the thirteenth to fifteenth centuries support this thesis; they were dominated by problems concerning trading and other commercial activities. By the end of the fifteenth century, the majority of mathematical works applied their ideas to economic problems.[11] But this explanation doesn't account for why these social needs were resolved in a specifically quantitative manner.

The uniqueness of quantification at the time was that it requires and inaugurates a level of abstraction away from immediate phenomenal experience. It requires, first, the projec-

---

[8] Crosby, *The Measure of Reality*, 41.

[9] Crosby, *The Measure of Reality*, 41–42.

[10] Crosby, *The Measure of Reality,* 62–63.

[11] Richard Hadden, *On the Shoulders of Merchants: Exchange and the Mathematical Conception of Nature in Early Modern Europe* (Albany: SUNY Press, 1994), 119–23. See also Frank Swetz, *Capitalism & Arithmetic: The New Math of the 15th Century* (La Salle: Open Court Publishing, 1987), 34–35.

tion of a homogeneous reality commensurable with measurement. If qualities and substances are heterogeneous, there can be no common measure to apply to them. What is necessary is a reduction of quality to quantity. Secondly, quantification requires an abstract scale with which to measure reality against. There is a double movement of abstraction – both the construction of a grid of reference, and an abstraction from the particularities of phenomenal reality. Neither of the two explanations given provides answers to these problems. To properly explain the quantitative revolution in thought, it is necessary to situate it within the social and economic context of the time.

§ THE MEDIEVAL ECONOMY

The eleventh and twelfth centuries had seen the integration of most of Europe into a system of exchange, and by the end of the thirteenth century, Europe and China had been linked together, forming the first proper world economic system.[12] This economic system spanned from northwestern Europe to the coasts of China, and hinged upon the Middle East as a passage for trade. It was comprised of a series of overlapping regional systems, and the entire network presupposed surplus products being available within domestic economies for shipment abroad. In turn, this surplus was premised upon a reasonably advanced economic system one which contained the seeds of modern capitalism.[13] Already, by the thirteenth century, there existed all the formative elements of capitalism: the wage-relation,[14] the commodity-form,[15] the proliferation of exchange, interest-bearing capital, and money as an emerg-

---

[12] Janet Abu-Lughod, *Before European Hegemony: The World System A.D. 1250-1350* (Oxford: Oxford University Press, 1989), 3.

[13] Michael Mann, *The Sources of Social Power, Vol. 1: A History of Power from the Beginning to A.D. 1760* (New York: Cambridge University Press, 1986), 435.

[14] Mann, *The Sources of Social Power*, 389–90.

[15] Mann, *The Sources of Social Power*, 398–99.

ing universal equivalent. For our purposes here, exchange relations and the emergence of money as a universal equivalent are the most important elements to consider.

In the first place, while the village and the manor continued to dominate local economic networks for some time, it was the exchange relations between towns, fairs and merchants that created the extensive economic networks across Europe and further.[16] By 1000 AD there was already an extensive trading network internal to Europe, passing from the northwestern corner into the southwestern Mediterranean region. This was a largely decentralized network, situated outside of the main states' control, but also underpinned by a common sense of values and norms provided by Christianity.[17] This proliferation of exchange relations made the emerging market economy a common, if still limited, phenomenon. The expansive spread of exchange also shaped local economies, imposing a division of labor between regions. Economies were by now beginning to move from a subsistence economy to one premised upon comparative advantages.

By this time, the economies of Europe were also well acquainted with the idea of money. The eleventh century saw the region of Italy become monetized, and by the twelfth and thirteenth centuries Britain and France had as well.[18] While

---

[16] Abu-Lughod, *Before European Hegemony*, 66–67. See also Mann, *The Sources of Social Power*, 394.

[17] Mann, *The Sources of Social Power*, 409.

[18] Joel Kaye, *Economy and Nature in the Fourteenth Century: Money, Market Exchange, and the Emergence of Scientific Thought* (Cambridge: Cambridge University Press, 2004) 16. Money appears to have arisen first in the Middle East, with Europe being a relatively late adopter (see Abu-Lughod, *Before European Hegemony*, 15.) Similarly, China, with its strong state, had the ability to produce paper money and guarantee its worth as early as the ninth century— centuries before Europe ever did. There is a clear instance here whereby money represents not some intrinsic value, but is instead a socially determined measure of value. This raises the question that further research would have to answer—namely, why did these

money has many functions, social and economic, of interest here is its function as a universal equivalent. In this function, money separates exchange value from the use value of particular commodities, and acts as an equivalent to any other commodity.[19] As Marx argues, the tension between use and exchange value within the commodity propels the search for an independent expression of value.[20] Money is the fulfillment of this search as an internal development of the commodity. But money never appears as such. To all physical appearances of course, money is just a piece of paper or some other material quality.

Economies were therefore increasingly dominated by commodity-exchange, and money was beginning to populate Europe in the late medieval era. Yet in establishing the relationship between the emerging market economies of this time, with the rise of quantification, we need to be able to determine the precise link for such thinking.

§ THE REAL ABSTRACTION OF COMMODITY EXCHANGE

Crucial here is Alfred Sohn-Rethel's work on real abstractions. According to Sohn-Rethel, the exchange of commodities is in reality an act of abstraction, even though it does not first appear as such to individual traders.[21] The act of exchange requires abstracting away from the physical qualities and use values of particular commodities, thus making heterogeneous

---

mathematical advances occur in Europe at a particular time, and not earlier in Muslim or Chinese areas? Or perhaps they did, but have gone unrecognized so far. Both these cases highlight questions that cannot be answered in the present discussion, but a comparative analysis of these areas and their mathematical development would be immensely fruitful for solidifying the notion of real abstraction.

[19] Alfred Sohn-Rethel, *Intellectual and Manual Labour: A Critique of Epistemology* (London: The Macmillan Press, 1978), 6.

[20] Karl Marx, *Capital, Vol. 1: A Critique of Political Economy*, trans. Ben Fowkes (Harmondsworth: Penguin Books, 1976), 181.

[21] Sohn-Rethel, *Intellectual and Manual Labour*, 26-27.

entities equivalent. What is named 'value' is simply this abstract equivalency that exists in reality without being actual. It is important to note that all of this happens outside of the mind of the participants. As Sohn-Rethel says, heterogeneous commodities "are equated by virtue of being exchanged, they are not exchanged by virtue of any equality which they possess."[22]

It is this abstraction within the act that Sohn-Rethel demonstrates provides the template for conceptual abstraction. The emergence of philosophy as the science of general concepts, and the exchange of commodities in the world, are intimately intertwined. The real abstractions of Greek coinage are mirrored by the conceptual abstractions of Parmenides. Similarly, he argues that Galileo's principle of inertia was formulated on the basis of the exchange abstraction.[23] It is the exchange relation that provides the phenomenal material for conceptual abstraction.

Yet while justifying the formal conceptual abstractions necessary for modern science, Sohn-Rethel leaves aside the content of modern science.[24] How and why did it take on a revolutionarily quantitative and mathematical content in the thirteenth and fourteenth centuries? If cognitive possibilities are constrained and made possible by the materiality of society, what changed to produce the revolution that brought about modern science? What made possible the quantification of reality?

---

[22] Sohn-Rethel, *Intellectual and Manual Labour*, 46.

[23] Sohn-Rethel, *Intellectual and Manual Labour*, 128.

[24] See Hadden, *On the Shoulders of Merchants*, 15. Sohn-Rethel's notion (and criticisms) of modern science also rely problematically on a strict separation between manual and intellectual labour. While intuitive to the public idea of science, such a separation breaks down when the practices of scientists are observed in action. For instance, see Bruno Latour, *Pandora's Hope: Essays on the Reality of Science Studies* (Cambridge, Mass.: Harvard University Press, 1999).

§ THE IDEAL ABSTRACTION OF VALUE AND NUMBER

The shift from a qualitative to quantitative world faced major conceptual hurdles to what numbers could be applied to. In particular, there were two conceptual restraints: first, heterogeneous substances were considered incommensurable; and second, number and magnitude had been conceptually separated since ancient times. The result was that there was no conception of general magnitude that could allow for the production of an abstract space for measurement and quantification.

The major conceptual hindrance was the separation of number and magnitude. After the Pythagoreans had encountered irrational ratios, these two notions had been separated as a way of overcoming conceptual contradictions.[25] Henceforth, for ancient mathematics multitude was that in virtue of which entities of the same kind could be compared, whereas number was multiples of a given unit. 'One' itself was not a number, however, since number was intrinsically multiple and one was indivisible into parts. On the one hand then, there was the continuity of magnitude, while on the other hand, there was the discreteness of number based upon multiples of one.[26]

The result was twofold. First, the separation of these concepts made magnitudes intrinsically unquantifiable. Magnitude was considered continuous and incapable of being represented by discrete numbers. Secondly, numbers could only apply to objects of the same kind, and became meaningless when compared across different substances. The numbers for each kind were ontologically grounded upon a different unit, making commensurability between them impossible. Heterogeneous forces were not compared against each other: time was compared with time, distance with distance, etc. The advance of modern mathematics was to abstract from the differ-

---

[25] Hadden, *On the Shoulders of Merchants*, 68–69.
[26] Hadden, *On the Shoulders of Merchants*, 70–71.

ent kinds of number and elaborate a general notion of number. On the basis of this, science could make equivalent these heterogeneous forces, thereby allowing the construction of mathematical equations to precisely state their relations.[27] Combinations of weight, force and speed were now thinkable. Similarly, overcoming the divide between magnitude and number allowed for the quantification of magnitude and the construction of the idea of general magnitude.

What was needed for ancient mathematics to transition to modern mathematics, with the latter's conception of general magnitude and an ontologically unproblematic concept of number, was a revolution in thought. What was required was an ideal abstraction from the particularities of individual entities.

Crucially, the materialist preconditions for this revolution were already available in the emerging centrality of commodity production and exchange relations. As Sohn-Rethel notes,

> The act of exchange has to be described as *abstract movement through abstract (homogenous, continuous, and empty) space and time of abstract substances (materially real but bare of sense-qualities) which thereby suffer no material change and which allow for none but quantitative differentiation (differentiation in abstract, non-dimensional quantity).*[28]

In other words, commodity exchange produces what Sohn-Rethel will elsewhere call an 'abstract nature.'[29]

What distinguished the late medieval era and why the mathematical conception of the world came to emerge at this time, was the working through of commercial problems using mathematical writings. The transition from the implicit practices involved in this real abstraction to the 'making explicit'

---

[27] Hadden, *On the Shoulders of* Merchants, 64.

[28] Sohn-Rethel, *Intellectual and Manual Labour*, 53.

[29] Sohn-Rethel, *Intellectual and Manual* Labour, 57.

of such logical spaces and their subsequent application to nature, took place primarily through the medium of mathematical treatises and textbooks. As Richard Hadden has demonstrated, in the late medieval period mathematicians were invariably concerned with calculating economic problems.[30] Without realizing it, these thinkers were calculating in practice on the basis of abstractions that would eventually form the same abstract space necessary for mathematizing nature. Without an explicit acknowledgement of it, these mathematicians were ignoring the division between magnitude and number, and ignoring the incommensurability between kinds of number. To a degree greater than ever before, it was simply a phenomenological given for these mathematicians that such postulates of ancient mathematics were no longer operative.

Eventually, these unconscious habits of thought, formed in the calculating of real abstractions involved in exchange, made their way into their perceptions of nature itself. Value, as the equivalency between different commodities is imperceptible. And as Hadden argues,

> Similarly body, pure matter, is imperceptible as such. The reckoning of the motion and effect of units of this substance demands a similar abstraction and homogenization of otherwise discretely perceptible properties of things.[31]

With the slow explication of implicit practices, the abstract nature of commodity exchange took hold and produced an abstract nature of bodies in motion. A non-empirical substrate for the world had been constructed. It was on the basis of this that the early moderns like Galileo, Descartes and Newton could begin to think of reality as a quantifiable, homogeneous and abstract space upon which to establish modern science.

---

[30] Hadden, *On the Shoulders of Merchants*, 83–114.
[31] Hadden, *On the Shoulders of Merchants*, 45.

§ GENESIS OF FINANCIAL QUANTIFICATION

Significantly for our purposes though, this advance in quantification was not based on finance but rather on the calculations involved in commercial trade. The medieval state of finance remained largely ad hoc and unquantified. At best, interest was calculated on various loans and debts, but this re-
lied only on basic arithmetic and was predominantly subject
to the whims of moral and legal arguments rather than any
sort of quantitative reason.[32] When interest was paid, it was
typically paid through the same substance that had been lent
out. Repayment was given "in kind"[33] for most of history, or
eventually through money (though money understood as a
means of exchange and not as self-generating capital). Medieval finance also neglected any numerical distinguishing of
maturities on loans beyond a basic ambiguous distinction
between short-term and long-term.[34]

Similarly, while options and futures had existed even during Aristotle's time, there was no market for such items and
no procedure for pricing them. A number was affixed to these
entities, but based on qualitative reason rather than quantitative calculation. As Joel Kaye argues, the basic problem was
this:

> Since [the lender's] profit is in the future he has no way
> of making a rational decision as to whether or how
> much he will benefit from the [lending], and both

[32] Kaye, *Economy and Nature in the Fourteenth Century*, 80–87. The
earliest known written laws were Sumerian and included precise
limits on how much interest could be charged on loans. See Sidney
Homer and Richard Sylla, *A History of Interest Rates,* 4th edn.
(Hoboken: John Wiley & Sons, 2005), Kindle Location 372–78.

[33] The term "in kind" has remained with us in the present era, and
suggests the historical separation of different kinds of substances,
values and magnitudes.

[34] Homer and Sylla, *A History of Interest Rates*, Kindle Location 276–
85.

equality and rationality are essential to proper, non-usurious economic transactions.[35]

What was necessary for financial—as opposed to commercial—quantification to arise was the ability to quantify and price the future itself. Finance being intrinsically temporal, this was a necessary condition. To my knowledge, the first act of making explicit a quantifiable commensurability between the present and the future is in the work of Peter John Olivi.[36] The crucial step of this shift was Olivi's argument for the reality of probability in issues of pricing.[37] Importantly, Olivi based this argument on his claim to be rationally transcribing existing economic practices. Since merchants already estimated a discounted real value to the probability of future profits, Olivi considered that in practice merchants were therefore implicitly giving reality to probability and future value. Despite the largely qualitative justification of pricing interest rates on loans, merchants were nevertheless suggesting in their actions the potential to quantify future value and probability. It was a form of quantification without metrology, or an application of numbers without measurement or calculation. Instead of the real abstraction of commodity exchange, what was taking place was the real abstraction of discounting future profits – an abstraction as crucial to capitalism as exchange. Present and future values were being made commensurable in a real abstraction that discounted future profits. On the basis of this practice, Olivi would go on to argue that the moral necessity of equality between capital lent out and capital returned was based not simply on an arithmetical calculation as had previously been thought. Rather, the equality of future value with present value was a geometrical concern, with a degree of lati-

---

[35] Kaye, *Economy and Nature in the Fourteenth Century*, 120.

[36] Olivi's work was spread primarily through the sermons of St. Bernadino of Siena, who often took directly from Olivi's writings without referencing them. See Kaye, *Economy and Nature in the Fourteenth Century*, 118.

[37] Kaye, *Economy and Nature in the Fourteenth Century*, 121.

tude given to randomness and the intrinsically probabilistic nature of the future.[38] Implicit here already is the geometrical diagrams of derivative pricing that will come to proliferate in today's financial world. With Olivi then, the idea of rationally justifying and quantifying future value and probability comes to be explicitly posed for the first time.

By the end of the medieval period, therefore, three components of modern financial quantification were in place. First, the idea of an abstract, homogeneous, quantifiable substrate situated behind otherwise incommensurable particulars. Second, the subsequent belief that anything could be quantified, even subjective orientations. Third, the emerging quantification of probability and future value. Both measurement and the application of numbers had been accomplished, if only in rough form. What was primarily missing was a rational means to determine the precise quantifications—that is to say, a means of calculation—and it was developments internal to mathematics that eventually brought this about.

§ THE METAPHYSICAL ABSTRACTION OF MODERN FINANCE

As these subsequent developments have been well cited by others, a schematic overview is all that is necessary here. Two aspects are particularly important: the calculation of randomness, and the calculation of a rational rate of return for risk. The first was carried out by an early French mathematician, Louis Bachelier. In his 1900 doctoral thesis, Bachelier was the first to model stochastic processes by focusing on stock price changes and their random fluctuations.[39] This provided the mathematical tools to quantify, and hence price, randomness itself. The second important step was carried out by William

---

[38] Kaye, *Economy and Nature in the Fourteenth Century*, 124.

[39] Louis Bachelier, "Theory of Speculation," in *Louis Bachelier's Theory of Speculation: The Origins of Modern Finance*, eds. Mark Davis and Alison Etheridge (Princeton: Princeton University Press, 2006), 117–182.

Sharpe and his capital asset pricing model (CAPM). On the basis of this model, it became possible to rationally relate risk to return, and to calculate a universal price for individual securities. The effect of both of these advances was to effectively make time and risk calculable in monetary terms.

These two advances were then synthesized by Fisher Black, Myron Scholes and Robert Merton in what came to be known as the Black-Scholes-Merton (BSM) equation. Combining the calculation of randomness with the calculation of a rational rate of return, the BSM equation allowed the rational pricing of options, futures, and eventually other derivatives.[40] This was an objective price in the precise Kantian sense that it presented a universally applicable condition for cognizing the price of a derivative. A materialist condition of quantification, to be sure, but one that nevertheless produced an objective value.

But despite the intended use of BSM to price derivatives, in practice traders have taken to using the models in a radically different way. Rather than derive a theoretical price, traders gradually began to use the equations to derive the "implied volatility"—meaning the level of variation that a security's price is expected to undergo. That is to say, the Black-Scholes-Merton equation was being reversed—given the market price, what level of volatility will solve the equation? The reason for this shift was the conceptual simplification that volatility brought about. As a theoretically produced entity, volatility managed to act as a common denominator behind the multiplicity of derivatives, strikes, maturities, and sectors. Quoting derivatives in terms of volatility rather than price allows traders to efficiently determine whether a derivative is mispriced and how it may be used to hedge their own position. Volatility quickly became the language of traders. While money was

---

[40] The adjective "rational" is apt, as even Merton's Nobel prize-winning paper was called "Theory of Rational Option Pricing." See Robert Merton, "Theory of Rational Option Pricing," *The Bell Journal of Economics and Management Science* 4.1 (1973): 141–83.

conceptualized by Marx as a general equivalent that manages to bring together otherwise heterogeneous commodities, in volatility we find an even more encompassing general equivalent. Price, for derivatives traders, was still too relative to time (i.e. maturity) and possibility (i.e. strike price). What was needed was an abstract equivalent that could make comparisons easy to accomplish between price, time, risk and possibility. Volatility came to serve this purpose, taking the abstractions of value even further than commodity exchange.

Metaphysically, therefore, with derivative valuations we have two expansions of real abstraction. First, the production of this general equivalent beyond money. This sort of valuation is not the pricing of a commodity, but rather the measuring of a possibility on that entity (or event). It is a further step beyond even the actual commodity itself. It is possibility itself, with all its temporal qualities which is being quantified and made comparable by virtue of financial models. Implied volatility is the measure of different currencies, different probabilities, different futures, and different time periods. Much like the medieval period saw the emergence of commodity traders in practice equating incommensurable commodities, today we see derivatives traders in practice equating incommensurable metaphysical aspects.

This leads us to the second expansion of contemporary abstraction: the world of derivative valuation has produced not merely a new measure, but an entire new abstract space. While there are independent valuation models for every asset class, and even independent models within asset classes, there is nevertheless a synthesizing function in the form of the no-arbitrage rule.[41] This fundamental rule of modern finance states that disproportionate rates of return on assets (adjusted for their risk) will have only a momentary existence. Risk-free profit opportunities will inevitably be arbitraged away, leaving

---

[41] Nassim Nicholas Taleb, "Foreword," in *The Volatility Surface: A Practitioner's Guide*, ed. Jim Gatheral (Hoboken: John Wiley & Sons, 2006), xxii.

only a smooth series of market prices consistent amongst all asset classes. There are, in other words, no irreducible gaps in the abstract space of derivative valuation. There is a common measure in volatility, and there is an equilibrium function in the no-arbitrage principle.

Three conclusions can be drawn from this sociological analysis so far: first, that there has been a positive feedback loop between the development of mathematics and the development of finance. Each reaches further into abstractions on the basis of developments in the other. The real abstraction of commodity exchange forms the conditions for the ideal abstractions of mathematical thought, which in turn make possible the metaphysical abstractions of modern finance.[42] For its part, modern finance draws upon the pure mathematics of stochastic calculus and probability theory in order to further develop valuation models. But whereas quantification originally arose out of social relations in the medieval era, today financial quantification has its own relative autonomy to shape the social relations of everyday life. The real abstractions of modern finance are abstractions of abstractions— what might be termed derivative abstractions. It is the internal developments of mathematics and finance that have led to the present situation of near total quantification.

This leads to the second conclusion: In conjunction with the historical analysis provided by Marxism, therefore, the historical analysis offered here gives new shape to the cyclical rhythms of financialization that periodically overcome capitalism. Rather than a mere repetition of past periods, there is also a progressive linear phenomenon as the quantification

---

[42] We can somewhat arbitrarily date the origins of the full resonance between quantification and finance to 1981, the year of the publication of what was arguably the first truly mathematical finance paper—that is to say, a piece that contained absolutely no economic concepts that were not formulated in mathematical terms. See Mark Davis and Alison Etheridge, "From Bachelier to Kreps, Harrison and Pliska," in *Louis Bachelier's Theory of* Speculation, eds. Davis and Etheridge, 114.

carried out by finance reaches new heights and incorporates new domains. What should be expected is that as finance progressively ties together new assets into its field of quantification, that the effects of financial crises will be correspondingly greater and have wider ramifications. This is not just a spatial expansion, as theories of global capitalism would suggest,[43] but rather a temporal and metaphysical expansion.

The third conclusion to be drawn from this analysis is that we can now give precise meaning to claims that modern day finance is abstract. It is abstract, yes, but not just in the sense of appearing separate from commodity production. It is more importantly abstract in the practices of the traders who everyday make time, currencies, possibilities and risk commensurable through their actions. If Marxist epistemology is to take seriously the materialist conditions for cognition, then finance today appears to be the cutting edge of this development.

§ FINANCIAL ABSTRACTION AND CRITIQUE

In conclusion, I will all too briefly try and raise the question of finance's possible limits. As with the spatial and resource limits of capitalist expansion, is there also a metaphysical limit? This is perhaps the crucial political import of Elie Ayache's work.[44] A former options trader and creator of financial models himself, Ayache's argument draws on Quentin Meillassoux's work on contingency in order to formulate precisely what eludes the financial quantification program. In the everyday activities of a trader using financial models, for Ayache the most metaphysically important is that of re-calibration. That is to say, taking the models and using them to reverse-

---

[43] For the classic statement of capitalism's intrinsic requirements to expand spatially, see David Harvey, *The Limits to Capital* (New York: Verso, 2006).

[44] Elie Ayache, *The Blank Swan: The End of Probability* (Hoboken: John Wiley & Sons, 2010).

engineer the level of volatility from the given market prices. This act reconfigures the set of possibilities used in the models, as the level of volatility changes. The practical requirement to re-calibrate demonstrates, first, the incapacity of even the most sophisticated models to price the future. There can be no absolute quantification of time, as not even the most monstrous probability distributions are capable of encompassing contingency itself. Secondly, it also necessitates a perspective shift—from a perspective internal to quantification, to a perspective internal to what Ayache (perhaps unfortunately) calls the 'market.' The former position sees contingency as a mere external irruption of chance, whereas the latter sees quantification as itself derivative to the fundamental field of contingency. In fact, contrary to those who see Ayache's work as an unwitting indictment of modern finance, the argument here is that Ayache is in fact the first to rigorously demonstrate the limits of capitalist valorization on a metaphysical level. There is necessarily something incommensurable to financial quantification, and this space is in fact the immanent origin that quantification regimes merely try to stratify after the event. From its empirical origins in medieval practices to its metaphysical culmination in derivatives valuation models, financial quantification demonstrates its own separation from being-in-itself.

Srnicek's Risk
Response to Nick Srnicek

Michael O'Rourke

In an August 2009 interview with Paul Ennis at *Another Heidegger Blog* Nick Srnicek, speculative heretic that he is, quite rightly asserts that, "Speculative Realism doesn't label a single set of positions" because "the four main contributors [Graham Harman, Quentin Meillassoux, Iain Hamilton Grant, Ray Brassier] to it are all vastly different, and there really is no common ground."[1] However, I want to suggest that Srnicek's work, at least in his contribution to our laboratory-atelier, "Abstraction and Value: The Medieval Origins of Financial Quantification," is closest to the critically speculative position of Meillassoux in *After Finitude*, a book which, in the same interview, Srnicek claims is "the best diagnosis of the problems with contemporary philosophy, and argued with a clarity that proves logic, surprise and wonder don't need to be mutually exclusive." Srnicek himself, at least in this interview, places his work within a post-Marxist faction of Speculative Realism which is broadly interested in and united by a common aim to reassess "agency in the light of neuroscience, eliminativism, and non-philosophy" as well as a

---

[1] Paul Ennis, "Interview with Nick Srnicek," *Another Hediegger Blog*, August 13, 2009, http://anotherheideggerblog.blogspot.com/2009/08/interview-with-nick-srnicek.html.

"focus on the concrete technical and material aspects of political economy." "Abstraction and Value," however, seems to be less obviously Latourian, or Laruellian or to have anything particularly to do with the eliminativist or non-philosophical positions we can discern in his other writing (or on his blog *The Accursed Share*).[2] Rather, Srnicek's basic post-Marxist thesis, the one advanced here, that the world political system is moving toward a more medieval type of political system depends—among other things—on a speculatively financial reading of Elie Ayache's reading of Meillassoux's *After Finitude*[3] in *The Blank Swan: The End of Probability*[4] to try to articulate what this different economic system will *do* to a medieval political system. What we have here is a sort of critically speculative, post-Marxist understanding of the economy. This is his risk.[5] And Ayache describes for us what this kind of creative political work might look like, might *do* in *The Blank Swan*:

> By travelling across the world with the necessity of contingency in our hand, we may verify no possibility and no necessity: we make the world *work*, we make *market* of the world, we make work, not state of the world; we exchange its unexchangeability against the unexchangeability of writing; we exceed it; we become at once posterior and original in it. We instate another

[2] See *The Accursed Share* [weblog], http://accursedshare.blogspot.com.

[3] Quentin Meillassoux, *After Finitude: An Essay on the Necessity of Contingency*, trans. Ray Brassier (London: Continuum, 2008).

[4] Elie Ayache, *The Blank Swan: The End of Probability* (Chichester: John Wiley & Sons, 2010), hereafter cited parenthetically by page number.

[5] This is by no means his only risk. Srnicek is not a medievalist so entering into this conversation with medievalists is an adventure, a risk, a set of speculations. And there is risk on both sides. In responding to him I take a double risk as someone who is neither a medievalist nor well versed in financial theory.

order of thought in it. We price it. (193)

And this is what Srnicek does: he instates "another order of thought." When Ennis asks Srnicek during their interview to ruminate upon potential future turns Speculative Realism might take, he responds that "the uptake of SR by other disciplines—notably animal studies [Donna Haraway], ecology [Timothy Morton], and even videogame studies [Ian Bogost]" potentializes the development of speculative realist splinter groups or collectivities within those very disciplines. But, what will possibly have surprised others, perhaps even Srnicek himself, is the impact on Speculative Realist thinking (or what Ennis has more recently called the "culture" of Speculative Realism[6]) of what Reza Negarestani has dubbed the two most "weaponized books" of 2010: *Re-Imagining War in the 21st Century: From Clausewitz to Network-Centric Warfare* by Manabrata Guha and *The Blank Swan: The End of Probability* by Elie Ayache who "has made a groundbreaking connection between metaphysics of contingency and the financial market."[7] Both books, Negarestani explains, "develop their analyses against the dominantly ideological and perhaps even superstitious backdrops of their respective fields, military/security studies [Guha] and finance [Ayache]. Ayache launches an elaborate assault on market-oriented ideologies and probabilistic philosophies."

My response to Srnicek's article will assess some of the overlaps between his own "weaponized" speculative financial thought and the speculative materialist thinking of Meillassoux and the radical speculation of Ayache, with whom Srnicek shares an emphasis on mathematics, metaphysics, price and so on. I am imagining, or staging, a kind of

[6] Paul Ennis, "The Speculative Terrain," *Academia.edu*, http://ucd-ie.academia.edu/PaulJohnEnnis/Papers/380565/The_Speculative_Terrain.

[7] Reza Negarestani, "Books of 2010," *Eliminative Culinarism*, http://blog.urbanomic.com/cyclon/archives/2010/08/index.html.

Pardoner's Tale—and Chaucer's text is precisely concerned with issues to do with gambling, money, conversion, the trader's body—with Srnicek, Meillassoux and Ayache (whatever the differences might be between the three) as the main protagonists. Trading, risk and adventuring are words which are familiar to the philosophy of finance even if, as Srnicek points out "the philosophically speculative nature of finance" is much less "well recognized." And Ayache illuminates the theatrical dimension to this: "The philosopher redeems his debt to philosophy and to the absolute, the circle of philosophical credit is closed and everybody goes home. By contrast, a true speculator never stops and his thought never stops differentiating. He is a revolutionary in Badiou's sense" (150). Srnicek's weaponized response to the "financial implosion" which takes a number of risks in speculative thought (a thought which ought not to be" teleological" and never to be made "thematic" according to Ayache [151]) retains only the ideas of "risk and differentiation."

The broad history of financial quantification which Srnicek sketches here begins from the medieval period and he argues that "it was the emergence of quantification in the late medieval period which would definitively change the nature of finance." Ayache would call this a rotation or a futural cut (we might even say a N/nick in time) which is how he refers to Meillassoux's "passage to the future" (152). However, Srnicek's stated aim, an adventurous one, is to "situate the current economic crisis in a wider historical perspective" than *The Blank Swan* can hope to do. (Ayache himself picks up on the word adventurous in Meillassoux's *After Finitude*: "The word adventurous holds my attention because of its obvious risky connotation and the faint suggestion that the missing speculative piece might not be found in the world or in its past but *in its future*" [147].)

To quickly run through Srnicek's historical picture we can repeat his assertions that: (a) "By the sixteenth century, a quantified vision of the world had become standard"; (b) "Quantification requires and inaugurates a level of abstraction away from immediate phenomenal experience" as well as "an abstract scale with which to measure reality against"; and (c) "Already, by the thirteenth century, there existed all the formative elements of capitalism," the "proliferation of exchange" and "money as an emerging universal equivalent" being the most pertinent examples (he notes, however, that "Money never appears as such": it is not phenomenalizable).

The rotation or the piece that has been missing is this: "What was necessary for financial—as opposed to commercial—quantification to arise was the ability to quantify and *price* the *future* itself." Further, he claims that, "What was primarily missing was a rational means to determine the precise quantifications—that is to say, a means of calculation—and it was developments internal to mathematics which eventually brought this about." In Part II of Ayache's *The Blank Swan*, "Absolute Contingency and the Return of Speculation" (123–93), we can see some similar preoccupations as he reads Meillassoux: price, futurity, absolute speculation, the necessity of contingency, and the ontologization of mathematics.

Ayache asserts that Meillassoux, with his ardent promotion of a nonmetaphysical speculation, has re-defined the term speculation which after *After Finitude* stands at a place that occupies the extreme opposite position to metaphysics and is much closer to the "pricing process" or "the writing process" or "risk." "In a word," he writes, he prices, he risks, "my claim is that speculation is regaining, at the hands of Meillassoux, its meaning from trading and risk exposure. It becomes a 'market,' the result of conversion" (144). He goes on to say later: "I believe he has redefined the word speculation, as I wonder whether to insist on speculation while insisting that speculation shall not aim at a metaphysical being does not come down, in the end, to maintaining speculation itself as *the only necessity*" (150).

Meillassoux's project is to produce a nonnegative or rather positive ontology underlying the necessity of contingency, what he calls "factial ontology"[8] and it is in mathematics and more specifically, following Badiou, in Cantor's notion of the transfinite, that Meillassoux locates this "specific positive condition guaranteeing the manifest stability of Chaos."[9] You may wonder, as Ayache does, what mathematics has got to do with this critical outpost of philosophy and it is here, Ayache explains, that Badiou's meta-ontology lends Meillassoux the support he needs: "One of Badiou's essential theses is the one in which he affirms the ontological scope of Cantor's theorem, in order to unveil the mathematical thinkability of the un-totalization of being-*qua*-being" (147).

Srnicek argues here that "it is not commodity exchange which acts as the spearhead of abstraction in today's economy, but instead a new form of quantification—derivative valu-ation" and that this derivative valuation is not "the pricing of a commodity, but rather the pricing of a possibility on that entity (or event)." Similarly, Meillassoux wants to think the absolute (speculation) and to think it *mathematically* and we cannot but be reminded of the fact that for Badiou, "ontology is nothing other than mathematics."[10] In *After Finitude* we read that, "The ontology of the enclosure of possibilities inevitably situates us within a world whose aversion to gravity is but the obverse of the fact that it only takes counting techniques seriously."[11] For Meillassoux we need to differ-entiate between frequency and gravity. For him, events *happen enough* and a philosophy of the event that recognizes its "incalculable, unpredictable" nature is the only one worthy of the name. The gravity of the history-changing event "*continues*," however, "*to be* mathematical."[12]

Meillassoux's thought, which is armed against metaphysics, has "no room for possibility" (149). Rather, the

[8] Meillassoux, *After Finitude*, 101.

[9] Meillassoux, *After Finitude*, 101.

[10] Alain Badiou, *Court Traité d'Ontologie Transitoire*, quoted in Aya-che, *The Blank Swan*, 156.

[11] Meillassoux, *After Finitude*, 108.

[12] Meillassoux, *After Finitude*, 108.

future, to which his critical speculative thought opens a passage, is what Ayache calls "the medium of contingency," not as an "index of possibility" but as what he calls the "*market*" (156, 150) (and this market, which he also terms "the space of writing," is, not unproblematically, "independent of chronological time" [127, 100]). Meillassoux's philosophy is conditioned by the Badiou-event and Meillassoux makes "the decision to embrace serious contingency, or the event" and to obtain "as a derivative consequence" of this move "the un-totalization of possibilities" (156). Srnicek's philosophy, his "*Conversion du regard*, conversion of our gaze" (Ayache, 174), is conditioned by what we might call the Quantification-event.

Srnicek writes, he prices, he risks: "On the basis of all this, the thesis here is that there has been a positive feedback loop between the development of mathematics and the development of finance. Each reaches further into abstractions on the basis of developments in the other. The real abstraction of commodity exchange makes possible the ideal abstractions of mathematical thought, which in turn make possible the metaphysical abstractions of modern finance." However, he admits that, "This near total quantification of empirical and metaphysical reality raises with urgency the question of its possible limits," and it is here, at the end of his presentation, that "the crucial political import of Elie Ayache's work" comes into play. Both Ayache and Srnicek, with their *absolutely* nonmetaphysical speculations, can agree that their shared world is "the ontologization of the necessity of contingency" (the nonnegative ontology Meillassoux was looking for), but Ayache seeks "to liberate Meillassoux's speculation *entirely from the weight of the past* and turn it entirely toward the future."

But what Srnicek's "ex-centred" (Ayache, 199) thinking (thought which falls out with the correlationist circle) seems to be arguing for is a different kind of gravity, for a feedback loop between the past and the future. By Ayache's lights, Meillassoux's explanation of the "manifest stability of laws in front of their contingency is not based on frequency but, cryptically, on gravity—not on the past, but on the future" (159). Yet, Meillassoux's own idea of radical speculation, his conception of what he calls "ex-centred" thought, in Ayache's view, is that speculation endows thought with "the power to think beyond or outside or *'out-time'* itself" (178). Critical speculation, radical speculation, absolute contingency (Meillassoux: "speculation that is exclusive of any metaphysics" [quoted in Ayache, 183]) cannot be chronological. And Srnicek highlights this very temporal problem in Ayache's work when he concludes that, "there can be no absolute quantification of time, as not even the most bizarre probability distributions are capable of encompassing contingency itself. Secondly, it also necessitates a perspective shift internal to what Ayache (perhaps unfortunately) calls the 'market'." The reason Ayache uses the word "market" is because the market is, for him, the *topos, "lieu géométrique"* (183), where Meillassoux's discourse can truly take place—the market, the medium of contingency, the mathematics of price "provides an alternative to possibility and probability and it transmits and mediates the cut, the rupture of contingency" (183). Similarly, Ayache adopts the word price because "Price is nonmetaphysical" (188). He goes on: "Price is material. Price is the thing; it is another word for 'necessity of contingency' . . . price is what exchanges the unexchange-ability of the world." Yet, coming back to the temporal knot, Ayache also says that "Absolute speculation now *embeds* contingency" and is the expression of absolute risk, "the continuous trading of thought" (181). Absolute speculation is "*without end*, and for this reason it literally takes place after the end, or after finitude" (181). Further, it "steps beyond the ending . . . beyond the end of metaphysics for the obvious anti-metaphysical reasons, but it also steps beyond the ending of the correlational discourse for anti-critical reasons—it exchanges the ending for *an end that can start*" (181). Absolute speculation is both *before* and *after* the end, turned entirely toward the past *and* the future.

Srnicek ends, or starts, with the bold claim that Ayache "is in fact the first to rigorously demonstrate the limits of capitalist valorization on a metaphysical level." We might also say that Srnicek is the first to rigorously demonstrate *the history* which pushes at the limits of capitalist valorization on a metaphysical level in both the past *and* the future. And if Srnicek is the Pardoner (and I am not saying he is a charlatan purveyor of false relics) in my theatrical unfolding, then "what I am saying is that the thought of absolute contingency, especially when it concerns the material world, is not materially tenable unless the trader's body (who has precisely got his body, this interval and instrument of exchange, as an advantage over the metaphysician) is thrown into the exchange" (Ayache, 190). In thinking "contingency as absolute with regard to the material world" (Ayache, 190), Srnicek is *thrown into the exchange*. And, if Meillassoux's speculation can only be meaningful, for Ayache, if it "runs over" (Ayache, 190) his body, then Srnicek's body—the writer's body—is truly the *topos* where we can carve out a space that is adapted to *factial* speculative financial thought.

Neroplatonism

Scott Wilson

> Perception is purely a matter of phantoms.
> Only now and then does this situation break
> down and lead to two real objects indirectly
> affecting one another by means of a third.
> And this is one form of what I call "allure."
>
> —Graham Harman, *Circus Philosophicus*

§ PREAMBLE: BATAILLE AND A.J. AYER

In a 2008 *Times Literary Supplement* review of Quentin Meillassoux's *After Finitude,* the founding text of Speculative Materialism, Simon Critchley takes Georges Bataille as an
example of the worst excesses of "correlationism." Critchley
mentions a notorious late night conversation between Bataille
and A.J. Ayer at which Merleau-Ponty and Giorgio Am-
brosini, the physicist who influenced Bataille's *The Accursed
Share,* were also present. This conversation, which went on
until 3 am, involved an argument as to whether or not you
could say that the "sun existed before man." Commenting on
"the abyss that separates French and English philosophy,"
Critchley writes:

> The thesis under discussion was very simple: did the
> sun exist before the appearance of humans? Ayer saw
> no reason to doubt that it did, whereas Bataille thought
> the whole proposition meaningless. For a philosopher
> committed to scientific realism, like Ayer, it makes ev-
> ident sense to utter ancestral statements such as "The
> sun existed prior to the appearance of humans,"
> whereas, for a correlationist like Bataille, more versed
> in Hegel and phenomenology, physical objects must be
> perceived by an observer in order to be said to exist.[1]

The anecdote is recounted by Bataille himself in a short lecture called "The Consequences of Nonknowledge."[2] The reason for the anecdote is not, however, to ridicule Ayer or
English philosophy, but on the contrary to disclose the limits
of Hegel and Absolute Knowledge. While, on the one hand,
there is no question that the statement "the sun existed before
man" "indicates the perfect non-sense that a reasonable proposition can assume" since there cannot be an object without a
subject, on the other hand this very non-sense makes us uneasy. We should also note what the sun means for Bataille in
relation to "man." "Man" has worshiped the sun, bathed in it,
sacrificed for it, organized all its "heliocentric" philosophical
metaphors around it, turned it into the Apollonian symbol of
order, reason, form, illumination, enlightenment and so on;
"Man" is inconceivable without the sun and vice versa.

Bataille writes, "Honestly, it seems to me that *insofar as we
remain within discursive considerations*, we might indefinitely
say that there could not have been a sun before man; however,
this also might make us uneasy: a proposition that isn't logically doubtful, but that makes the mind uneasy, induces in us

---

[1] Simon Critchley, "Back to the Great Outdoors," *Times Literary Supplement*, February 28, 2009: 28.

[2] Georges Bataille, "The Consequences of Nonknowledge," in *The Unfinished System of Nonknowledge*, ed. Stuart Kendall (Minne-apolis: University of Minnesota Press, 2001), 112 [111–18].

an imbalance: an object independent of any subject."[3] It is this latter idea of an object independent of any subject that fascinates Bataille, as indeed it does Graham Harman, of course. The failure of language to convey that which isn't logically doubtful in a form that is both perfect and yet non-sense opens up an abyss not just between French and English philosophy but between himself and the world: "I myself am in a world I recognise as profoundly inaccessible to me."[4] Bataille, or the body that went by that name, was not however inaccessible to the world that began to transform it into dust in 1962.

As we know, for Meillassoux the cosmos is accessible, but primarily through mathematics. Only mathematics, it seems, can grasp the laws and forms of the cosmos that are inaccessible to discourse (narrowly conceived) and pre-exist both "man" and the sun. Since we must therefore also say that mathematics pre-exists man, what of that sonic form of maths known as music? Certainly, I would suggest, if we regard music as an open system with the minimal yet quite conventional definition of "organized sound" where, of course, the principle of organization—form—does not originate in human culture. Again this idea is far from unknown; figures as diverse as Stockhausen and Steven Spielberg have speculated that aliens communicate through music.

§ BASE IDEALISM

The point I wish to make in this essay, speculatively and play-

---

[3] Bataille, "The Consequences of Nonknowledge," 112, my emphasis.
[4] Bataille, "The Consequences of Nonknowledge," 113. It is perfectly possible to posit that language itself pre-exists both man and the sun, logically, scientifically and speculatively in the sense that: 1) language produces the very categories of subject and object, man and sun, that makes such differentiations possible; 2) in the sense that modern humans are an evolutionary product of the invention of language and other systems of signification and symbolization; and that 3) there may well have been and currently may be very many alien languages out there in the cosmos.

fully titled "Neroplatonism," is that it is the heteronomy of form itself that produces the "unease" through which we do not not know the heterogeneity of objects and the worlds they inhabit. And here Bataille is an interesting figure, in both his medievalism and in his speculation on matter and form. The short piece "Base Materialism and Gnosticism" points to Bataille's affinities with the Gnostics, close rivals of the Neoplatonists, but hostile, it is assumed, in part because the former regard base matter as an "*active* principle having its own eternal autonomous existence as darkness," a conception that perhaps could be said to currently have cosmic correlates in the mathematical intuition or formal necessity of dark matter and dark energy.[5]

In contrast, it is often suggested that for the Neoplatonists matter is quite different and merely a passive receptacle or a question of simple privation. But on closer inspection this is not always the case. Plotinus states quite clearly that to call matter a receptacle or simply privation would be to define it, and matter is pure indeterminacy, formlessness; a darkness within all perceptible darkness, matter lies beyond even the apprehension of shapelessness, colourlessness and sizelessness. It is the imperceptible darkness at the heart of being and between beings: the pure indeterminacy of (non)relation between and inherent to forms and objects.

Even as late as Marcilio Ficino's *Platonic Theology*, matter is, on the one hand, that formlessness (*informe*) of absolute passivity, the double negative (*nonnihil*) on the (non)basis of which all forms of life act and move, and on the other, "the stream of Lethe" in which an active form is "overwhelmed [by matter], as by something infecting it."[6] Uncannily like Aristotle's prime mover that does not itself move or possess any par-

---

[5] Georges Bataille, *Visions of Excess: Selected Writings 1927-1939*, ed. Allan Stoekl (Minneapolis: University of Minnesota Press, 1985), 46.
[6] Marcilio Ficino, *Platonic Theology*, trans. Michael J. B. Allen, ed. James Hankins, 6 vols. (Cambridge: Harvard University Press, 2001-2006), 5:I.III.16.

ticular form, formless matter is also the locus of all mutability, decay and dissolution. Both good and evil, absolutely passive yet obscurely active and infectious, matter is for Ficino an alterity that ironically, in disclosing the insufficiency of being, can only *be* an idea: the pure Idea of what it is not.

Thus also for Bataille, the twentieth-century Gnostic taking up arms against latter day Platonists, base matter is associated with formlessness: "All of philosophy has no other goal: it is a matter of giving a frock coat to what is, a mathematical frock coat. On the other hand, affirming that the universe resembles nothing and is only *formless* amounts to saying that the universe is something like a spider or spit."[7] An easy objection can be made to this, whether or not one wears a mathematical frock coat. To say that the universe is something like a spider or spit is *precisely* to give it a form, the form of a spider or spit, of course. But here Bataille is ironically moving from the Gnostic tautology of "base matter" to the more Neoplationic (or at least Petrarchan) realm of affect that can only be conveyed in oxymoron. Spit and spiders are formless forms in the sense that they are phobic objects whose powers of horror reduce many people to a state of abjection beyond all rational control or determination. This is the formlessness of the universe for Bataille, a formlessness that arises as an effect of a form that it is impossible to grasp, an impossibility precisely missed through mathematical formularization. A spider or a gob of spit is not its mathematical form even though it does indeed have a form and this form, beyond the threshold of sense, reduces us (or some of us) to formlessness. As if it were inhabited by an active principle of base matter having its own autonomous existence as darkness, form exerts an allure that is simultaneously a power of horror.

Oxymoron, as the Petrarchan conceit par excellence, is a striking hyperbolic comparison in which, for example, the beloved's black eyes are the formless forms of delightful agony; incomparably compared to the sun, the icy fire of the "*bel*

---

[7] Georges Bataille, *Visions of Excess*, 31.

nero" of Laura's eyes are the unfathomable source of the Petrarachan conception of love—a Neoplatonism that as such is always also a Neroplatonism: a Platonism that finds its truth in the black eyes of its beloved. Neroplatonic love involves, to quote *Rime* 37 of Petrarch's *Canzionere*, that "Strange pleasure that in human minds is often found, to love whatever strange thing brings the thickest cloud of sighs!" ["Novo piacer che ne gli ingegni / Spesse volte si trova, / D'amar qual cosa nova / Più folta schiera di sospiri accoglia!"].[8]

As I understand it, speculative realism requires that one's speculations be grounded in scientific realism, however elaborate they may become, such that, for example, allowing the realist contention that God does not exist does not preclude the possibility that he may come to be in the future (see Meillassoux's thesis on "Divine Inexistence" in Harman's *Quentin Meillassoux*).[9] Following suit, then, and drawing on the medieval and Renaissance convention of the "elaborate conceit" that allows one to toy with the devices of science, I am going to suggest that Petrarchan Neroplatonism shows that love is not just a form of madness or folly (this is after all highly conventional), not just an affliction caused by an external nonhuman force (again this is a totally conventional idea), but that it is a neurological (or perhaps better, a "nerological") condition that allows us to explore the heteronomy between form and perception. In this sense "nerological" love is a form of agnosia like amusia or prosopagnosia.[10] These afflictions can be placed under the sign of oxymoron because the former

---

[8] Petrarch, "*Rime* 37," in *Petrarch's Lyric Poems: The* Rime Sparse *and other Poems*, ed. Robert M. During (Cambridge: Harvard University Press, 1976), 65–68.

[9] Graham Harman, *Quentin Meillassoux: Philosophy in the Making* (Edinburgh: Edinburgh University Press, 2011).

[10] For a discussion of love's relation to prosopagnosia see Scott Wilson, "Prosopopeia to Prosopagnosia: Dante on Facebook," in *On the Love of Commentary*, eds. Nicola Masciandaro and Scott Wilson, special issue of *Glossator: The Theory and Practice of the Commentary*, 5 (2011): 19–56

denotes musical noise while the latter concerns faceless faces.

Amusia never concerns simply a case of tone deafness or indifference to music; it does not describe a world of silence so much as the perception of often agonizing noise where there is music. For Vladimir Nabokov, for example, listening to a string quartet felt like being "flayed alive."[11] While the experience is one of formlessness, what produces the experience is a specific form. It is not the nonperception of music, but the perception of music as painful noise. The notion of amusia also therefore presupposes that music can disclose a fissure in the brain's model of external reality that frames phenomenal experience, hinting at a reality outside that model: the unknown impulse that generates painful "amusic." The "malfunction" of the system of perception and aural object recognition, the disjunction between the brain and its reality, is betrayed by the a-musical repetition of noise. Similarly, for prosopagnosia, the non-recognition of faces remains predicated upon an abstract model of the face. Confusion, distress, meaninglessness is predicated upon the perception of an abstract face-shape. For the sufferer of prosopagnosia faces are objects that do not correlate to an empathic personality, but are mysterious things. Neuroscientist Martha J. Farah writes, "object recognition is accomplished by repeatedly transforming the retinal imput into stimulus representations with increasingly greater abstraction."[12] In its positing of a highly generic face comprised of a blazon of conventional features (golden hair, black eyes, ruby lips etc.), there could be said to be something prosopagnosic about the poetry of courtly love even though the praise of the beloved's face is both the condition and the means of the production of poetic subjectivity. To quote Petrarchan scholar Isabella Bertoletti, "Petrarch relies on the enumeration of a limited number of formularized discrete physical attributes that he re-iterates hypnotically,

---

[11] Oliver Sacks, *Musicophilia: Tales of Music and the Brain* (London: Picador, 2007), 101.

[12] Martha J. Farah, *Visual Agnosia* (Cambridge: MIT Press, 2004), 3.

attributes which never come together as a portrait."[13] Love it seems therefore, like prosopagnosia, involves with regard to the face a different relation between form and perception, in which the face-object is an "inhuman partner" that exerts a strange allure that is both fascinating and horrifying. In Neroplatonic love, then, we have the experience of agony, distress, catastrophe predicated not just on the general, abstract form of a beautiful face, but in particular, the piercing "*bel nero*" of its gaze, to which the lover returns hypnotically. These eyes, the paradoxical light of the Ideal that emerges from impenetrable blackness only to reduce its object to formless agony, are both the cause and effect of the prosopagnosia of neroplatonic love.

Both amusia and prosopagnosia are examples of associative agnosia "in which perception seems adequate to allow recognition, and yet recognition cannot take place."[14] In Tauber's phrase, it involves "a normal percept stripped of its meaning."[15] Agnosias like amusia are useful for neuroscience in ascertaining the contingent and modular (evolutionary) nature of perceptual apparatuses and neural "knowledge" systems that abstract and pattern the object-"stuff" of perception. At the limit, the loss of certain phenomenal "qualities" may imply the emergence of new forms, and indeed new forms of knowledge.[16] Neuroscience, then, in its general discussion of the agnosias (and there are many different kinds) seems to be operating with quasi- if not neo-platonic categories that involve a clear distinction between form and matter or, in their words, between neuro-computational forms that give shape to the base "stuff" of perception that lacks form. To quote Farah,

---

[13]Isabella Bertoletti, "Petrarch's *Rerum Vulgarium Fragmenta*: Mourning Laura," *Quaderni d'italianistica* 23.2 (2002): 26 [25–43].

[14] Farah, *Visual Agnosia*, 2.

[15] Farah, *Visual Agnosia*, 2.

[16] Thomas Metzinger, *Being No One: The Self-Model Theory of Subjectivity* (Cambridge, MA: MIT Press, 2004), 8.

Early vision has been characterised as representing "stuff" rather than "things," meaning that the visual system initially extracts information about local visual properties before computing the larger scale structure of the image. In many ways, visual form agnosia can be described as preserved stuff vision in the absence of thing vision. What is striking about visual form agnosia is the complex nature of the stuff that can be represented in the absence of things. The perception of depth, velocity, acuity, and especially color (as opposed to wavelength), which are at least roughly intact in many visual form agnostics, requires considerable cortical computation. These computations yield a kind of rich but *formless* (my emphasis) goo, which requires some additional and separately lesionable grouping process to represent objects.[17]

It is this other neural grouping, or faculty of the mind, rather than perception per se, that has the facility of apprehending the form of things or Ideas supposed to shape the formless gooey stuff of perception. The question, therefore, concerns the formal relation between inside and outside. While apprehension of the order of things seems to be primarily a process of intellection, it would not be scientifically realist to presume that form is solely an effect or trick of the mind in contradistinction to the formless gooey stuff made perceptible by our senses out of impulses coming from whatever is out there. The dark matter of perceptible reality requires considerable computational power *even before* it can be rendered into the "formless goo" out of which the faculty of the mind is able to perceive or apprehend or intuit the "platonic" or mathematizable Ideas that inhabit it, no doubt as an effect of evolutionary adaptation. In this new Neoplatonic neuroscience, then, reality is only perceptible as an Idea recognized by certain neural groupings in the brain out of the goo of spurious perceptions

---

[17] Farah, *Visual Agnosia*, 19.

computed by other areas of the brain crunched from the mass of data introduced by the senses. The brain can only reconstruct or represent the Idea out of a mass of spurious computations of matter. Ideas are a play of form and formlessness in the brain predicated upon some imperceptible "base" matter with its own autonomous reality. Ironically, this structure is similar to the way Plotinus suggests we can intuit the existence of matter itself divest of any Idea or heterogeneous to any particular form.

In Plotinus's account matter escapes all rational apprehension and can only be intuited, as Plato himself suggests, through "spurious reasoning." In his account he relies on the metaphor of darkness:

> The eye is aware of darkness as a base capable of receiving any colour not yet seen against it: so the Mind, putting aside all attributes perceptible to sense—all that corresponds to light—comes upon a residuum which it cannot bring under determination: it is thus the state of the eye which, when directed towards darkness, has in some way become identical with the object of its spurious vision.[18]

For matter to be intuited, therefore, both the eye and the Mind have to construct a (spurious) vision of darkness (or formless goo, let's say) in order to sense something within it, the darker darkness of matter itself. "With what is perceptible to it," that is, the eye/mind, says Plotinus, "there is presented something else: what it can directly apprehend it sets on one side as its own; but the something else which Reason rejects, this, the dim, it knows dimly, this, the dark, it knows darkly, this it knows in a sort of non-knowing."[19]

---

[18] Plotinus, *The Enneads*, ed. John Dillon (Harmondsworth: Penguin Classics, 2005), 99.

[19] Plotinus, *The Enneads*, 100.

The darkness, or in Bataille's terms, the base materiality of the unknown knowns of perception perhaps accounts for the possibility of changes in the Ideas that shape perceiving and thinking beings in their relation with their own reality. The forms of life and matter are indeed essentially Ideas in the mind, but as such there could be no change in phenomenal reality unless immanent to those forms were not at the same time some "active principle" having its own "autonomous existence as darkness."[20] It is through the agency of such an active principle in the formlessness of form that changes in phenomenal reality may occur in the "advent" of strange new forms, thus obviating the need for a theory of *ex nihilo* creation (see Meillassoux in Harman's *Quentin Meillassoux*).[21] What is interesting, then, about the apparent Neoplatonism of neuroscience with regard to agnosias like amusia and prosopagnosia is that it is in the very form itself that the effect of formlessness or radical indetermination is felt and known. Indetermination is determined, somehow, on the very basis of form; a deeper formlessness is determined by the very indetermination immanent to form: that is, impossibly, form *is* formlessness, music *is* noise, a face *is* a faceless void, and sovereign beauty the terror of base matter.

§ THE SPECIOUS VISION OF DEATH

One of the most beautiful poems in Petrarch's *Canzoniere* is *Rime 323*. It is a Visions of Ruin poem that re-iterates Ovidian themes and images from *Rime 23* but also laments the trauma of love in a fuller development of the lines from *Rime 37* where love's strange pleasure is "to love whatever strange thing brings the thickest cloud of sighs!" It is a poem, like all of them ultimately, about death and writing. It suggests, one could propose somewhat anachronistically, that poetry's creation of a new or strange thing (*cosa nova*), that is to say new

---

[20] Bataille, *Visions of Excess*, 46.
[21] Harman, *Quentin Meillassoux*, 184–85.

and strange thoughts and feelings in the formation of new neural circuits, arises as an effect of love's trauma; the mental disorder or catastrophe that is love, and the death that it prefigures and anticipates.

In *Rime* 323 the strange/new pleasure is elaborated in six emblematic visions of ruin and mourning traditionally associated with the death of Laura from the plague on 6 April 1348, the same month and day as his *innamoramento*, his falling in love, as he writes in *Rime* 211 (see also 336).[22] Six visions of ruinous beauty and the beauty of ruin offer complex forms of always reversible allegory. The hind, the ship, the laurel tree, the fountain, the phoenix and the Bella Donna are "all emblems for Laura [that] at sometime or other also stands for the lover, and vice versa. If Laura is the laurel, the lover turns into a laurel; if she is the beautiful deer he is hunting, he is Acteaon (and, again, in 323 she is torn apart by dogs); if he becomes a fountain of tears, she is a fountain of inspiration (but is it Narcissus's pool?) . . . the myths are constantly being transformed."[23] Narcissus is certainly referenced in the final emblem. While the snake bite of course recalls Eurydice, she falls bowed like a flower when plucked.

It has often been noted that the myth of Narcissus, from Ovid to Freud, provides the classical pattern for the psychic structure of love and love poetry. It is indeed also the structure of Neoplatonism, assuming we recognise the Neoplatonic universe as the Empire of the One. In a wry remark on the Neoplatonism of scientific reason, Jacques Lacan affirms that yes, of course, "we proceed on the basis of the One. . . . The One engenders science," but not, he quickly adds, in the sense of measurement, that is not what is important. Rather, "what distinguishes modern science . . . is precisely the function of

---

[22] The convergence between the dates is also noted in 30, 50, 62, 79, 101, 107, 1 18, 122, 145, 212, 221, 266, 271, 278, 364, ranging from 1334 to 1358.

[23] Robert M. During, "Introduction," in Petrarch, *Petrarch's Lyric Poems*, 32.

the One, the One in so far as it is only there, we can assume, to represent solitude—the fact that the One doesn't truly knot itself with anything that resembles the sexual Other."[24] The insistence of the Other which, as we know from Lacan, does not exist, is an effect of the "One-missing."[25] It is for this very reason that the One can be said to be both transcendent and immanent to the many, the worlds of objects which exist but with which there is no relation. Or rather, there are only indirect relations by means of a third, the principle of the many, the obscure form(s), both alluring and dissonant, that articulates the two and denotes the impossibility of their complementarity, harmony or synthesis.

"Perception is purely a matter of [alluring] phantoms," writes Graham Harman, by means of which two real objects indirectly affect one another in the absence of any direct relation or recognition: a face, for example, and some water.[26] Less often noted than its function as the paradigm of romance, the myth of Narcissus is the first recorded instance of prosopagnosia. Narcissisus's love for his own reflection must be predicated on the fact that he fails to recognise the face as his own. And this is indeed how the myth is sometimes translated. Dryden, for example, writes:

> For as his own bright image he survey'd,
> He fell in love with the fantastick shade;
> And o'er the fair resemblance hung unmov'd,
> Nor knew, fond youth! it was himself he lov'd.[27]

---

[24] Jacques Lacan, *Encore*: Seminar XX, trans. Bruce Fink. (New York: W.W. Norton, 1999), 128.

[25] Lacan, *Encore*, 129.

[26] Graham Harman, "Offshore Drilling Rig," in *Circus Philosophicus* (London: Zero Books, 2010), and *The Quadruple Object* (London: Zero Books, 2011).

[27] John Dryden, *Fables Ancient and Modern Translated into Verse by John Dryden* [1700] (London: Kessinger Books, 2003), 89 (Book III).

But after all, what kind of sublime idiot would pine away at an image if he knew it to be his own? At the heart of the myth of Narcissus, hidden it seems from view, is the tale of a profound alienation predicated upon a disjunction, a radical heteronomy between perception and form, eye and brain, subject and object. Yet Narcissus looks upon himself as something strange and new, someone or something utterly not himself that he cannot not love even though it brings the thickest cloud of sighs (not least from Echo's "amusical" song that is the dissonant echo of Narcissus's visual agnosia). Each of Petrarch's reversible emblems in *Rime* 323 take this Narcissistic structure but disclose the radical heteronomy at the heart of the myth.

The key to this is perhaps the emblem of the phoenix that, here, does not rise again from the ashes of death. Classical symbol of re-birth and resurrection, the phoenix is described in explicitly Neoplatonic form as the celestial immortality of Form itself, the Idea that breathes new life into dead matter. But here it commits suicide, destroys itself in the face of the preceding visions of ruin. "All things," it seems, "fly towards their end," even the Ideas that animate them. There is a darker principle that determines the fate even of form, the indeterminacy that is represented by the Idea of death. Death is only ever an Idea, of course; it is not something that we can actually experience. Death does not mean anything to science; it is just the transformation of matter. Matter does not die even when it turns to dust. As an Idea death is related to its opposite, eternity, and as such is no doubt a form of consolation, a promise that there is indeed truly an end to this interminable life and the horror of eternity. The latter is a horror that might well be linked to the horror of the "eternal autonomous existence of darkness" of Bataille's Gnostic intuition of base matter—the matter that that inhabits us all just as much as it inhabits the Idea of death that veils matter's transformative, putrefying power, even the matter of Bataille's own body that turned to dust after 1962. The Idea of death is a spurious vision, but through it one "comes across a residuum which it cannot bring under determination."[28] Looking deep into the beautiful black, "*bel nero*" eyes of death one becomes somehow identical with the strange new thing [*cose nove*] behind it, the force of exteriority that transforms the psyche: the indeterminate determination of all indeterminacy.

Given this radical indetermination, death is not final, is not the end, as Petrarch writes in the final lines of *Rime 328*, in which the dead black eyes of Laura address his own eyes and speak to him: "Her beautiful eyes . . . with chaste, strange shining said to my eyes: 'Peace be with You, dear friends; never again here, no, but we shall see each other again elsewhere'" ["Li occhi belli . . . Dicean lor con faville oneste et nove: / Rimanetevi in pace, o cari amici: / Qui mai più, no, rivedremne altrove"].[29]

§ CODA: THE NUMBER AND THE BEAST

Meillassoux's follow up to *After Finitude*, his *Le Nombre et la sirène* (2011), seeks to ground his idea of the absolute in the secrecy of numerical code in an elaborate commentary on Stéphane Mallarmé's 1897 poem, "Un coup de dés jamais n'abolira le hasard." Meillassoux undertakes a remarkable numerological analysis of the poem in a manner not seen since the days of Alastair Fowler and Thomas P. Roche.[30] (see Fowler 1970 and Roche 1989). Through a painstaking task of counting and re-counting the words of the poem, Meillassoux lights upon the number 707 that coincides with the word "*sacre*" that appears just before the final 7 word line of the poem, "*Toute pensée émet un Coup de Dés*" [All Thought expresses a throw of the dice]. The poem thereby "performatively" sa-

---

[28] Plotinus, *The Enneads*, 99.

[29] Petrarch, *Petrarch's Lyric Poems*, 328: 9, 12–14.

[30] Alastair Fowler, *Triumphal Forms: Structural Patterns in Elizabethan Poetry* (Cambridge: Cambridge University Press, 1970), and Thomas P. Roche, *Petrarch and the English Sonnet Sequences* (New York: AMS Press, 1989).

cralises the number, much of which is made by Meillassoux.[31] The number is both a cipher for the future of poetry and a figure for chance itself. Poised between the "7" that is the sign of chance and the "7" of the classic French alexandrine meter is the 0 that symbolizes the abyss that yawns open in the absence of God, giving way to the eternal contingency of hyper-chaos.

The code 707 is also the number of the "*ultérieur démon immémorial*" who appears earlier in the poem at the moment where the ship's master is about to be engulfed by the sea at the point of casting his dice. For Meillassoux this *démon* is both the ancestral demon of poetry and the demonic spirit of the "catastrophic" rupture of its mighty line (although the alexandrine has 12 syllables, its caesura falls after the sixth syllable, thus it can be considered a mute "seventh"), a break also symbolic of the cleavage between classic and free verse represented by Mallarmé's own poetry.[32] This break is also, of course, coterminous with the death of God that nevertheless threatens to found "*la perdition*" on earth.[33]

Given the question raised by the poem concerning "*LE NOMBRE*" and its existence, and whether or not it is an *hallucination éparse d'agonie*, and moreover notwithstanding Meillassoux's painstaking attempts to count it, this intensely symbolist poem is no doubt also referring to another literary demon. Indeed, not simply a demon but the apocalyptic beast of the sea that is encoded with another number that its author calls on the reader to enumerate: "Here is wisdom. Let him who has understanding calculate the number of the beast, for it is the number of a man: His number is 666" (Rev. 13:18). This seven-headed beast, ennobled with its own "*lucide et sei-gneuriale aigrette*" of crowns each bearing the name of blas-

---

[31] Quentin Meillassoux, *Le Nombre et la sirène: Un déchiffrage du 'Un coup de dés de Mallarmé* (Paris: Fayard, 2011), 46.

[32] Meillassoux, *Le Nombre et la sirène,* 42.

[33] Stéphane Mallarmé, *Selected Poetry and Prose*, ed. Mary Ann Caws (New York: New Directions, 1982), 123.

phemy, rises out of the sea in the *Book of Revelations* heralding the end of days. In Revelation 17 he even bears on his back a Siren, the woman who embodies the mystery of the fate of those who see the beast that was "and is not," the equivocal beast that shall "ascend out of the bottomless pit, and go into perdition: and they that dwell on the earth shall wonder, whose names were not written in the book of life from the foundation of the world, when they behold the beast that was, and is not, and yet is." (Rev. 17:8).

A dice throw that did not abolish chance might be one that came up six after six after six, for as Meillassoux insists absolute chance—contingency—has nothing to do with probability.[34] 666. These were the numbers that came up for Petrarch the poet, with devastating effects. April 6, the date of Petrarch's *innamoramento* and Laura's death from the plague in 1348, lies at the heart of the *Canzoniere's* elaborate numerological system. For example in *Rime* 323, the six emblematic visions of Laura's death are conveyed in 12 lines each (3+3x2); the whole sequence itself comprises of 366 poems, 6x60+6. The miraculous birth of beauty and perfection, its horrifying putrefaction in the blackest of deaths and the whole architecture of the *Rime sparse* are signified by the number 6. Throughout its history, of course, from the Troubadours to André Breton's *L'Amour fou*, love has been regarded as a mental disturbance, madness, folly, one of the most common symptoms of which is a numerological obsession with dates and numbers. For Dante Alighieri, it was the number 9. For Petrarch, the number 6 repeated three times encompasses the poetry of love and death; it is the code of the *bel nero* of the eyes of death's spurious vision in which all kinds of speculative possibilities of the new and the strange may be glimpsed.

It is also, of course, the number of the beast which for the Preterian theologians unmistakably meant "*Neron Kaiser*," the Emperor Nero, hatred for whom consumed St John the Divine, author of *Revelations*. In contrast, for Kabbalistic Juda-

---

[34] See Meillassoux, *After Finitude* (London: Continuum, 2008), 105.

ism 666 represents the perfection of the world given the six days of creation, the six cardinal directions and the numerical value of a letter in God's name. The code for all blasphemy, persecution and evil, for hatred and the apocalypse, is also the code for love and the love of perfection, for Divine form. Is this pure chance? Is this an effect of the essential meaning-lessness of numbers, whose enigmas enflame the amorous intensities of mystics and psychotics? But how far away is this from the claims made for mathematical knowledge of the universe and its laws, as if algebraic formulae were likewise the means through which God speaks to scientists in His own language. In the absence of God and indeed faith in science, yet giving up on neither perhaps, we can no doubt take the number 666 as another sign—not of contingency, but of that base matter that inhabits the horror of its Idea.

PORTFOLIO:

PHOTOGRAPHS: NYC LABORATORY

16 SEPTEMBER 2011

BY ÖYKÜ TEKTEN

New York City.09.16.2011

Transmission by Sponge
Aristotle's *Poetics*

Anna Kłosowska

> Trees write their autobiographies in circles
>   each year,
> pausing briefly each spring to weep over
>   what they have written. I guess that's life.

> —Spencer Reece, from "Ghazals for Spring"

§ AVERROES ON THE ELEVATOR

The history of transmission of Aristotle in the West is surprisingly complex, and it attaches (but what doesn't?) to period distinctions between medieval and modern.[1] For instance, the

I want to thank Eileen Joy for her tireless work on this volume and symposia, and for help in writing. My thanks to the Averroes Group, a transdisciplinary, multi-institution collaboration that enabled a group of scholars to simultaneously read the *Poetics* and other texts in Greek (Steve Nimis and Evan Hayes), Arabic (Elizabeth Bergman and Karla Mallette), and Latin. My grateful thanks for inspiration and comments to speakers and colleagues who attended the London and New York symposia, and the supporting institutions, including King's College London, The Graduate Center (CUNY), and Miami University. This work would not be possible without the intellectual propagation of Aristotle's *Physics* is contemporary with the rise of instrumentaria, that is, making things to measure other things, but also production of musical instruments. The first graduated thermometers appear throughout Europe around the turn of the sixteenth century, roughly the same time when the writing of poetry and playing musical instruments become both more popular and more specialized. In that period, lutes become more widespread as middle class possessions, leading historians to catalogue lutes as a means to establish the rise of early modern middle class in Paris. This is the period of specialization when teaching, writing and publishing music is decoupled from writing poetry. That transformative time for *Physics* is also when some intellectuals move away from the traditional Averroes's commentary on Aristotle's *Poetics* and increasingly rely on direct translations from the Greek.

In turn, when Louis le Roy gives the first direct French translation of *Politics* in 1566, he introduces the text *via* better known Plato's *Symposium* and *Republic*, the latter sketchily known but apparently a relatively commonplace reference due to its scandalous ideas (common ownership of wives and children as a foundation of strong democracy).[2] In his preface

---

challenge and momentum, as well as the collegial support and criticism, of the Petropunk Collective and BABEL Working Group.

[1] The transmission of Aristotle's *Poetics* is the subject of Karla Mallette's excellent article, "Beyond Mimesis: Aristotle's *Poetics* in the Medieval Mediterranean," *PMLA* 124 (2009): 583–91.

[2] Louis Le Roy, *De l'origine, antiquité, progres, excellence, et utilité de l'art politique. Ensemble les Legislateurs plus renommez qui l'ont premierement prattiquée, et des autheurs illustres qui en ont escrit, specialement de Platon et Aristote, avec le sommaire et conference de leurs Politiques traduittes de Grec en François, et eclarcies d'expositions pour les accommoder aux meurs et affaires de ce temps* (Paris: Frederic Morel, 1567), hereafter cited parenthetically by folio number. On Le Roy, see Marie Gaille-Nikodimov, "Un humaniste peut-il inventer? L'idée d'un progrès de l'art politique chez Louis Le Roy," *Laboratoire italien* 6 (2006): 55–77. See also Werner L. Gundersheimer, *The Life and Works of Louis Le Roy* (Geneva: Droz, 1966), 47-58. Nicole Oresme's first French commentary/gloss and

(published separately and dedicated to the powerful royal minister Claude de l'Aubespine, while he dedicated *Politics* to the king) Le Roy highlights a discontinuity between political science and other fields:

> Grammar, Poetics, Rhetoric and Dialectic have been treated by an infinite number of persons. . . . Mathematics has never been better known. . . . Physics and Medicine . . . have not been more perfected among ancient Greeks and Arabs than they are now . . . military discipline . . . architecture, painting, music are almost restored to their original state; and it is impossible to work more on eloquence and civil law. But Politics. . . was left behind without receiving any light of learning. (Le Roy, *De l'origine*, 4r-5v)

The metaphor of elevators seems a good way to visualize how Aristotelian texts were bundled and carried across time. In brief, there are two elevators, the small one with texts preserved in Syriac, translated and commented in Arabic (*Poetics, Organon*, and some other texts), the big one with Greek texts, about four times bigger. It makes sense, because in the second half of the thirteenth century this bigger elevator has to lift Thomas Aquinas (as we know, the Angelic Doctor was no Kate Moss), and also because he walks in with everything that was missing from the other elevator, for instance *Politics*. At the Renaissance, everyone exits and regroups.

Today I will tell a story with the same suspects: Averroes (1126-1198) commenting on Syriac versions in Arabic and his Latin translator Hermannus Alemannus; roughly contempo-

---

translation (1370-1374) from William of Moerbeke's Latin was sponsored by Charles V; see Susan M. Babbit, *Oresme's* Livre de Politiques *and the France of Charles V* (Philadelphia: The American Philosophical Society, 1985), 7–31, and Nicole Oresme, *Le Livre de Politiques d'Aristote,* ed. Albert Douglas Menut (Philadelphia: The American Philosophical Society, 1970).

rary with Hermannus, Thomas Aquinas with William of Moerbeke, the translator of Aristotle from Greek to Latin. However, I will focus more closely on *Poetics*, resulting in a peculiar narrative of transmission. As we may recall, William of Moerbeke's big-elevator translation was the preferred basis of all of the medieval Aristotle, with the notable exception of William's translation of *Poetics* and *On Animals*. William's *Poetics* only survives in one early copy. This means that *Poetics* is almost always on the petite elevator. This peculiarity is related to the fact that there was little interest in *Poetics* before the Renaissance, in comparison with the more popular texts, such as the *Rhetoric* and *Analytics*. Meanwhile, on the big elevator, Hermannus Alemannus's translations from Arabic were surpassed by William's translations from Greek by the order of twenty, judging by extant copies: there exist five early-ish extant manuscripts of Hermann's *Rhetoric* versus one hundred of William's. This gap was both created and subsequently amplified by the university system: *Poetics* was not usually a university text, whereas *Rhetoric* and *Analytics* were.

As this overview of transmission illustrates, to focus on *Poetics* is to focus, in essence, on an exception. As early as *any* Latin translations of Aristotle were made—Hermannus's in Toledo, 1240-56, William's in Corinth beginning with *Politics* in 1260, possibly at Thomas Aquinas's request—there was the understanding that Arabic commentaries were not translated directly from the Greek (in fact, *Politics* did not have an Arabic version), and from then on, almost all of the Aristotle circulating in Latin—all that mattered for the university canon— was directly translated from the Greek. All, that is, with the notable exception of *Poetics*, which was not a standard university text. Unlike commentaries on other books of Aristotle, abundant throughout, commentaries on *Poetics* proliferated mostly in the fifteenth and nineteenth centuries. The two main traditions of *Poetics,* Arabic and Greek, are easy to tell apart because they have a different definition of tragedy. Two versions of *Poetics*, medieval and modern, or Arabic and Greek, emerge. This history of reception does not correspond to the present (modern/postmodern) currency of Aristotle's works, where *Nicomachean Ethics*, *Politics*, and *Poetics* dominate, followed by *Rhetorics, Metaphysics*, and *Physics*.[3]

To illustrate the forces that shaped accounts (not the reality) of Aristotle's transmission, I will start with two images, from Jorge Luis Borges and Ernest Renan. Everyone remembers Borges's story of how Averroes mistranslated Aristotle's definition of tragedy:

> Few things more beautiful and more pathetic are recorded in history than this Arab physician's dedication to the thoughts of a man separated from him by fourteen centuries; to these intricate difficulties we should add that Averroes, ignorant of Syriac and of Greek, was working with the translation of a translation. The night before, two doubtful words had halted him at the beginning of the *Poetics*. These words were *tragedy* and *comedy*. He had encountered them years before in the third book of the *Rhetoric*; no one in the whole world of Islam could conjuncture what they meant. In vain he had exhausted the pages. . . . these two arcane words

---

[3] An "Identities" gadget in WorldCat (http://www.worldcat. org/identities/) shows a timeline and association cloud for all titles. It is still in development (for example, the input dates corresponding to two different eras, i.e. dates in Christian and Muslim calendars, have not been converted yet to one calendar in the database, creating a spike of mysterious commentaries by Averroes . . . some 700 years before his birth!), but it promises to help with questions concerning transmission. Another gadget shows the network of identities: http:// experimental.worldcat.org/IDNetwork/index.html. The ease of access to some information that we used to have to configure on our fingers reminds me of a comment about a book on scansion in *Beowulf* (pre-computers), where the author thanks his graduate students for entering and collating data on index cards. For a similar story, see Andrew Prescott, "Images in History, *Making History* [website], School of Advanced Study, University of London: http://www.history.ac.uk/makinghistory/resources/articles/images_ history.html.

pullullated throughout the text of the *Poetics*; it was impossible to elude them.[4]

Averroes works until dark and then goes to a dinner party where a traveler returned from China describes a masked theatrical performance he witnessed there. No one can understand his description, because no one has ever been in a theater. In spite of listening, at this propitious moment (Julian Yates, in this volume, would call it *kairos*, the right time), to the eyewitness account of theater, which could have been the key to decoding Aristotle's numerous references to Greek theater (theater is the main example in *Poetics*, alongside the epic)—a version of "open, Sesame!" that would have unlocked the treasures of this work—Averroes is defeated in his attempts to translate and more poignantly, given that Borges imagines the correct answer was right before him, is also defeated in his attempts to do as little as to imagine a reality outside his "orb." In the story's epilogue, Borges speaks of his own parallel defeat. The fictional Aristotle vanishes as Borges begins to doubt his own powers of conjuring the past: "I felt that the work was mocking me. I felt that Averroes, wanting to imagine what a drama is without ever having suspected what a theater is, was no more absurd than I, wanting to imagine Averroes."[5]

The second image comes from Ernest Renan's well-known 1882 Sorbonne lecture, "What is a Nation?" Renan wrote about Averroes and Aristotle early in his career, in the 1850s. He is an Orientalist from Saidian caricature, a great seeker of pure origins that, emphatically, were not Semitic (and yet, he was raked over the coals by French antisemites for his alleged Semitic sympathies).[6] Renan's hallmark in his day was equal

---

[4] Jorge Luis Borges, "Averroes' Search," in *Labyrinths: Selected Stories and Other Writings*, ed. Donald A. Yates and James E. Irby (1962; repr. New York: New Directions: 2007), 155 [148–55].

[5] Borges, "Averroes' Search," 155.

[6] Edward Said, *Orientalism* (1978; repr. New York: Vintage, 1994), discusses Renan in Chap. 2, "Orientalist Structures and Restruc-

opportunity effrontery: he held that "Judaism and Christianity will both disappear" (*Histoire du peuple d'Israël,* 1887), and he was criticized by both the left and right—by the latter, for anticlericalism and for not being enough of a racist, in other

---

tures," 113–200, at 123–48. Renan's anti-religious sentiment was not entirely out of touch with the previous generation of Jewish Enlightenment-inspired intellectuals, but in advocating a departure from religion after 1850, Renan is out of step with a movement of return to tradition in Jewish French community, a return provoked among others by a rise of antisemitism. Seen from a twentieth-century perspective, Renan is a favorite source of ultraconservatives and virulent antisemites (with Auguste Comte, he is a favorite of Charles Maurras, 1868-1952). This makes Renan "the chief scientific sponsor of the Aryan myth in France who later became an almost official ideologist of the Third Reich" (Léon Poliakov, *The Aryan Myth: A History of Racist and Nationalist Ideas in Europe* [New York ; Basic Books, 1974], 206; see also Gerald Tulchinsky, "Goldwin Smith: Victorian Canadian Antisemite," in *Antisemitism in Canada: History and Interpretation*, ed. Alan T. Davies [Waterloo: Wilfrid Laurier University Press, 1999], 67–92, at 74–75). For an overview of the nineteenth-century invention of the binary Jewish vs. Greek, see Tessa Rajak, *The Jewish Dialogue with Greece and Rome* (Leiden: Brill, 2002), 535–58 ("Jews and Greeks: The Invention and Exploitation of Polarities in the Nineteenth Century"). For a concise discussion of Jewish identities in nineteenth-century France in a European context, see Maurice Samuels, *Inventing the Israelite: Jewish Fiction in Nineteenth-Century France* (Stanford: Stanford University Press, 2010), especially the Introduction, 1–36, and Conclusion, 239–61. One of the complexities of French history of race relations is that the Third Republic, which brought the separation of Church and State and also free public education, among other initiatives, also escalated colonialism and antisemitism (see comments on Renan in Aimé Césaire, *Discours sur le colonialisme* [Paris: Présence Africaine, 2010]). Racism was shared by both the proponents and opponents of colonialism; this is emblematic in the well-known *mot* that the right-wing journalist Paul Deroulède notoriously flung against then-president Jules Ferry (responsible for the escalation of colonialism): "I have lost two sisters [Alsace and Lorraine], you give me twenty housemaids [colonies]" ["J'ai perdu deux soeurs, vous me donnez vingt domestiques"].

words, for thinking of "blood" or race as a construct, not a reality.[7] And yet, the catastrophic consequences of Renan's "liberal" ideas are terribly obvious, from the twentieth-century perspective, in what directly follows the above quote: "The work of the Jew will have its end; the work of the Greek—in other words, science and civilization, rational, ex-perimental . . . will last forever" (*Histoire du peuple d'Israël*, 1887).[8] This is but one example of a discourse that fed antise-mitic ideologies. However, at the time, Renan was more likely seen as an anti-clerical figure than a racist. In his inaugural lecture at the Collège de France, "On the Semitic Contribu-tions in History of Civilization," he referred to Jesus as "an incomparable man," leading to Renan's abrupt dismissal from the Collège where he had just been appointed (1862); he was just as promptly reinstated when the regime changed to one that was secular and anti-clerical, at the beginning of the Third Republic (1871).[9]

---

[7] See for instance Henri Alexandre Wallon, "Sur le monothéisme considéré par M. Renan comme déterminant le caractère général des races sémitiques," *L'Institut, Journal Universel des sicences et des sociétés savantes en France et à l'étranger. IIe section: sciences historiques, archéologiques et Philosophiques* 24:283/284 (July-August 1859) (report on the séances of July 8 and 15): 85–87, also published separately as Henri Alexandre Wallon, *Du monothéisme chez les races sémitiques* (Paris: Simon Raçon, 1859). See also Henri Desportes and François Bournand, with a preface by J. de Biez, *Ernest Renan: Sa Vie et Son Oeuvre* (Paris: Tolra, 1893). That book, dedicated to the Pope to console him on "the public burial given by the government of catholic France to an apostate," denounces Renan for being pro-Jewish; what particularly galls de Biez is Renan's reference to "Juifs Gaulois." If Renan publicly maintains that one can be both French (i.e., *Gaulois*) and Jewish, it is, the book alleges, purely out of financial motive, since his publishers are Calmann-Lévy (ix and 235).

[8] Ernest Renan, *Oeuvres Complètes*, ed. Henriette Psichari (Paris: Calmann-Lévy, 1953), 6 vols, 6:1517.

[9] Ernest Renan, *De la part des peuples Sémitiques dans l'histoire de la civilisation* (Paris: Lévy, 1862). On the reception of this lecture, see

In the well-known 1882 "Nation" speech, inspired by
Moritz Lazarus's "Was Heiss National?" (an influence Renan
failed to acknowledge; yet it seems that Lazarus, the author of
Die Ethik des Judenthums, among others, should be credited
with the defining idea of Renan's arguably best known text),
Renan defines nation-making (the emergence of proper European nations from their medieval matrix) as a dynamic of
remembering and forgetting:

> Forgetting, and I would even say historical error, are
> an essential factor of nation formation, and thus the
> progress of historical scholarship is often a danger to a
> nationality. Historical investigation brings to the light,
> in fact, violent acts that took place at the origin of all
> political formations, even those whose consequences
> were the most beneficial. Unity is always achieved bru-
> tally.[10]

Renan's point is that we are not slaves to our race, language,
religion, geography or even interest: nation is a soul, it is a
love affair, a social contract that transcends origins.

Borges's Averroes represents the Arabic or medieval for-
getting-what-tragedy-is, but Borges's text also refracts other
facets of the Averroes legend. Sometimes Averroes is the emblem of the Occident or Maghreb (Al Garb al Andalus, or
"West of the Vandals"?), with the secular and rational West-
erners as opposed to the religious Easterners. This geography
conflates Western Arabs or Maghrebis with Western Europeans, and Al Andalus with Northern Europe. The Averroes of

---

Hippolyte Taine, *Life and Letters of Hippolyte Taine, 1853-1870,*
trans. R. L. Devonshire (Westminster: Constable, 1904), 190. See also
Robert Chabanne, "L'affaire Renan et la politique religieuse du
Second Empire," *Annales de faculté de droit et des sciences
économiques de l'Université de Lyon II, 1972-3* (Paris: LGD, 1974), 35,
and Wallon, *Du monothéisme chez les races sémitiques*, 54.

[10] Ernest Renan, *Qu'est-ce qu'une nation?* (Paris: Calmann Lévy,
1882), 8.

that tradition is the author of the *Incoherence of the Incoherence of Philosophy* (*Tahafut Altahafut Alfalasifaa*), a polemic with Abu Hamid Al-Ghazali, whose *Incoherence of Philosophy* was written in Baghdad in 1098. Al-Ghazali demonstrated that Greek-influenced philosophers such as the great interpreter of Aristotle, the Sunni Persian Ibn Sinna/Avicenna (980-1037; wrote both in Arabic and in Persian), failed to attain certitude through dialectical methods, thus removing the need for the study of Greek philosophy under Islam. Averroes's polemic argued for the study of the Greek tradition by showing that Al-Ghazali used the methods he denounced to arrive at his conclusions. Another Averroes is a figure of civil disobedience, exiled by the Caliph Al-Mansur who has fallen under the sway of Islamist clerics. But throughout the centuries which are our focus here, Averroes was known in the Arab world primarily for his commentaries on Avicenna and Aristotle's *Logic*, until 1885, when an edition of his more polemical text, *Tahafut Altahafut Alfalasifaa*, Averroes's reply to Al-Ghazali, appeared in English in Cairo.

§ THE POETRY OF THE ARABS, DANTE, AND PETRARCH'S CONDESCENSION

Given the little interest in the East in Averroes's commentary to *Poetics*, how did it fare in the West? As Averroes's editor Charles E. Butterworth says, "Thanks to Saint Thomas Aquinas and Dante, [Averroes] is well known as *the* commentator on Aristotle."[11] A very enjoyable account of the transmission of Aristotle's *Poetics* in the Middle Ages is Karla Mallette's in her *European Modernity and the Arab Mediterranean* (2010). Mallette pulls together parts of a story split between disciplines that don't talk to each other, and therefore it has not been taught quite the way she does. All medievalists recall

---

[11] Charles E. Butterworth, "Averroes," in: *Philosophy of Education: An Encyclopedia*, ed. Joseph James Chambliss (New York: Garland, 1996), 43-44, at 43.

from their training some form of "Arabs translated Aristotle" or "troubadour love poetry—with its Platonic and homoerotic substrates—comes from the Arabs," but that's it. The work was done by magic, as if in an Arthurian legend. In contrast, Mallette's account draws a precise map of what happened and when. There are three *loci* on this map: first, Aristotle's *Poetics*; second, Dante's *Divine Comedy*; and third, Petrarch.

At least since the late eighteenth century, contemporary with Dante's canonization as the father of Italian literature, there was a notion that a swarm of similarities links Dante's *Commedia* to the so-call "Book of the Ladder," or the *Dream* (*Mi'raj*) of Mohammed, where he climbs the ladder and visits Heaven. At the same time, the father of Italian literature being both un-original and, *horresco referrens*, copying from Islam, didn't go over very well, which is why this notion about the sources of the *Commedia* flourished in Spain and not Italy. The philological proof that there was a Latin and medieval French translation of the Arabic text that circulated in the Middle Ages and could have been known by Dante and his contemporaries did not surface until 1949, six centuries after that translation from Arabic was created and, sadly, six years after the death of the scholar who most persistently advanced the thesis of resemblance between Dante's text and Mohammed's *Mi'raj*.[12] Along with the modern edition of 1949, there came a list of references to the "Book of the Ladder" in Spanish, Italian and French from the ninth to the fifteenth centuries, "with a chapter . . . on the thirteenth century philosophers of the Oxford school for good measure" (46). While Mallette acknowledges, "I would be remiss if I didn't report that scholarly consensus has not been reached" (46) (on whether Dante was, or was not, aware of the Arab sources), she also concludes that we are looking at a porous Mediterra-

---

[12] Karla Mallette, *European Modernity and the Arab Mediterranean: Toward a New Philology and a Counter-Orientalism* (Philadelphia: University of Pennsylvania Press, 2010), 44; hereafter referred to parenthetically, by page number.

nean Middle Ages, not a compartmentalized Arab Middle Ages here and a Christian Middle Ages over there, perhaps with some occasional exchange going on.

Mallette's second case is Petrarch, who famously writes to his physician: "The Arabs! You know them as doctors; I know them as poets. Nothing more insipid, nothing softer, nothing more flaccid, nothing more obscene" (46–47). The question here has usually been, as Mallette notes, "How could Petrarch have known Arabic poetry, of which the Middle Ages had not the slightest notion?" (47). But that, precisely, was not the case. Again, philological proof in the form of the source text did not surface until 1982, when a scholar noted that this formulation and the vocabulary Petrarch uses, and that Dante used before him when talking about the Arabs, comes from none other but Averroes's assessment of some Arabic poetry in Averroes's commentary on Aristotle's *Poetics*, as it is translated by Hermannus Alemannus in Toledo in 1256. How did it make its way to Petrarch? Hermannus's translation survives in twenty-four manuscripts and it is entrenched in the Western canon thanks to its influence on such major authors as Aquinas (1225-1274), Roger Bacon (1214-1294), and Coluccio Salutati (1331-1406). As we have said before, *Poetics* was not a standard university text; however, it was available. To the extent that *Poetics* was bundled with *Logic* in the *Organon*, it was taught, although it was considered somewhat useless. As Mallette summarizes, this ensured transmission at major universities (albeit far from the ubiquity that characterized other philosophical texts), and "numerous florilegia excerpted important passages from it as cribs for instructors, students, and armchair philosophers. Jean de Fayt, a scholar and preacher who was in Avignon at the same time as Petrarch, produced one such florilegium, apparently for use at the University of Paris" (49).[13]

---

[13] Mallette adds: "It . . . may have provided Petrarch with a crash course in Arabic poetics. Jean's selection of citations from Hermannus's translation includes Averroes' denunciation of the

Let us recall that Hermannus's translation of Averroes was filtered through Arabic and Persian poetic traditions. Closely following Averroes, Hermannus translates tragedy as "poetry of vituperation" (or satire) and comedy as eulogy (or "poetry of praise"). Also, apparently Averroes did not inherit Homer. Although Syriac Christian tradition did have Homer all along, and some of it may have come from Baghdad, it surfaced in the West later, after Averroes, and was then excerpted in Arabic. In saying that the Syriac Christian tradition had access to Homer, I mean both Homer circulating in Syriac translation, and Homer in Greek. For example, among the earlier manuscripts of Homer's *Iliad* is a Syriac palimpsest, also containing Euclid, where the *Iliad* is overwritten with a Syriac text. Its 19th-century editor suspects that the volume was part of a book purchase brought from Baghdad in 931.[14] So, for the excerpts from Sophocles and Homer in Aristotle, Averroes substituted the Persian and Arabic poetry canon as well as the Qur'an. Forty-three of these Persian and Arabic poetry examples were translated by Hermannus. There are even successful attempts at translating puns; however, proper names are usually only transliterated or dropped altogether. Using a prevailing thirteenth-century Western poetic style, Hermannus rhymes lines that are loosely rhythmically related to each other and that use stressed meter, while the Arabic poetry he was translating, like Greek and Latin poetry, did not rhyme and was based on the long/short syllable, not on stressed and unstressed distinction. Hermannus himself says that the poetry interpolations were the reason for choosing Averroes as his source instead of another Arabic translation. Renan cites: "Wanting to put my hand to a translation of *Poetics,* I found so much difficulty in it because of the difference in meters between Greek and Arabic, that I despaired of ever finishing. I

---

poetry of the Arabs: it is a 'provocation to the coital act, disguised and prettified with the name of love'" (49).

[14] *Fragments of the* Iliad *of Homer from a Syriac Palimpsest,* ed. William Cureton (London: The British Museum, 1851), v–vi.

therefore took Averroes's edition."[15] Mallette sums up: "Petrarch—who had a demonstrable professional interest in the poetry of the Arabs: 'you know them as doctors, I know them as poets'—could have derived double value from Hermannus's treatise" (53). First, he could have found there, and adopted as his own, Averroes's condemnation of Arabic poets as immoral. Second, he could have found there the poetic examples themselves, which were anthologized by Jean de Fayt and others (53).

Commenting on Petrarch's (and Averroes's) condescension towards bad Arab poets, Mallette reminds us that Petrarch had a similarly condescending attitude towards Dante's poetry, which he likewise claimed to hate and ignore at the same time: "in a notorious letter to Boccaccio, [Petrarch] vehemently denied feeling envy for the poet . . . whose work he could not avoid knowing although he stated emphatically that he had never read it" (53). Identical to what he says to his doctor about Arabic poetry, Petrarch "told Boccaccio that he hadn't sought out Dante's books, yet he claimed familiarity with Dante's writing" (53). In Mallette's account, Petrarch "created a literary modernity by consigning Dante and the Arabs equally to the ungainly, mongrel, medieval past and moving into the wide literary and intellectual space he thus created" (54).

In the case of *Poetics*, this negotiation, this freeing oneself from the twin weight of the medieval and the Arabic, took another two or three centuries. Interestingly, in the sixteenth century, both commentaries on Petrarch and translations of *Poetics* directly from the Greek are the domain of Protestant writers such as Lodovico Castelvetro.[16] And when Tasso will

---

[15] "Assumpsi ergo editionem Averod determinativam dicti operis Aristotelis, secundum quod ipse aliquid intelligibile elicere potuit ad ipso": Ernest Renan, *Averroès et l'averroïsme* (Paris: Michel Lévy Frères, 1866), 212.

[16] Bartélémy d'Herbelot de Molainville (1625-1695), who held the chair of Syriac at the Collège de France (1692-1695), in his dictionary *Bibliothèque orientale* lists Abu Bishr Matta (or Matthew, indicating

attack Castelvetro in his own commentary on "heroic poems," he will specifically affirm the continuity between Averroes and the Catholic tradition of *Poetics* regarding the role of virtue. When Castelvetro tries to uncouple "virtue" and "poetry of praise" from the definition of tragedy, Tasso objects:

> Castelvetro undoubtedly erred when he said that the Heroic poet should not praise, because if the heroic poet celebrates virtue he ought to elevate it with praise [*con le lodi*] unto Heavens; therefore Saint Basil says, that Homer's *Iliad* is none other than a praise [*lode*] of virtue, and Averroes in the commentary on poetry expresses the same opinion, and Plutarch in the book where he writes of the ways of understanding poets, where he also teaches that poets must not blame. . . . otherwise it would be possible to harm with the example of the things imitated, and to make the lesson of the poets very dangerous. . . . leaving the followers of Castelvetro to their own opinion, we will follow that of Polybus, Damascene, Saint Basil, Averroes, Plutarch, and Aristotle himself.[17]

It is not inaccurate to say, with Władysław Tatarkiewicz, that "Aristotle and his *Poetics* were subjected to a peculiar kind of

---

that he would be a Rumi ["Roman"], that is, a Greek Syriac) as the translator of Aristotle's *On Interpretation* (in Arabic, *Bari Arminias*, from Greek *Peri Hermeneuion*) and *Poetics* from Greek to Arabic; Herbelot, *Bibliothèque orientale, ou Dictionnaire universel contenant tout ce qui fait connoître les peuples de l'Orient* (The Hague: Neaulme and van Daalen, 1777), Vol. 1, 74 [article: "Abu Bashar Matta"].

[17]Quoted in O. B. Hardison, "Poetics: Aristotle and Averroes," in *Poetics and Praxis: Understanding and Imagination, The Collected Essays of O. B. Hardison Jr.*, ed. Arthur F. Kinney (Athens: University of Georgia Press, 1997), 35 [21–36]. My own translation of Torquato Tasso, *Discorsi del sig. Torquato Tasso del poema heroico, Al'illustrissimo e reverendissimo signor cardinale Aldobrandino, libro primo* (Naples: Stigliola, 1594), 87.

fate: in Antiquity his influence was slight; in the Middle Ages, it was great, though his *Poetics* was still unknown; then at the Renaissance, it became known, but was widely misunderstood."[18]

Keep in mind that Hermannus translated Averroes's twelfth-century commentary on *Poetics* in 1256, and "he also translated Al Farabi's and Averroes's commentaries on Aristotle's *Rhetoric* around the same time," forming "a small library of rhetorical works" (Mallette, 48–49). I cite Mallette again:

> The Greek text of Aristotle's *Poetics* came to Italy, along with a flood of other Greek manuscripts, following the fall of Constantinople to the Ottoman Turks in 1453. A Latin translation made directly from the Greek appeared in 1498, and a Greek edition of the text was published in 1508. During the course of the sixteenth century, no fewer than eight translations (into Latin or Italian) or reprints of translations were made directly from the Greek. But during the same century, between 1481 and 1600, the Hermannus Alemannus translation —along with Latin translations of Hebrew translations of Averroes's commentary—appeared in *ten* editions and reprints. It took a century of debate and negotiation for the notion that Aristotle's Greek should be viewed as the *correct* version of the *Poetics*—the most proximate and most relevant to European letters—to establish itself in the intellectual circles of Europe.
>
> And once the Averroes-Hermannus treatise had been superseded, memory of it gradually faded. (63)

---

[18] Wladyslaw Tatarkiewicz, *History of Aesthetics* (London: Continuum, 2005), 3 vols., 3:175.

It was apparently unknown to major figures who worked on Dante's Islamic connections and Petrarch's Arab question, says Mallette:

> A thirteenth-century Latin translation of Aristotle's *Poetics* made directly from the Greek by William of Moerbeke was published in a modern edition before Hermannus's version, despite the fact that medieval readers seemed not much interested in that text: it lay uncopied on a library shelf, forgotten until its discovery by twentieth-century scholars. (63)

By contrast, Mallette reminds us, Hermannus's translation was only published as a companion volume to the second edition of William's translation. Hermannus's translation was judged "completely illegible" by Ernest Renan, who wrote on Averroes in the 1850s-1860s (Renan also cites Roger Bacon's contempt for Hermannus's "squalid" Latin).[19] How could Renan make that comment is an interesting question, since Hermann's translation is very easy to read and nearly identical to Averroes's Arabic version. Renan excelled in Greek and Latin as a schoolboy, and he also studied Hebrew, Syriac and Arabic. His sister Henrietta, who lived in Germany, introduced him to Heinrich Ewald, "the father of philology," who published *Hebrew Grammar* in German 1827 and a Latin essay on the "meter of Arabic poetry" in 1825.

Indeed, it is the Greek that is pretty much illegible. *Poetics* makes a free use of pronouns, making its definitions dependent on conjunctures derived not only from *Poetics,* but the whole Aristotelian canon. Thus, any proper translation of *Poetics* (for example, the English Loeb translation) is always a commentary (often silent, like in Loeb, where it substitutes nouns for pronouns), much like in Averroes.

Let us pause for a moment and see what Renan says about the Western tradition. Renan unfolds the narrative of "inexo-

---

[19] Renan, *Averroès et l'averroïsme,* 82.

rable progress,"[20] where the improvement is made by returning to the unadulterated origins, a golden age. This timeline
can also be superposed on a ladder going from Semitic to non-
Semitic peoples, which Renan presents in his inaugural lecture
at Collège de France:

> We often hear of Arabian science and philosophy, and
> it is true that during one or two centuries in the Middle
> Ages, the Arabs were our masters, but only, however,
> until the discovery of the Greek originals. This Arabian
> science and philosophy was but a poor translation of
> Greek science and philosophy. As soon as authentic
> Greece arises, these miserable translations become use-
> less, and it is not without reason that all the philolo-
> gists of the Renaissance undertake a veritable crusade
> against them. Moreover, on close examination, we find
> that this Arabian science had nothing of the Arab in it.
> Its foundation is purely Greek; among those who orig-
> inated it, there is not one real Semite, they were Span-
> iards and Persians writing in Arabic. The Jews of the
> Middle Ages acted also as simple interpreters of phi-
> losophy. The Jewish philosophy of that epoch is un-
> modified Arabic. One page of Roger Bacon contains
> more of the true scientific spirit than does all that se-
> cond-hand science, worthy of respect, certainly, as a
> link of tradition, but destitute of all noble originality.[21]

So, in Renan's version, "the false Aristotle of the Arabs and
the commentators of the Middle Ages, is the first to fall under
the blows of the Hellenists of the fifteenth and sixteenth cen-

---

[20] Ernest Renan, "The part of the Semitic peoples in the History of
Civilization," in Ernest Renan, *Studies of Religious History and
Criticism. Authorized Translation from the French*, trans. Octavius
Brooks Frothingham (New York: Carleton, 1864), 169 [109–68];
translation of "Etudes d'histoire religieuse" and other essays.
[21]Renan, "The part of the Semitic peoples in the History of Civilization," 157.

turies, and to give place to an authentic and original Aristotle."[22] In order to create that narrative, there was a lot of forgetting, which we must undo.

First, as we have seen in Tasso's attack on Castelvetro, "these miserable [Arabic] translations" are far from "becoming useless" as soon as Greek sources become available. Quite the opposite, Averroes's moral commentary inspired by Islam was valued by the Christian counter-Reformation although Greek sources were widely available. It appears that the Protestants launched a critique, and the counter-Reformation entrenched itself in a counter-critique (Tasso), but this dynamic can in no way be described as a "crusade" with all that implies of anti-Arab Christian sentiment. On the contrary, it was a veritable ecumenical *fête* for Tasso who, as we saw, puts Averroes right next to Saint Basil (Church) and Plutarch (Classical Western tradition).

Second, it is very inaccurate to say that "the Arabs were our masters, but only, however, until the discovery of the Greek originals," for one or two centuries. As we saw, at least in the case of *Poetics*, the "discovery" of Greek originals (their translation into Latin and popularization in Western university system, assisted by the influence of Thomas Aquinas) was practically simultaneous (down to a few decades) with the "discovery" of the Arabic commentaries. The misperception that there was a "change of guard" over time from Arabic commentaries to Greek primary sources is an illusion. Sequential substitution of Arabic tradition by Greek in Latin West imagined by Renan did not take place in actuality.

Third, when Renan says, "this Arabian science and philosophy was but a poor translation of Greek science and philosophy," he sounds petty. Both Loeb and Averroes's translation silently comment on *Poetics*, without which *Poetics* would hardly be legible. But if Renan calls Arabic translations poor, Jews derivative, and cites Bacon as the one true original, it is

---

[22] Renan, "The part of the Semitic peoples in the History of Civilization," 169.

not consciously because he is a racist, but because he opposes reason to religion. Renan's ideas of race and its attendant idiom (i.e., race characteristics) evolve and are complex and fluid. He is an opportunist racist, while his overarching interpretive motivation is anti-clericalism. Sometimes he opposes Greeks to Semites, but at other times he deplores that Islam is no longer moderated by the rationalist tendencies of "astute and intellectual" Arabs and "speculative" Persians, but has abandoned "rational culture" under the sway of "Barbarians (Turks and Berbers)."[23] Further in the "Nation" essay, Renan says that Semites—Phoenicians and, in the Middle Ages, Arabs and Jews—invented trade and luxury, while moral edification and social progress is a collaboration between all races, although "delicacy of moral sense . . . seems to be the especial endowment of the Germanic and Celtic races," that is, the French (Renan was proud of his distinctive Breton origins).[24] It is that racist discourse that Aimé Césaire denounces when he cites Renan's 1871 *La réforme intellectuelle et morale en France* in his *Discours sur le colonialisme*, including Renan's passages on the ideas of the "regeneration of the inferior or degenerate races by the superior races" as "part of the providential order of humanity" and of the "Negro" as the "race of the tillers of the soil."[25] Again, I want to stress that Renan's greatest preoccupation is rationalism vs. clericalism.

Renan's most bizarrely racist statement—"this Arabian science had nothing of the Arab in it. Its foundation is purely Greek; among those who originated it, there is not one real Semite, they were Spaniards and Persians writing in Arabic"— is like having your cake and eating it, too: either Averroes's translation was Arab (and superseded by the Greek, in Renan's narrative) or it was Spanish/Persian: we can't have it

---

[23] Renan, *Averroes et l'averroïsme*, 16–17.

[24] Renan, "The part of the Semitic peoples in the History of Civilization," 158.

[25] On Césaire and Renan, see Robert C. Young, *Colonial Desire: Hybridity in Theory, Culture, and Race* (London: Routledge, 1995), 65–66.

both ways. Averroes, who lived in Cordoba, criticized the immoral "poetry of the Arabs" and also used the classical (pre-Arab) Persian poetic tradition to illustrate his translation of Aristotle's *Poetics*. This makes him Spanish and Persian when it suits Renan, and Arab at other times; but let us unpack this cultural heritage. Arabs conquered the Persians but adopted their culture, not unlike the Romans did to the Greeks. Arab moralists commented on the inherent dangers of such assimilation, but to little effect. It seems undeniable that, as Mallette points out, Averroes is *verbatim* the source of Petrarch's comment on the immoral poetry of the Arabs. So, it is the popularizer of Arab/Spanish/Persian/Greek, Averroes, that gives Petrarch the meme of contempt for Arab poetry, making it rather useless as an example of the march from Arab inferiority to Spanish/Persian/Greek superiority. Add Averroes's polemic in favor of Greek philosophy and throw in Abu Bishr Mata (Matthew, i.e., a Christian), the "Rumi" (Roman, i.e., Eastern Roman Empire or Byzantine Greek) speaker of Syriac who translated Aristotle into Arabic (and translated tragedy as poetry of praise; the second part of *Poetics* on comedy was lost by his time), and you get a Western tradition of *Poetics* where no one, but no one, can see a linear "march" (much less a crusade), but rather a cluster of interconnected random fragments—or, to push Karla Malette's porous Middle Ages metaphor further into Mediterranean and oceanic modes . . . a sponge.

Cosmic Eggs, or Events Before
Anything

J. Allan Mitchell

If it is a question of where to begin, medieval embryology and
cosmogony answer speculatively, starting at the *very* beginning: they return the human to the site of so many primordial,
intestinal involvements in the world—or rather, the very conception of *worlds* from "mere seeds and hopes," as Ovid puts
it in the *Metamorphoses*.[1] At one end of the spectrum, embry-
ological narratives effectively reverse engineer the organism,
tracing back through time a fluid and concatenating series of
molecular events, topological movements, and intensities that
may be missed only because they result in such solid-seeming
entities. In the fourteenth century, Nicole Oresme marvels at
the contingencies involved in the process, expressing surprise
that a human being comes about at all, since "error can happen from many causes but only in one way can it complete all
things successfully—and for this one way many things are
required." Even when things pan out, the wrenching epigenet-
ic change undergone by the embryo is extreme: "between
[Socrates] at his birth and at his maturity . . . there is surely a

---

[1] Ovid, *Metamorphoses, Books IX-XV,* trans. Frank Justus Miller; rev.
G. P. Goold, Loeb Classical Library (Cambridge: Harvard University
Press, 1984), XV, ll. 216–17 [381].

greater difference, if you consider it well, than there is between a pig and a dog at birth, or between an ass and a horse or mule, or a crow and an eagle, or between a wolf and a dog, all of which are of different species."[2] It is as if the human were originally constituted as some kind of menagerie, especially in light of the Aristotelian thesis that the embryo moves through successive stages of micro-speciation (vegetal, animal, human). At the other end of the spectrum, medieval cosmogony regularly describes a cosmic birth that is equally fraught: an account of everything originally abandoned to chaotic flux before being resolved into the developed Ptolemaism that we all associate with the Middle Ages. The methodological challenge of beginning is the same, tarrying with seminal, gestational moments anterior to being. It is to speculate about what is *not yet*, rather than what *is*.

To be specific, such speculations put in abeyance Augustine's "seminal reasons" or Aristotle's "entelechy," residing within an immanent unfolding or folding of things, attending precisely to the *fold* that precedes and produces all life forms. It was Aristotle who set out the epistemological policy according to which, "when we are dealing with definite and ordered products of nature, we must not say that each *is* of a certain quality because it *becomes* so, rather that they *become* so and so because they *are* so and so, for the process of becoming attends upon being and is for the sake of being, not vice versa."[3] Presenting the alternatives, Aristotle sees there is a choice to be made: it is a matter of finding the "fittest mode" of analysis for the subject matter.[4] Augustine's "seminal reasons" are

---

[2] *Nicole Oresme and the Marvels of Nature: A Study of his* De causis mirabilium *with Critical Edition, Translation, and Commentary*, ed. and trans. Bert Hansen (Toronto: Pontifical Institute of Mediaeval Studies, 1985), 241 and 233.

[3] Aristotle, *Generation of Animals*, trans. A. Platt in *The Complete Works of Aristotle: Revised Oxford Translation*, Vol. 1, rev. and ed. Jonathan Barnes (Princeton: Princeton University Press, 1984), 778b [1204].

[4] Aristotle, *Parts of Animals*, trans. W. Ogle in *The Complete Works*,

equally teleological. But narratives of gestation and growth take time to get to the *telos* and, in their temporality, emphasize a different modality, which is the indetermination of the organism. Embryogenesis and cosmogenesis expose—to borrow Derrida's pregnant phrase—the "*seminal* adventure of the trace."[5] Talk of embryos and eggs is where one can eavesdrop on a conversation that is quite unlike any other. It exposes the limitrophic nature of being, generating terms of reference for thinking about novelty, creaturely specificity, but also the generic matrix out of which anything arises. If this sounds like a chicken-and-egg dilemma, then indeed, it always is. The problem was addressed in a seriocomic dialogue composed by a fifth-century contemporary of Augustine: "You jest about what you suppose to be a triviality, in asking whether the hen came first from the egg or the egg from the hen," says one of the interlocutors around the table in Macrobius' *Saturnalia*, "but the point should be regarded as one of importance—one worthy of discussion and careful discussion at that."[6] Medieval writers tended to think so, too; at least, they allowed for some chaos to enter into their ontological systems, if only temporarily. What happens when we think this chaos through to the beginning?

My interest in the possibilities has found additional stimulus in one of the more lyrical passages in Quentin Meillassoux's *After Finitude,* which posits a so-called speculative thesis, i.e., the absoluteness of contingency, as a kind of hyper-chaos:

> Our absolute, in effect, is nothing other than an extreme form of chaos, a *hyper-Chaos*, for which nothing is or would seem to be, impossible, not even the un-

Vol. 1, 640b1 [996].

[5] Jacques Derrida, "Structure, Sign, and Play in the Discourse of the Human Sciences," *Writing and Difference*, trans. Alan Bass (London: Routledge, 1978), 292.

[6] Macrobius, *The Saturnalia*, trans. Percival Vaughn Davies (New York: Columbia University Press, 1969), VII.16.2 [512].

thinkable. . . . If we look through the aperture which we have opened up onto the absolute, what we see there is a rather menacing power—something insensible, and capable of destroying both things and worlds, of bringing forth monstrous absurdities, yet also of never doing anything, of realizing every dream, but also every nightmare, of engendering random and frenetic transformations, or conversely, of producing a universe that remains motionless down to its ultimate recesses, like a cloud bearing the fiercest storms, then the eeriest bright spells, if only for an interval of disquieting calm.[7]

Hyper-chaos is intended as a necessary corrective to modernist correlations of mind and matter (to be brief), and I take it to be a rigorous formulation with limited scope outside of Meillassoux's own disciplinary coordinates. That is, I do not expect much in the way of historical consciousness here. But the description cannot help but recall an archaic cosmic *mise-en-scène*, and it turns out that Meillassoux is not entirely indifferent to history either, for there is at the end of the book a whole Ptolemaic-Galilean-Copernican thematics; in short, a faint medievalism to which I will return. But to begin with, what is recognizable in Meillassoux's absolute contingency is not just the turbid chaos but also an old philosophical attraction to thinking a zero-degree primordiality from which all arises. It is in some sense the exemplary scene of potentiality, and always has been.

Yet that is not the orthodox view of intellectual history, and Meillassoux is hardly out to change things. And so speculative medievalism has something to do. In what follows I want to do three things, some of them simultaneously: First, I should recall evidence for cosmic birth that runs from Greco-Roman antiquity through to the late medieval Neoplatonists,

---

[7] Quentin Meillassoux, *After Finitude*, trans. Ray Brassier (London: Continuum, 2009), 64.

and as inherited by a fourteenth-century English poet, John Gower. Second, I want to think through the micro and macro scales of the cosmos. Gower is particularly lucid about the resultant disequilibrium of the Ptolemaic universe. Third, I will conclude with some meta-critical observations about the problem with adopting Meillassoux's brand of speculation. I recommend instead hyper-Ptolemaism.

§ ON COSMIC BIRTH

Cosmogony was a site from which to ponder the emergent complexity of a proto-universe, as though it were a huge living organism, the *Welt als Makranthropos* having a life cycle paralleling that of human creatures (*anthropos*). The seeds of the notion are traceable to Orphic mythology, and have origins in Empedocles' and Lucretius' analogies of the world to an animated mortal being, which is later accompanied by the Platonic doctrine of the world-soul (*animus mundi*).[8] As Bernardus Silvestris eventually says: "Mundus quidem est animal," the universe is an animal.[9] This is a picture of all the parts working together organically for the consistency of the whole, but it implies more than simple unity and isomorphism of parts and whole. Medieval Platonists composed mythopoetic histories for the cosmic organism developing over time, starting as a relatively amorphous embryonic body that grows by degrees. Cosmogony constitutes a kind of zoogony. In this formulation there is an implicit rejection of Plato's eternity of

---

[8] See George Perrigo Conger, *Theories of Macrocosms and Microcosms in the History of Philosophy* (New York: Columbia University Press, 1922); and Myrto Garani, *Empedocles Redivivus: Poetry and Analogy in Lucretius* (New York: Routledge, 2007), 71ff.

[9] Bernardus Silvestris, *The Cosmographia*, trans. Winthrop Wetherbee (New York: Columbia University Press, 1973), 88; Bernardus Silvestris, *Cosmographia*, ed. Peter Dronke (Leiden: E. J. Brill, 1978), 118; compare with Plato, *Timaeus*, trans. Donald J. Zeyl, in *Complete Works,* ed. John Cooper (Indianapolis: Hackett Publishing Company, 1997), 33b–34a [1238].

the world that would appeal to later medieval thinkers (especially after the Parisian Condemnations of 1277). At the same time, it poses difficulties by introducing radical changes of growth and decay. While presupposing entelechy, the unfolding may be messier than one had hoped. The cosmos grows out of something it may never overcome, toward something it perhaps should *not* become. Also, the quasi-personification may betray hints of vitalism or animism that are theologically suspect.

Such are some implications of commonplace images of the world as egg, embryo, infant, or rebellious child. The cosmic egg was handed down from Greco-Roman antiquity through Macrobius to Albertus Magnus, Peter Abelard, William of Conches, and Hildegard of Bingen.[10] Plato's *Timaeus* and Ovid's *Metamorphoses* gave the idea genuine traction with their respective interests in chaos, generation, and corruption. Although neither employs the figure itself, Ovid's name was later etymologized "ovum dividens" (he who distinguishes the egg), a superb honorific.[11] What the egg means in any given context was carefully specified. Some drew a fairly basic structural analogy based on the four elements and physical geography. Caxton translated the prose *Ovide moralisé*: "The yolk signefyeth the erth. The white signefyeth the see, that goþ rounded about & closeth the earthe. And the pellete [membrane], þat is ordeyned aboue þe other tweyne aforsayd, signefyeth the heuen. In this manner hath Ouyd manifested and shewd the ordenaunce of the elements by an egge."[12] In

---

[10] See Peter Dronke, *Fabula: Explorations into the Uses of Myth in Medieval Platonism* (Leiden: E. J. Brill, 1985), 79–99 and Appendix A.

[11] See Ana Pairet, "Recasting the *Metamorphoses* in Fourteenth-Century France: The Challenges of the *Ovide moralisé*," in *Ovid in the Middle Ages,* ed. James G. Clark et al. (Cambridge: Cambridge University Press, 2011), 92.

[12] *The Middle English Text of* Caxton's Ovid, *Book I,* edited from Cambridge, Magdalene College, Old Library, MS F.4.34, with a Parallel Text of the "Ovide moralisé en prose II," edited from Paris,

one of the most intriguing examples, Hildegard of Bingen's world egg is an image of a surging, pulsing, roiling mass of fire and wind brought together to become—however unlikely—an ordered universe under the auspices of divine providence.[13] Who can escape the plasticity and fragility of the medium? And is the feminine origin of the egg not a rival to patriocentric genealogy? In any case, the egg is the scandal of the transitional lifeform. Nor is it human.

The issue has a long antiquity, going back at least to the satirical treatment of the Orphic egg in Aristophanes' *The Birds*. There, a chorus of birds, with a comical air of superiority, addresses an audience of mere humans: "In the beginning . . . there was no Earth, no Air, no Sky. It was in the boundless womb of Erebus that the first egg was laid by black-winged Night."[14] Of course birds *would* imagine the world hatching from an egg. They are seen to invent a self-serving cosmogony, a natural alibi for their winged species superiority. The avian analogy is less convenient for the human, with its non-anthropocentric, *inhuman* resonance. Much later, Pseudo-Clement would write that chaos forms the egg out of which is hatched the androgynous four elements.[15]

William of Conches expresses something of the vexed yet constructive nature of zoogony, writing about how "the configuration of our world resembles that of an egg." More interesting than the oviform shape is the picture of the coagulating elements. Everything originated in a plenum he calls "one large body," almost a monadic unity, but it is called "*chaos* by the philosophers, which can be translated as 'confusion.'"[16]

Bibliothèque Nationale, MS fonds français 137, ed. Diane Rumrich (Heidelberg: Winter, 2011), 61.

[13] Hildegard of Bingen, *Scivias*, trans. Mother Columbia Hart and Jane Bishop (New York: Paulist Press, 1990), 93ff.

[14] Aristophanes, *The Birds*, trans. David Barrett and Alan Sommerstein (New York: Penguin, 2003) ll. 692, 694–95 [177–78].

[15] Dronke, *Fabula*, 83–85.

[16] William of Conches, *A Dialogue on Natural Philosophy (Dragmaticon Philosophiae)*, trans. Italo Ronca and Matthew Curr

Invoking the authority of Ovid on the primordial soup, he speaks of the way elements were eventually sorted and bound together, taking up forms in tentative arrangements.

One final example is Bernardus Silvestris' *Cosmographia*, which produces a startling vision of ongoing cosmogenesis, not with a cosmic egg analogy as such, but keeping with the idea of biological generation. In the beginning there was a discordant, teeming mass of Hyle.[17] Hyle is the "the inexhaustible womb of generation, [. . .] the foundation of substance," the chaos-mother of creation. Aristotle coined the Greek ὕλη to designate matter (*hyle*) relative to form (*morphe*), but Bernardus shifts the emphasis to primordial plasma that is *formless*, initially only seeking form. And so it comes to pass. Divine intellect produces amity between the elements, generating species and fabricating a "cosmic soul," Entelecheia. An infant "megacosmos" is born from the fertile material matrix. His second book treats the coming of the "microcosmos," the creation of the human. Yet both micro and macro hylomorphs are beset by difficulties. Primordial matter is not totally contained, and so the cosmos amounts to what Peter Dronke calls an "*enfant sauvage*," a wayward child.[18] The fecundity in matter is moralized as something hostile, an irrepressible sublunary materiality. In the end, the best that can be done is for things to pass in and out of existence, endlessly receding from and emerging into forms. There is generation and corruption. Chaos has not been eliminated but transferred, becoming one natural move among others. Meillassoux does not seem so far away.

(Notre Dame: Notre Dame Press, 1997), 17.

[17] Bernardus Silvestris, *The Cosmographia*, 67–68. On *hyle* and *silva* see Brian Stock, *Myth and Science in the Twelfth Century: A Study of Bernard Silvester* (Princeton: Princeton University Press, 1972), 97ff.

[18] Bernardus Silvestris, *Cosmographia*, 30.

§ TOTALIZING ECOLOGIES

The larger point of these examples is to paint a total picture of the universe as something of an *unfinished* totality, composed of fluctuating intensities and heterogeneous extensities that end up leaving a legacy of cosmic disequilibrium. Granted, premodern cosmology aspires to holism, harmony, autarchy. But equilibrium was an optimistic ideal asserted against so much that was known to exist (and exist unknown), and against a profound sense of the residual, humiliating chaos. In the seventh book of his *Confessio Amantis*, John Gower returns to the originary moment of creation with a description that relies heavily on the Neoplatonists:

> For yit withouten eny forme
> Was that matiere universal,
> Which hihte Ylem in special.
> Of Ylem, as I am enformed,
> These elementz ben mad and formed,
> Of Ylem elementz they hote
> After the Scole of Aristote,
> Of whiche if more I schal reherce,
> Foure elementz ther ben diverse.[19]

He goes on to describe the ordering of the universe forthwith, and his picture ends up (to cut a long story short) looking a lot like the Ptolemaic diagrams we all know. Here the four elements, the complexions, the seven planets, and the fixed stars all revolve around a stationary center. The human occupies pride of place in the constellation, not just by virtue of his physical centrality on earth but also by means of isomorphism. But in the ordinary course of nature, as John Gower knew, bodies sicken and die, a problem he diagnoses as a

---

[19] John Gower, *Confessio Amantis,* Vol. 2 of *The English Works of John Gower*, ed. G. C. Macaulay (Oxford: Clarendon Press, 1899-1902), VII.214–22 [239].

postlapsarian one exemplified first in the human make-up:

> It may ferst proeve upon a man;
> The which, for his complexioun
> Is mad upon divisioun
> Of cold, of hot, of moist, of drye,
> He mot be verray kynde dye:
> For the contraire of his astat
> Stant evermore in such debat,
> Til that o part be overcome,
> Ther may no final pes be nome.
> Bot other wise, if a man were
> Mad al togedre of o matiere
> Withouten interrupcioun,
> Ther scholde no corrupcioun
> Engendre upon that unite:
> Bot for ther is diversite
> Withinne himself, he may noght laste,
> That he ne deieth ate laste.[20]

The greater world too is composed of a concomitant division of elements, with all the human disorder occasioning major upheavals: "And whan this litel world mistorneth, / The grete world al overtorneth" (Prol. 954–58). He goes on in the Prologue:

> For as the man hath passioun
> Of seknesse, in comparisoun
> So soffren othre creatures.
> Lo, ferst the hevenly figures,
> The Sonne and Mone eclipsen bothe,
> And ben with mannes senne wrothe;
> The purest Eir for Senne alofte
> Hath ben and is corrupt fulofte,
> Right now the hyhe wyndes blowe,

---

[20] John Gower, *Confessio Amantis,* Vol. 1, Prol. 974–90 [31–32].

And anon after thei ben lowe,
Now clowdy and now clier it is:
So may it proeven wel be this,
A mannes Senne is forto hate,
Which makth the welkne to debate.
And forto se the proprete
Of every thyng in his degree,
Benethe forth among ous hiere
Al stant aliche in this matiere:
The See now ebbeth, now it floweth,
The lond now welketh, now it groweth,
Now be the Trees with leves grene,
Now thei be bare and nothing sene,
Now be the lusti somer floures,
Now be the stormy wynter shoures,
Now be the daies, now the nyhtes,
So stant ther nothing al upryhtes,
Now it is lyht, now it is derk;
And thus stant al the worldes werk
After the disposicioun
Of man and his condicioun.[21]

Here we find no neutral background or foreground—all elements are equally "there," as T. Morton would say—meeting a condition of the *ecological thought*.[22] Of course, ecologists are unlikely to attribute the corruption of the oceans and atmosphere to original sin, but as we enter the Anthropocene in the recognition that humans have irrevocably transformed the earth's ecosystems, the idea of a maladaptive chaotic condition is an improvement on what usually passes for a cosmos. Gower's holism affords a much-needed view of the total catastrophe. Without the whole, there can be no chaos.

---

[21] John Gower, *Confessio Amantis*, vol. 1, Prol. 913–44 [30–31].

[22] Timothy Morton, *The Ecological Thought* (Cambridge: Harvard University Press, 2010), 28 et passim.

§ MEDIEVAL FUTURES

Gower's *ylem* has a long history but an even more significant, and odd, future career, for as it turns out two mid-century physicists – George Gamow and Ralph Alpher—appropriated the term for their new theory. Gower's formulation appealed to Alpher who, around 1948, found a reference in *Webster's Dictionary*, and promptly celebrated his discovery by purchasing a bottle of Cointreau and relabeling it YLEM.[23] Now on display at the Smithsonian Air & Space Museum, this bottle of spirits would become a reminder of the original chemistry of the emerging proto-universe, when, during an initial hot gaseous phase, a jumble of protons, neutrons, and electrons were busy synthesizing to create the elements. Given the curious accident of history, it is perhaps worth putting medieval cosmogony in dialogue with modern physics and philosophy more generally. To what extent, in a post-Copernican, post-Newtonian universe, can the imagined dimensions and dynamics of premodern explanatory models ever be considered relevant, even *real*? Of course, medieval and modern cosmologies are worlds apart, but premodern speculations can sometimes have a weird future; an element here or there may make the quantum leap from there to here, background becomes foreground. And where they diverge in *matters of fact* they can agree on *matters of concern*.[24]

This is a roundabout way to return to Meillassoux's hyperchaos, a remedy for what he sees as modern malaise he associates with (of all things) Ptolemaism. In his final chapter, entitled "Ptolemy's Revenge," he argues that today thought has

---

[23] See John David North, *Cosmos: An Illustrated History of Astronomy and Cosmology* (Chicago: University of Chicago Press, 2008), 651; Helge Kragh, *Cosmology and Controversy: The Historical Development of Two Theories of the Universe* (Princeton: Princeton University Press, 1996), 114; and George Gamow, *The Creation of the Universe* (New York: Viking Press, 1952), 54.

[24] Bruno Latour, "An Attempt at a 'Compositionist Manifesto,'" in *New Literary History* 41.3 (2010): 478 [471–90].

not realized the full extent of the Galilean-Copernican revolution. Science attempts to reformat the world by mathematical means, while Kantian philosophy rallies a "Ptolemaic counter-revolution," ever recentralizing the human observer.[25]   But why insist on casting the debate in these terms? The problem for the intellectual historian who wishes to think along with Meillassoux is this: he is a vigorous promoter of periodization, dividing time into epochs before and after Kant (on the far side of which stands a naive, pre-critical, dogmatic metaphysics and, on the other side, an enlightened critique). As it happens, this is very unlike the way some others engaged in affiliated "speculative realist" projects now tend to privilege the premodern. Think of Latour's "we have never been modern," and more recently, Harman's recovery of early modern occasionalist philosophy.

In Meillassoux's account, however, medieval discourses would be disqualified from the speculative scene, shunted into a benighted pre-scientific past. "Certainly," he concedes, "humans did not have to wait for the advent of empirical science in order to produce accounts of what had preceded human existence – whether in the shape of Cyclopes, Titans, or Gods. But the fundamental dimension presented by modern science from the moment of its inception was the fact that its assertions could become part of a *cognitive process*. They were no longer of the order of myths, theogonies, or fabulations, and instead became *hypotheses* susceptible to corroboration or refutation by actual experiments."[26] Here is just the latest iteration of Burkhardtian mythology about how the brambles of faith had to be cleared away for reason to flourish in the modern period. Leaving aside whether medieval science is all monsters and myths (refuted by a causal glance at the mathematical rigor of Ptolemaic astronomy, or by acquaintance with the sophisticated trigonometry of the astrolabe), it is notable that Meillassoux cannot sustain the courage of his convictions. For

---

[25] Meillassoux, *After Finitude,* 117–18.

[26] Meillassoux, *After Finitude,* 113–14.

while he goes on to describe the Galilean-Copernican revolution and the modern introduction of mathematization and empiricism that is proper to science, he simultaneously shows that modern thought is not critical enough, either.

Meillassoux seems clear-sighted about the prospects that lie ahead *if* speculation is allowed to return to the past. As it stands, he forces a provisional adoption of the metrics of scientific modernism and cool reflexive reason of Kant, all of which must be overcome on the way to something yet uncorrelated and hyper-chaotic. In other words, his speculative gesture is grounded in a modernism he everywhere should have wished to discard. He makes a very specific historical argument, but one that fails to do justice to the premodern situation *and* produces the modern situation he wants to transcend.

§ HYPER-PTOLEMAISM, OR THE FARAWAY NEARBY

Perhaps *transcendence* is the real problem here. The impulse to jettison the past is understandable, but in this case instead of affording speculative freedom to hypothesize we are left with another dogma. What is lost to history in Meillassoux's account?

Consider one final example. Celestial influence is only the most obvious vantage from which to spot the degree to which bodies—embryonic and astronomic—are entangled and reticulated across time and space. In the evocative language of the Middle English *De Spermate*, the human *proceeds* to the universe: "wherof the soule of man, as in his reason goeth furth to the vniuersite." The soul has a share in the wider world that exists. At conception and throughout a pregnancy the planets rule over specific months in the gestational cycle, and the embryo contracts benign and malign planetary and zodiacal influences, undertaking "to transferre the propirtes of planetis and signs." The developing creature is expressly a nexus where manifold elements are conjoined, folded, "ligat, bounden, and

joined in planetis and signes, nexed to the iiij elementis."[27]
The emphasis falls on what lies between bodies, and how they
are laced together for good or ill. Here is anthropocentrism,
but an anthropocentrism without human separatism.

A typical manuscript image for use in medieval phleboto-
my shows a "bloodletting man" whose body is a hub from
which radial points draw lines of connection to the heavens;
each bloodletting point of the diseased body stands in relation
to the relevant stars, producing an image of a fully entangled,
environed human creature. It is a meshwork without the
healthy symmetry on display in Leonardo's Vitruvian Man
(which such an illustration is likely to conjure up), showing
instead a set of specific somatic relationships between a disor-
dered body and radiant heavenly bodies. The human is constitutively local and trans-local, distributed across a range of
assemblages. Biology and astrology belong to a larger totality,
but they are not totally themselves. They are *virtually elsewhere*. They are medieval. They are hyper-Ptolemaic.

---

[27] Paivi Pahta, ed., *Medieval Embryology in the Vernacular* (Helsinki:
Société néophilologique, 1998), 199–201 and 251.

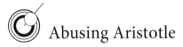 Abusing Aristotle

Kellie Robertson

'Speculative' in contemporary usage often denotes something that is not grounded in fact, not based in the "actual world." This is a term of suspicion for some (as in the phrase "merely speculative") and of approval for others (as in the introduction to *Towards Speculative Realism*, where the philosopher Graham Harman asserts that "speculative" serves as a kind of homeopathic inoculation of realism, ensuring that realism is not equated with an interest in "a dull commonsense realism of genuine trees and billiard balls existing outside the mind, but a darker form of 'weird realism' bearing little resemblance to the presuppositions of everyday life").[1] Yet in medieval scholastic usage, this term was frequently used to denote the very material science of physics, a science whose goal was to describe and analyze everyday experience, the "dull commonsense realism" of things. Ockham, in the prologue to his commentary on Aristotle's *Physics*, describes the overlap between physics and metaphysics, asserting that physics is also "primarily speculative."[2] Thus, for Ockham and his contemporaries, looking at a rock was just as speculative an endeavor

---

[1] Graham Harman, *Towards Speculative Realism: Essays and Lectures* (Winchester: Zero Books, 2010), 2.

[2] William Ockham, *Ockham on Aristotle's Physics: A Translation of Ockham's Brevis summa libri physicorum*, trans. Julian A. Davies (St. Bonaventure: The Franciscan Institute, 1989), 5.

as imagining how that rock was transformed by your looking into a mental or intentional object. What I find useful about the recent turn to speculative realism is that it reminds us of the speculative nature of both the physical sciences and moral philosophy. This paper is in part a meditation on how the "specters of Aristotle" (*pace* Derrida) haunt the modern intellectual divide that seeks to partition off the "dull" physical world from our metaphysical engagement with it.

Medieval scholasticism is often imagined as being virtually synonymous with Aristotelianism, but the scholastic relation to him was often ambivalent, sometimes openly hostile. Aristotle was not always viewed as the wise *magister*, although his writings formed the core of the arts curriculum from the thirteenth century onwards. His pervasiveness apparently prompted a backlash. This reaction is witnessed by the well-known figure of the so-called *Aristote chevauchée*, or mounted Aristotle, that depicts the wise philosopher yielding to carnal desire. On his hands and knees, he is portrayed being "ridden" about a garden by Alexander's crop-wielding mistress, Phyllis. A figure for the spirit overcome by the flesh, wisdom by concupiscence, this cautionary Aristotle appears on many varieties of household goods as well as in literary *fabliaux* and sermon exempla.[3]

Abusing Aristotle has a long, varied, and even, on occasion, entertaining history. The ubiquity of this image of Phyllis topping Aristotle says less about putative medieval gender relations and rather more about the re-appropriation of Aristotle by male scholastic culture. It is no coincidence that this image really takes hold in the thirteenth century, a time when Aristotle's influence was starting to transform the majority of universities across Europe. If Phyllis was the most visible Aristotle-abuser of the Middle Ages, she was by no means alone: many ecclesiastic officials, concerned about pagan knowledge infiltrating the university curriculum, began to denounce both

---

[3] On the mounted Aristotle tradition, see Susan L. Smith, *The Power of Women: A Topos in Medieval Art and Literature* (Philadelphia: University of Pennsylvania Press, 1995).

the philosophy and the man. While the 1277 condemnations of Aristotle's natural philosophy were the most well-known and far-reaching censure of Aristotle, his legacy provoked all kinds of local pamphlet wars, including a debate over the ultimate resting place of his soul, that gave rise to a genre of quodlibetal questions under the rubric, "Utrum Aristoteles sit salvatus." Unsurprisingly, most conservative theologians packed him off to hell.[4]

If, as Tolstoy reminds us, every family is unhappy in its own way, so too every age engages in a family romance with Aristotle that, more often than not, ends unhappily (albeit in distinctively different ways). As the medieval ardor for Aristotle cooled--abruptly or gradually depending on which historian of science you believe--early modern attacks on Aristotle took the form of unhappiness with his ostensible animism and teleological naiveté, not to mention his "popish" sensibility. This sentiment is expressed most succinctly in an analogy attributed to Martin Luther: "In a word, Aristotle is to divinity as darkness is to light."[5] While I'm tempted to spend the rest

---

[4] On the controversies surrounding Aristotle, see Fernand van Steenberghen, *Aristotle in the West* (Louvain: Nauwelaerts, 1955), and Edward Grant, "Science and Theology in the Middle Ages," in *The Nature of Natural Philosophy in the Later Middle Ages* (Washington, D.C.: Catholic University of America Press, 2010). On the quodlibetal question genre, see Anton-Hermann Chroust, "A Contribution to the Medieval Discussion: Utrum Aristoteles sit salvatus," *Journal of the History of Ideas* 6 (1945): 231–38, and Ruedi Imbach, "Aristoteles in Der Holle: Eine anonyme Quaestio 'Utrum Aristotiles sit salvatus' im co. Vat. Lat 1012 (127 ra-127 va) zum Jenseitsschicksal des Stagiriten," in *Peregrina Curiositas: Eine Reise durch den orbis antiquus: Zu Ehren von Dirk van Damme*, ed. Dirk van Damme, Andreas Kessler, Thomas Ricklin and Gregor Wurst (Freiburg: Universitätsverlag, Göttingen: Vandenhoeck & Ruprecht, 1994).

[5] Proposition 50 of Luther's 97 theses posted in 1517. An English version of these theses can be found in Martin Luther, *Martin Luther's Basic Theological Writings*, trans. Timothy F. Lull (Minneapolis: Fortress Press, 1989). On the reception of Aristotle in the early modern period more generally, see Stephen Gaukroger, *The Emer-*

of my essay quoting a string of mean, pithy Aristotelian epithets from the seventeenth century, I'll instead address one question raised by the *longue durée* of unease with all or part of the Aristotelian project: how relevant is this project, in the form re-articulated by medieval scholasticism, to the challenges, ethical and scientific, that we face today? To answer this, I'll address the "return" to Aristotle in two very different strains of recent philosophical thought: the school of "revolutionary Aristotelianism" spawned by the writings of Alasdair MacIntyre, which are concerned with redefining a pragmatic ethics, and Graham Harman's "weird Aristotelianism," a realist ontology that seeks a middle path between contemporary versions of monism (the Deleuzo-Guattarian/eliminativist camp) and correlationism (whether associated with Hegelian idealism or deconstruction). This paper will describe the ways in which these two strains of what might be called "neo-Aristotelianism" are both a return to and a departure from the late medieval scholastic Aristotle, a tradition that MacIntyre and Harman both self-consciously attempt to recuperate in characteristic, and characteristically extraordinary, ways.

§ COMRADE ARISTOTLE

The decline in reputation suffered by Aristotle in the early modern period and the Enlightenment was to last a substantial while. If we look at the relatively rough evidence provided by Google's ngram viewer—a tool that has definite limitations—we can discern, at least in rough outline, Aristotle's fortunes in print over several centuries [Figure 1].[6] While an

---

gence of a Scientific Culture: Science and the Shaping of Modernity, 1210-1685 (Oxford: Clarendon, 2006), and Steven Shapin, *The Scientific Revolution* (Chicago: University of Chicago Press, 1996).

[6] The Ngram tool can be found at http://books.google.com/ngrams (accessed 31 January 2012). For a discussion of the uses and limitations of this tool, see Jean-Baptiste Michel, Yuan Kui Shen, Aviva Presser Aiden, Adrian Veres, Matthew K. Gray, William Brockman, The Google Books Team, Joseph P. Pickett, Dale Hoiberg, Dan Clancy, Peter Norvig, Jon Orwant, Steven Pinker, Martin A. Nowak, and

uptick is evident at the end of the twentieth century, this up-ward trend is still only relatively significant when compared, for instance, to the frequency with which Plato is cited [Figure 2]. This statistical snapshot suggests that Aristotle's "print footprint" re-expands dramatically in the 1980s.

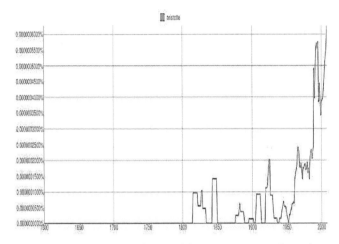

Figure 1. Google ngram, 'Aristotle' as percentage of words in print in the Google Books corpus, 1600-2008

Speculation on what lead to the growing citation of Aristotle at this particular cultural moment aside, it is the case that the publication of Alasdair MacIntyre's *After Virtue* in 1981 was part of a broader resurgence of interest in Aristotle.[7] The pro-logue to that book suggests a post-apocalyptic, *Riddley Walk-er*-esque scenario wherein a civilization must piece back to-gether its cultural values from a few remaining fragments, an

Erez Lieberman Aiden, "Quantitative Analysis of Culture Using Mil-lions of Digitized Books," *Science*, December 16, 2010; doi: 10.1126/science.1199644.

[7] Alasdair MacIntyre, *After Virtue: A Study in Moral Theory*, 2nd edn. (Notre Dame: University of Notre Dame Press, 1984); hereafter cited parenthetically in text, by page number.

archaeological project that necessarily results in a partial rendering of its past-directed present. Polemically, the rest of the book argues that this scenario is analogous to the state of contemporary ethics, since the received "language of morality" (2) in which philosophers regularly trade is but a piecemeal, incoherent thing, according to MacIntyre; at best, it is merely relativist, at worst, instrumental and "emotivist."

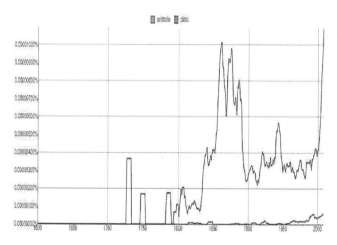

Figure 2. Google ngram, 'Aristotle' vs. 'Plato' as percentage of words in print in the Google Books corpus, 1600-2008

According to MacIntyre, this fragmentary state of knowledge is the direct result of what was lost in the transition from medieval to early modern, from Catholic to Protestant: the end-directed drive of the *Nicomachean Ethics* that transformed "human-nature-as-it-happens-to-be" into "human-nature-as-it-could-be-if-it-realized-its-*telos*" (51). In MacIntyre's narrative, Protestantism vitiated ethical teleology, and in doing so, man was denied "any comprehension of [his] true end" (51); consequently, moral pronouncements no longer have purchase on what is verifiably true or false. Reason, emptied of any explanatory power in theology, is shunted off to experimental science, an "anti-Aristotelian science" that sets "strict boundaries to the powers of reason" (52) and, since it could not legitimately speak about ends, confines itself only to describing the means in ever-increasing detail. Thus MacIntyre concludes:

> Hence the eighteenth-century moral philosophers engaged in what was an inevitably unsuccessful project; for they did indeed attempt to find a rational basis for their moral beliefs in a particular understanding of human nature, while inheriting a set of moral injunctions on the one hand and a conception of human nature on the other which had been expressly designed to be discrepant with each other. . . . They inherited incoherent fragments of a once coherent scheme of thought and action and, since they did not recognise their own peculiar historical and cultural situation, they could not recognise the impossible and quixotic character of their self-appointed task. (53)

The Enlightenment said that man was an innately rational creature, but that his moral sense was not rationally directed towards an innate goal. On this view, modernity (and modern liberalism in particular) is not just false-consciousness (as in Latour) but a willful blindness to its own historical position. Modernity is the petulant tragedy of a child putting together a puzzle that has lost some of its pieces, but who insists on continuing in the face of this knowledge.

Critics either praise MacIntyre for an anti-capitalist vision that seeks to repair the antinomy of the modern world through a return to Aristotelian values or they critique him as a naïf communitarian who romanticizes pre-modern ethics, a retrograde crank in the tradition of Thomas Carlyle.[8] Despite

---

[8] Examples of critics who find MacIntyre's model useful would include Peter McMylor, *Alasdair MacIntyre: Critic of Modernity* (London: Routledge, 1993). More critical responses include, for example, Martha Nussbaum, "Recoiling from Reason," *New York Review of Books* 36 (1989): 36–42; and Gary Kitchen, "Alasdair MacIntyre: The

such criticisms, MacIntyre's work has spawned a movement of so-called "revolutionary Aristotelianism."[9] As the political application of MacIntyre's "ethics of virtue," this movement argues that, since capitalism writ large prevents us from seeing our shared values, we must train our vision on the local, on working for the common rather than the individual profit in ways that facilitate asking questions about character and moral choice that capitalism, by design, prevents us from asking.

So does "revolutionary Aristotelianism" qualify as Aristotle abuse? I will admit to being enticed by the idea of "revolutionary Aristotelianism"; at least enough to get the t-shirt were there to be one. Like many recent historians, MacIntyre is indignant at the early modern treatment of Aristotle, claiming that the medieval scholastic Aristotle—Aquinas's Aristotle—is the "true" Aristotle. Yet the Aristotle that emerges from his account of the Middle Ages—what he refers to as "the predecessor culture"—may not look immediately familiar to medieval historians of scholasticism either. It would perhaps come across as a bit too "William Morris-y": on this view, Aristotle stands for intimate communities engaged in reciprocal economic and ethical exchanges on a small scale, a philosophical vision of community with which MacIntyre combats the paradoxes of modern liberal society. The problem with this Aristotle is less that it is historically "inaccurate" than that it is partial in the way that MacIntyre accuses post-Enlightenment philosophy of being partial. His scholastic Aristotle is primarily the Aristotle of the *Ethics* seasoned with occasional dashes of the *Rhetoric* and the *Politics*. Yet for Aquinas and his contemporaries, Aristotle was also the author of numerous treatises of natural philosophy; the Aristotelian world was one in which metaphysical moral values and physical movements both operated according to similar laws, a

---

Epitaph of Modernity," *Philosophy & Social Criticism* 23 (1997): 71–98.

[9] See the articles collected in Paul Blackledge and Kelvin Knight, eds., *Virtue and Politics: Alasdair MacIntyre's Revolutionary Aristotelianism* (Notre Dame: University of Notre Dame Press, 2011).

model of inclination that drew rocks as well as souls towards their respective natural places.

MacIntyre's diagnosis of the disorder of contemporary ethics points to a rupture between the medieval and the early modern, but what is lost is not necessarily a shared sense of teleological ethics, a consensus on the "facts of human nature," but instead this analogous relation between the everyday and the transcendent. The seventeenth century largely discards the physical basis of Aristotle's philosophy only to preserve the metaphysical. Out went the *Physics*, *On the Heavens*, *On Meteorology*, and the *Generation of Animals*, while the *Ethics* and the *Politics* were keepers. MacIntyre turns away from the real implications of his apocalyptic fable, and his later work is similarly amnesiac on the relation of natural science and moral ethics. As the scholastics regularly maintained, both physics and metaphysics are "speculative" sciences, domains of knowledge constituted through practical reasoning (*ratio practica*) and demonstration (*demonstratio*).

§ WEIRD ARISTOTLE

The recent turn to speculative realism in continental philosophy has also revived Aristotle's reputation as a relevant philosopher. The philosopher Graham Harman has recently suggested on his blog that we embrace a "weird Aristotelianism." He writes:

> Here is my proposal: German Idealism has had its moment in the sun in continental circles. We now need a *weird Aristotle*. (I add the adjective "weird" not just for perversity's sake, but because Aristotle can easily be turned into a bore in the wrong hands).[10]

---

[10] Graham Harman, "Nice Cairo Evening Scene" [weblog post], Object Oriented Ontology, January 5, 2011: http://doctorzamalek2. wordpress.com/2011/01/05/nice-cairo-evening-scene/.

By "weird Aristotle," Harman means, in part, an Aristotle not distorted by what he identifies as the occasionally self-serving framework of twentieth-century continental thought. Like MacIntyre, Harman is rightfully indignant about the way Aristotle has been represented in this tradition: the philosopher is synonymous with all that is tedious and obsolete. And when Aristotle is not being made redundant, he is suffering a perhaps worse fate: "the greatest Aristotelian of modern times, Leibniz, has been allowed into contemporary discourse only through Deleuze's utter falsification of his position."[11] You can hear the branches snapping as Harman sets up the philosophical brush burning necessary before he can launch into his own re-appropriation of the *Physics* and the *Metaphysics*. Deleuze-bashing aside, Harman's real use for Aristotle is as a stick with which to beat post-Kantian, specifically Hegelian Idealism—the belief that, to differing degrees, mind filters our access to the material world, and thus the material has no "real" independent existence. Harman's rehabilitation of Aristotelian substance allows him to imagine a physical thing—a rock, a baseball, a weapon of mass destruction—in all the glory of its concreteness as opposed to the view of empiricists such as David Hume who would reduce a material object to, in Harman's memorable idiom, an "internal diamond encrusted with an accidental grime of relations."[12]

For Harman, Aristotle is a useful tool to prevent not just the reduction of things to "mere relations" but also to prevent the opposite view that reality precedes relations. In Harman's essay "On the Undermining of Objects: Grant, Bruno, and Radical Philosophy," he contrasts these two opposing tendencies and explains why he considers them to be equally misdirected.[13] Harman has dubbed these tendencies "undermining"

---

[11] Harman, "Nice Cairo Evening Scene."

[12] Harman, *Towards Speculative Realism*, 150.

[13] Graham Harman, "On the Undermining of Objects: Grant, Bruno, and Radical Philosophy," in *The Speculative Turn: Continental Materialism and Realism*, eds. Levi R. Bryant, Nick Srnicek, and Graham Harman (Melbourne, Australia: re.press, 2011), 21–40.

and "overmining." Philosophy "undermines" the object by claiming that there is some further physical particle to which a thing may always be reduced. On this view matter is the "deeper principle" to which appeal is always made. Schools of this type would include atomism and more recently, eliminativism, the reduction of subjective experience to biological phenomena. On the opposite view, philosophy "overmines" the object by privileging relationalism over reality. Being is only or primarily relational, and our access to these relations is most often described in terms of language's ability to represent thought. Here we would find a continuum from Idealism to most flavors of social constructionism (including deconstruction). In different ways, both of these schools of thought attempt to "eliminate the object" from philosophy according to Harman.

In rejecting these two umbrella approaches to objects, Harman needs another approach, and this is where Aristotle comes in handy. While Harman's talk elaborates his position more fully, I will just say that what most interests me about Harman's turn to Aristotle is that it depends on a revised version of Aristotelian substantial forms. In Aristotelian hylomorphism, substance is composed of both matter and form, joined together in such a way that neither properly precedes the other. Matter is not merely inert stuff because it contains within it the potential susceptibility to form; likewise, form as actuality is not wholly "immaterial" because a given form is limited by a predisposition to certain types of matter.[14] This ontological mixing was what got Aristotle accused of being an animist and a panpsychist in the early modern period, a period in which matter became purely passive and physical as opposed to the lively medieval substance indissolubly linked

---

[14] For a detailed discussion of substance ontology, see Anneliese Maier, *On the Threshold of Exact Science: Selected Writings of Anneliese Maier on Late Medieval Natural Philosophy*, trans. Steven D. Sargent (Philadelphia: University of Pennsylvania Press, 1982); and Mary Louise Gill, *Aristotle on Substance: The Paradox of Unity* (Princeton: Princeton University Press, 1989).

to the active immateriality of form. The beautiful simplicity of the Aristotelian model as interpreted by the scholastics is that it applies equally to the world of physics (it explains how the matter of an acorn remains continuous with the matter of the oak) as well as metaphysics (it explains the soul as the necessary spiritual form of the human body). Suffice to say that few philosophers have taken substantial forms seriously since the Enlightenment. For Harman, Aristotelian substance lets him re-think the Enlightenment separation of matter and form in ways that allow active and passive qualities to be smuggled back and forth across the de-militarized border between the human and the non-human, the animate and the inanimate (just as it did for medieval scholastics). Harman's twist, however, will be to redefine the idea of "form" in a way that allows for the reality of collective entities—objects composed of objects—a maneuver that may or may not qualify as Aristotle "abuse." What the historian R. H. Tawney famously said of Marx—that he was the "last scholastic"—may perhaps now be said of Harman.

Harman's return to the Aristotelian idea of form as the basis of his ontology is radical, perverse, and, to my mind, promising for several reasons. First, it opens up a space in the history of philosophy for reconsidering scholastic theories of hylomorphism as part of a longer genealogy of materialism, a genealogy from which the Middle Ages is regularly excluded.[15] Even without Harman's twist, his analysis shows the ways in which certain aspects of hylomorphism are compatible with a realist ontology. Second, I think it allows us a new way to return to the notion of teleology that is not *a priori* a reductive one. In doing so, it re-opens a door that was kicked shut, initially, by early modern writers such as Bacon, who mocked Aristotle's human-sized, end-directed notions of becoming as

---

[15] See Kellie Robertson, "Medieval Materialism: A Manifesto," *Exemplaria* 22:2 (2010): 99–118. Harman himself dislikes the term 'materialism,' and claims that what he does is "realism without materialism"; see Levi Bryant, Nick Srnicek, and Graham Harman, "Toward a Speculative Philosophy," in *The Speculative Turn*, 9 [1–18].

the worst kind of anthropocentrism. More recently, the prejudice against teleology has been re-affirmed in the work of Deleuze and Guatttari and those who advocate a "flat ontology," one where becoming has no direction and, therefore, leaves open a world of infinite possibility. On this view, teleology is seen as oppressive or, at least, like Aristotle himself, boring. Flat ontology, in doing away with the problem of determinism, raises other problems, such as how to explain how a specific thing comes into existence—why this instead of that? Finally, and most importantly, it has the potential to do what MacIntyre's "revolutionary Aristotelianism" promised but did not deliver: it makes possible a philosophy where ethics and physics share mutually informing principles. The existing separation of the two, a legacy of the Enlightenment, is one of the many consequences of a Cartesian dualism that rendered matter purely physical and hence passive. A neo-Aristotelian physics would seem to offer a currently unfashionable but useful starting point for opening a dialogue with philosophies enamored of something transcendental like God, form, mind, language, or, more recently, becoming. The challenge for Harman and the rest of those working in the speculative realist vineyard is to articulate what kinds of ethics arise from this weird Aristotelian physics. Precisely how weird would Aristotle need to be in order to make such an ethics possible?

For Harman, Aristotle has become a rallying point for those who want to revive philosophical problems left unresolved by centuries of post-Kantian Idealism. In particular, Aristotle has been seen as one potential answer to the failures of what Quentin Meillassoux has termed "correlationism"— the idea that "if I claim to think of an object beyond thought, then I am thinking it, and thereby turning it into a correlate of thought in spite of myself. Hence the object is nothing more than its accessibility to humans."[16] The insidious effects of correlationism in both its Hegelian and deconstructive forms

---

[16] Harman, "On the Undermining of Objects," 22.

can be combated, according to Harman, with a return to Aristotelian ideas of potentiality—the potentiality of matter to receive certain kinds of forms as outlined in the *Physics*, which granted physical objects autonomous relations with other objects outside of their relations with the human. Aristotle seems to be one of the lighted exits through which we can "get back to the great outdoors" in Meillassoux's phrase, an exterior essentially lost in post-Kantian philosophy. These recent metaphysical conflicts reprise the medieval debate over Aristotelian physics to the extent that they both ask "what is really real?" Is it the physical object in itself or some surrogate object to which it points—whether this "object" is Plato's transcendent Idea, a Christian God, or an intentional object in the human mind. There is thus a surprising through-line from the medieval inheritance of Aristotle to its most recent realist avatars. What both the medieval and the modern debates demonstrate is that there is never a shortage of partisans who want to keep Aristotle weird, and, if given time, perhaps even make him truly revolutionary.

Lynx-Eyed Aristotle
Response to Kellie Robertson

Drew Daniel

And now for some catty remarks. In the Prologue to the *Expositio super viii (octo) libros Physicorum*, William of Ockham pounces upon a particularly jarring image with which to praise Aristotle's exceptional status among the philosophers:

> The most accomplished man to have appeared among them is Aristotle, outstanding as a man of no slight or insignificant learning. With the eyes of a lynx, as it were, he explored the deep secrets of nature and revealed to posterity the hidden truths of natural philosophy.[1]

I'm placing this image of the lynx-eyed Aristotle beside Kellie Robertson's learned and capacious essay because Ockham's queer construction of a nocturnal, feline Aristotle further supplements her archive of medieval Aristotles: the infidel, the physicist, the S&M bottom engaged in a brisk session of pony-play with a rampant Phyllis, but more importantly, the thinker of a hylomorphic metaphysics whose enduring alterity might help to pry us out of present predicaments. Joining this

---

[1] William of Ockham, "On the Notion of Knowledge or Science," *Philosophical Writings* (Edinburgh: Thomas Nelson, 1957), 3.

company, scenting the air with paws extended and pupils dilated wide, Ockham's lynx-eyed Aristotle stands poised to forage for what lies hidden within the dark world of physical nature that Graham Harman's project has plumbed so fiercely. Since Kellie's paper is both historical in its exposition of the past archive of these medieval Aristotles and proleptic in its sense of how that history might reinforce and prepare the way for Graham's own paper today, I want to cut left and simply flag some key, portable points in Kellie's paper that I found most generative. These points—hers not mine—potentially help to anchor a particularly life-saving rope bridge that we might throw across some wide gaps in philosophical history.

Did I just say "philosophical history"? Uh oh. That tiny phrase prompts a cruelly basic question that we haven't the time to unpack today but which Kellie's paper raises for me regardless: Quite simply, why think about philosophy historically at all? This I take to be a common enough gut reaction, and Jonathan Barnes is at least usefully frank in his statement that "the philosophical justification for studying the history of philosophy is not a justification for studying the *history* of philosophy at all: it is a reason for pretending that the subject has no history."[2] How could a "weird Aristotle" not only exemplify the mutual impasse of a methodological Chinese finger-puzzle (philosophy's resistance to history; history's resistance to philosophy), but also help us to think in new ways about the puzzle's reach and shape? It is here that the example of Kellie's paper is so suggestive. When Robertson points out that MacIntyre's Aristotle is simultaneously Aquinas's Aristotle (hence unoriginal) and yet also, and I love this phrase, "too William Morris-y" (hence deviating badly from the original, not hence sounding like Morrissey), we can sense a usefully polychronic pileup of possible Aristotles in play, thanks to her acute powers of analysis and quick-draw wit. Naïve histori-

---

[2] Jonathan Barnes, "Introduction," *The Cambridge Companion to Aristotle*, ed. Jonathan Barnes (Cambridge: Cambridge University Press, 1995), xvii.

cists might well get cranky and want to ask, well, which is it really: Aquinas or Morris? Is MacIntyre's "revolutionary Aristotelianism" unoriginal and hence not recognizably "revolutionary" enough or is it too original and hence not recognizably "Aristotelian" enough? I am not accusing Kellie of hypocrisy—far from it— in both detecting the provenance and trajectory of Aristotle's dissemination while at the same time permitting and encouraging abuse and transformation and "weirding." As any S&M practitioner could tell you, there is good abuse and there is bad abuse. MacIntyre's indignation *does* sit oddly with his own re-fashioning. How can you defend from modernization the very thing that you are yourself modernizing? When Robertson calls him out for this, the hypocrisy is not hers but his.

Yet here I want to encourage Kellie to go further with the set of instincts that permit her to say that MacIntyre's Aristotle "bears very little resemblance to the one with which [she is] familiar," and to speculate about what grounds that instinct of familiarity further. Can one call for a "weird" Aristotle without in the process running the risk of such a defacement? I would predict that Kellie's answer would be: "Very well, so be it, but it should be done like this" with an ostensive finger pointing towards Mr. Harman. If MacIntyre's Aristotle is an infelicitous cross-breed of Aquinas and William Morris, are there other splicings and genetic experiments which could prove more generative? And would they be generative because they openly celebrated a perversion or deviation in relation to what we take to be Aristotle's positions (themselves fugitive creatures, rarely housebroken for long), or because their return to Aristotle would be strategically perverse in relation to prevailing correlationist paradigms? Is Aristotle weird to us because of our own Kantian and phenomenological preoccupations, or is Aristotle, as it were, weird to the bone?

Getting shakier still, dare we call Kellie out about the substantial cause of her familiarity with what does or does not look like Aristotle and ask what Aristotle's Aristotle, the origin and ratio from which such deviations are to be measured and "weirdnesses" show up as weird, actually looks and sounds like? To pose such a question sounds bad, rude, simplistic. In the credulous and conservative climate in which Aristotle's prose is lovingly described by its own admirers as having the texture of "chop'd hay," to cite Thomas Gray's immortal phrase, do we really want to raise up the particularly paternal spectre of What Aristotle Originally Intended?[3] To invoke authorial intentions in this manner seems so very not weird. Like calling one's self "a man's man," to ask after "Aristotle's Aristotle" sounds presumptuous. But just as surely as one cannot have a snub nose without having a nose in the first place, one cannot have a weird Aristotle without having an Aristotle.[4]

To continue to press here, and it is a pressure which I take Kellie Robertson's own thinking to have made available, let us ask: what would happen if we applied Aristotelian metaphysics to the problem of Aristotle's own variability across the history of philosophy itself? Looking into Book Delta of the *Metaphysics*, we are told that:

> Things are called substances in two ways: a substance is whatever is an ultimate subject, which is

---

[3] The phrase appears in a 1746 letter to Thomas Wharton: "In the first Place he is the hardest Author by far I ever meddled with. Then he has a dry Conciseness, that makes one imagine one is perusing a Table of Contents rather than a Book; it tastes for all the World like chop'd Hay, or rather like chop'd Logic; for he has a violent Affection to that Art, being in some Sort his own Invention; so that he often loses himself in little trifling Distinctions and verbal Niceties, and what is worse leaves you to extricate yourself as you can" (Thomas Gray, *Essays and Criticisms by Thomas Gray*, ed. C.S. Northrup [Boston: D. C. Heath, 1911], 143).

[4] For a fuller account of snubbed noses, see D. M. Balme's "Appendix 2: the Snub," attached to his article "Aristotle's biology was not essentialist" in *Philosophical Issues in Aristotle's Biology*, eds. Allan Gotthelf and James G. Lennox (Cambridge: Cambridge University Press, 1987), 306.

no longer said of anything else; and a substance is a
this-and-so which is also separable.[5]

What would an account of philosophical history modeled
upon the tension between these two ways of thinking substance look like? How can Aristotle function as both an ultimate subject, the horizon of Kellie Robertson's familiarity as
she sizes up what MacIntryre and Harman are up to, and yet
also be subject to the separability which might permit the
work of "weirding" to take place? I have in mind not just the
doctrinal history of the dissemination of hylomorphism as
one particularly influential peace treaty between form and
matter along the road from Empedocles and Plato to the present. Rather, how would an intellectual history operate and
argue which tried to think the primary temporality of an auto-
potentializing *ousia* with variable expressions piling up over
time after that primary moment?

If scholastic thinkers pursued with uncommon, even ex-
hausting rigor, the distinction between *dunamis* (potency)
and *energeia* (act), between what an entity can potentially do
and what an entity is actually doing, then perhaps the relationship between these two terms can help us to realize that in
some sense, Aristotle's Aristotle has been in front of us all
along, and he was always "weird." The quick and dirty, perhaps sophistical trial run would tell us that, like the malleable
bronze material so beloved of ontological thought experiments which can become a bust of a Greek philosopher or can
be melted and reformed into bullets, if we take up Aristotle
and treat him as a kind of philosophico-historical *ousia*, then
Aristotle's "substantial form" persists within and across all
that can possibly be done to and with him: each interpretation
actualizes a potential Aristotle already contained, already
germinal, within his essence. This seemingly pre-emptive
scripting of what can be done with Aristotle is articulated into

---

[5] Aristotle, *Metaphysics*, in *The Works of Aristotle*. ed. W.D. Ross
(Oxford: Clarendon Press, 1928), 1017b23–25.

Aristotle's own substance as an "ultimate subject," and couldn't be otherwise. This doesn't delimit Kellie Robertson's capacity to demur from the appeal of MacIntyre's Aristotle on all sorts of grounds, from the philosophical to the aesthetic, or to prefer Harman's Aristotle precisely because of its weirdness. Nor is this quite the "teleological" history that certain kinds of Aristotle, had we succumbed to them, would have led us to expect, and which kneejerk opponents to thinking essences on behalf of now stale critiques of "essentialism" stand poised to decry. For this Aristotle—can I call it Robertsonian?—is counterfactually in excess of the entire sequence of Aristotelianisms up to the present moment: at once cumulatively packed with the full history of its own dissemination and yet weirdly poised to potentially phase-shift into unimaginable shapes as the particular separability of "this" Aristotle continues to move and change. Our temporal moment cannot conclude, cannot bring to an end, what we can expect from this substantial form's futurity. So I want to thank Kellie Robertson for leading me to wonder if a weirder Aristotle might itself model a weird new way to stop pretending that philosophy has no history without thereby surrendering philosophy up to a purely or merely historicist capture: if the readings that Kellie resurrects and Graham promises are any indication, we are going to be left with a far less reliable, less stolid and less reassuring figure than the bearded bust collecting dust in the recesses of the library. If I may close with a wretched homonymic pun, perhaps it is time to trade the plural "links" of an exhausted correlationism forever shuttling between mind and world for the singular "lynx" of the manifestly weird, unashamedly speculative, medieval Aristotle of William of Ockham: the lynx-eyed predator who stares into the conceptual darkness of the physical world and tracks the substance of his prey.

Shakespeare's Kitchen Archives

Julian Yates

> The continuity of all agents in space and time is not given to [compositionists] as it was to the naturalists: they have to compose it, slowly and progressively. And moreover to compose it from discontinuous pieces. . . . [C]onsequences overwhelm their causes, and this over-flow has to be respected everywhere, in every domain, in every discipline, and for every type of entity.
>
> —Bruno Latour, "An Attempt at a Compositionist Manifesto"

> No transportation without transformation.
>
> —Bruno Latour, *Aramis or the Love of Technology*

These words you are reading, some of which I read aloud once upon a speculatively medieval afternoon in New York City—and which I find myself compelled now to rewrite—what *are* they? What were they? And what have they become by their translation and so transformation from paper to essay, from colloquium to whichever media now hosts them? Perhaps, by their end, they will have the flavor of a manifesto. But if so, it will not be in the arch/modern sense that Bruno Latour sets to one side even as he attempts his own "Compositionist Manifesto." There will be no "war cries intended to speed up the movement, ridicule the Philistines, castigate the reactionaries."[1] Like his, the words I wrote and now rewrite "have something in common" with such rallying calls, "namely the *search for the Common*." "The thirst for the Common World is what there is of communism in compositionism," he observes, "with this small but crucial difference: that it has to be slowly composed." The compositionist has to entertain competing and divergent, wandering agencies. Her manifestos remain therefore subject to failure, deformation, and transformation by the "discontinuous pieces" they attempt to host, by the overflow of entities and agencies they register. What then do they produce? To what do they amount? "Prospects," merely, boasts Latour—projections, speculative possibilities. Composing "carries with it the pungent but ecologically correct smell of 'compost'," a scene of slow cooking, of fermentation, percolation," the active 'de-composition' of many invisible actors."[2]

In offering you this essay as a composting of the old, an archive whose difference from the paper captures something of its flavor, I should explain that my aim is to reach after a type of writing that takes its cue from the things it stages and combines. If any of the words you read here bear repeating, then perhaps, that will be because they were a 'recipe,' a speculative gathering of ingredients and the setting into motion of *things* for which I served as the occasion, but for which I could not claim to be sole author, even as the words were at one time historical, came from my mouth, on a certain day. This essay archives the paper. Such is its relation to that occasion or performance. As you read, supplying your voice instead of mine, understand that these are words that search after things they do not quite yet know—a composition, a

---

[1] Bruno Latour, "An Attempt at a Compositionist Manifesto," *New Literary History* 41.3 (Summer 2010): 472 [471–90].
[2] Latour, "Compositionist Manifesto," 474.

recipe, an archive, a compost-heap, a project/ion. Welcome to this archive (and its ash).[3]

§ OF RECIPES AND THE PLAY-TEXTS: EVERYDAY METAPHYSICS

In what follows I assume a provisional or working analogy between recipes and play-scripts, regarding both forms as projective, expressing, that is, a desire or a vector to become other than they are. I am interested in the practical metaphysics (cooking and play-acting) to which such texts, "freeze-framed" as they may be, disconnected therefore from a chain of making to which they belong, allude, and which they may be said to archive either before or after the fact of performance.[4] Recipes and play-texts designate actants in a cascade (ingredients and *personae*) that will lead to the production of some other thing—a 'dish,' 'a play,' which has or will have been, and which may be, again, and which remains, always and again, for the very first time, different from itself, and, by that difference, the same. Leftovers that both precede and post-date their projections, the recipe or play-text offer us a strange sort of archive. Do they constitute castings, exoskeletons, pre or post-fossils, traces of a several becoming? Even as their freeze framing embeds them in a problem of presence and absence, in a concern with the trace or the impression left by things on various substrates, to restate and so to archive the Derridean problematic, they remain, still, relays or translational nodes that do not belong to any particular time, a

---

[3] In *Archive Fever* ash figures what remains secret and is indexed to the processes of forgetting, erasure, and fragmentation that attend to the archive: Jacques Derrida, *Archive Fever: A Freudian Impression*, trans. Eric Prenowitz (Chicago: University of Chicago Press, 1996), 100–1.

[4] On the fracturing of chains of reference and the inhospitability of the "freeze frame," see "Thou Shalt Not Freeze Frame, Or How Not to Misunderstand the Science and Religion Debate," in Bruno Latour, *On the Modern Cult of the Factish Gods* (Durham: Duke University Press, 2010), 99–123.

switchboard emitting different orders of time effects for all occasions. Freeze framed mediators, both recipe and play-text remain joinable by their incompletion, a possible haunt for the reader turned specter, the reader become host to a set of routines past that speak us even as we speak them.

As my language indicates I describe these textual forms from the vantage point afforded by Latour's modeling of mechanisms of translation in the sciences and his recasting of questions of reference as chains of mediators, "reference" 'circulating' or percolating through the chain as long as it is not interrupted, and failing when the chain is broken.[5] In Latour's vocabulary, recipes and play-texts exist as mediators in a chain of translations that seek to make something repeatable, that enable some *thing* to endure by its difference from itself and by the noise it is able to tolerate, as it remains differently the same. A strategic difference between the Latour's positing of a parliament of things, however, and the projects of many of us housed in the humanities resides in the way we find ourselves oriented to our objects of study. Tuned to things past, to the fragments of chains of making long since severed or attenuated, partially interrupted, and so to actor networks that have dropped actants as they have added new ones, we are obliged to deal with the objects that result from these dropped connections. It is these texts or traces, these partial connections that we take as our points of departure. We serve then, in Latour's terms, as 'avatars' of the freeze frame, or, to speak an allied language, "vicars of [lost] causations" or causations gone missing.[6] Our object remains always the archive of a practice, the remnants of some thing, which, by our joining, we re/activate, alive to the ways the figure of the archive itself

---

[5] On "circulating reference," see in particular Bruno Latour, *Pandora's Hope: Essays on the Reality of Science Studies*, trans. Catherine Porter (Cambridge: Harvard University Press, 1999), 24–79; and on translation, Bruno Latour, *Aramis or the Love of Technology*, trans. Catherine Porter (Cambridge: Harvard University Press, 1993), 119.

[6] Graham Harman, "On Vicarious Causation," *Collapse* II (2007): 171–205.

as actor-network enables certain modes of joining and disables others, makes certain worlds or prospects un/thinkable.

The phrase "everyday" or "practical metaphysics" (the everydayness poached from Michel de Certeau) suggests a strategy of composition, then, of the recipe or play-text, as a mode of knowing, and as offering an epistemology tuned to the difficulties posed by humanities work that wishes to own its connection to Actor Network Theory (ANT) and Object Oriented Ontology (OOO). Such work requires, I think, a certain generic play/playfulness, and an orientation to textual remains that understands the practice we name reading as a mode of joining with practices as they have been archived, as they have been freeze framed, and caught in various substrates. Less a charnel house than an *oubliette*, less a Protestant drama of the elect and the preterit than a purgatorial catholicism that retains all even as all is lost, the script I seek to imagine plays archival work out as a mode of inquiry content to forgo the Judgment Day poetics of resurrection and bad messianism for a more humdrum 'everyday metaphysics' that models the efforts of humanistic study as a making available of you and I as screens that register the effects of such sensual objects named "past" that attract.[7] In what follows I broach the co-incidence or co-imbrication of matters of cuisine and moral philosophy; try my hand at pastry; and then follow one of Shakespeare's cooks into his own stage world— all in order to discover what such a trajectory or composing might elicit.

§ *DRAMATIS PERSONAE*: TITUS, IRÈNE, BRUNO, AND ME

At a certain point, the analogy between recipe and play-script, kitchen, and stage breaks down. Indeed, it begins to do so

---

[7] For an allied argument for the human become "screen," see Julian Yates, "It's (for) You: The Tele-T/r/opical Post-human," *post-medieval: a journal of medieval cultural studies* 1.1/2 (Spring/Summer 2010): 223–34.

almost immediately. Shakespeare's plays, as we receive them, already anticipate the correlation, deploying the metaphysics of the kitchen in order to render the metaphysics of the stage. The kitchen is deployed as one register with which to explore the vagaries of action, agency, and making as they intersect with those scripts on offer that seek to answer the age-old question of moral philosophy, dieting, and social theory in the West: "How to live well?" A minimal emblem for this analogy, to which I will return, might be the stage direction that accompanies the re-entrance of the revenging Titus in Act 5, Scene 3 of *Titus Andronicus*:

Titus: Welcome, my gracious lord; welcome dread queen; welcome, ye war-like Goths; welcome Lucius; and welcome all. Although the cheer be poor, 'twill fill your stomachs; please you eat of it.

Saturnius: Why are thou this attired, Andronicus?

Titus: Because I would be sure to have all well, to entertain your highness and your empress.

Tamora: We are beholding to you, good Andronicus.[8]

Trumpets sound. Enter Titus "like a cook, placing dishes." Titus arrogates to himself the off-stage routines of the kitchen, and sets the stage for a return to power, for the renewed efficacy of his erstwhile unsuccessful acts of contrition, intercession, and now revenge. Give him his due, lackluster viciousness that he is, Emperor Saturninus poses the right question: why is Titus "thus attired" (5.3.30)? "Because I would be sure to have all well," he answers "To entertain your highness and your empress" (5.3.31–32). Titus' lines read now

---

[8] William Shakespeare, *Titus Andronicus*, ed. Alan Hughes (Cambridge: Cambridge University Press, 1994), 5.3.25–33. Subsequent references appear parenthetically in the text.

as grisly irony or black comedy, but to an audience tuned to Greek and Roman traditions, the matter of hospitality and the question of "wellness" voiced in his spoken desire to "have all well" indicates that he remains embarked on answering the question 'how to live well.' Indebted to the cannibalistic revenge plot of the story of Procne and to Seneca's *Thyestes*, *Titus Andronicus* plays out the classical script as it is allied to questions of government and the mutually extensive well-being of individual and social bodies. The play puzzles this moral philosophical problem in the world of broken tables, poisonous or cannibal kitchens, and the mistaken, pretended, malicious or failed acts of hospitality that constitute Titus's Rome.[9]

That Titus aims to answer this question with a pie, with a food item that announces itself as an event, as feast food, but which is indexed to a problem of insides and outsides, of the instability of knowing, takes me into the kitchen where I find the true occasion for this paper: the sentiments expressed by the *persona* named "Irène," a 1970s Parisian clerical worker and housewife who scandalously does not enjoy cooking. Her words, which capture an order of kitchen metaphysics, of knowledge crafted in and by cooking, were recorded in an interview that forms part of Luce Giard, Pierre Mayol, and Michel de Certeau's second volume of *The Practice of Everyday Life*—"living and cooking." Here are two passages from the interview. The first concerns Irène's attempts at pastry:

Marie: And the custards, did you make them all by yourself, or . . . ?

Irène: Oh yes! Yes, yes, yes, all by myself. There I at least have my sister's recipes. We spent some spring vacations in the country with my sister; there were

---

[9] My reading of *Titus Andronicus* is indebted to Katherine A. Rowe's *Dead Hands: Fictions of Agency: Renaissance to Modern* (Stanford: Stanford University Press, 1999), 52–85.

many children who loved custard, so she used to make them every day. We had fresh milk from a farmer next door, so it was really nice. She used to make five pints of custard every day, sometimes caramel, or vanilla, or chocolate, and I started to make some too. Sometimes they're not bad at all.

Jean: Yes, I managed to get some down!

Irène: It's so happened that I've made some pies, but pretty rarely, because there too, you [Jean] don't really like them. . . a pie crust isn't too complicated to make (*then, in a hesitating tone*) that might be within my reach.[10]

The second expresses her dis/comfort with the kitchen and with cooking in general:

Irène: "When I make things that are too complicated, I worry and I ruin everything, so it's to my advantage to make simple things. When it comes down to it, cooking worries me. I don't know why?"

Marie: "In the end, I think it's much more a question of being accustomed to making complicated things, more elaborate things, in any case.[11]

In the interview and analysis that follows, Giard and Mayol minister to what they perceive to be a felt lack of expertise, a failed exposure to the physics of the kitchen whose mastery eludes Irène even as she gets by with what, though it goes unnamed, we imagine is a pre-made pie-crust (sigh!). They read

---

[10] Michel de Certeau, Luce Giard, Pierre Mayol, *The Practice of Everyday Life*, Vol. 2: *Living and Cooking*, trans. Timothy Tomasik (Minneapolis: University of Minnesota Press, 1998), 231.

[11] de Certeau, Giard, Mayol, *The Practice*, 225.

her as one of an increasing number of women alienated from their culinary past and adrift in the kitchen, much like the city-dwellers adrift in a Paris whose infrastructures of neighborliness and hospitality that once defined and gave character to each *arrondissement* have entered a slow decay.[12] In doing so, they miss, I think, the way Irène's comments might be read as more than a confession or even as more than the performance of a confession—such as when she observes the following, tantalizing *praeteritio*: "When it comes down to it, cooking worries me. I don't know why?" In articulating this worry in a finite statement of non-knowledge, Irène momentarily retards the conversation. She slows things down, introducing a little idiocy or gap into the proceedings as Isabelle Stengers might put it, an opening on to another order of discussion.[13] "It's a question," says Marie, "of being accustomed to making complicated things, more elaborate things." The kitchen borders the compost heap, we might observe. The exposure to chance forces and diverging agencies lies in the essence of its routines and recipes. Some will fail. Accustom yourself to such failures. Relax. Let's pause with Irène, therefore, and take up Marie's invitation to custom, to practice, by projecting Irène's ambiguously stated desire to try her hand at pastry into our own test kitchen, provided by a series of textual surrogates: a sixteenth-century recipe for pastry; and then the play in which Shakespeare comes closest to putting a kitchen on stage, *Titus Andronicus*. Along the way, I'll engage in a running conversation with the modeling of agency and making on offer from Bruno Latour, to see what the four of us, Irène, Bruno, Titus, and I can learn.

---

[12] de Certeau, Giard, Mayol, *The Practice*, 151–211.

[13] Isabelle Stengers, "The Cosmopolitical Proposal," in *Making Things Public: Atmospheres of Democracy*, eds. Bruno Latour and Peter Weibel (Cambridge: MIT Press, 2005), 994.

§ GESTURE SEQUENCES 1

You may want to wash your hands. We're heading into the kitchen to make pastry or a "fine paste," following a receipt or recipe from the second part to Thomas Dawson's *The Good Huswife's Jewell* (1597):

> To make a fine paste.
> Take faire flower and wheate & the yolkes of egges with sweet butter melted, mixing all these together with your hands, til it be brought to a past, & then make your coffins whether it be for pyes or tartes, then you may put Saffron and suger if you have it a sweet paste, having respect to the true seasoning some use to put to their paste Beefe or mutton broth, and some creame.[14]

Beyond the lack of quantities, several things may strike you about the phraseology of this recipe as it differs from other recipes you have absorbed into the habit knowledge or memory of your muscles. The open-ended infinitive in the title, "to make a fine paste" foregrounds the verb, the "doing" of the cooking that will be done. It gestures forwards to a future: the production of "a fine paste," not "fine paste" *per se*, but "*a* fine paste," *a* finite "paste," that will be the product of *your* hands (or of the metonyms / servants you put to work). The recipe posits itself as a set of routines for managing the vagaries of time and place and ingredients that results always in, and by its difference from, the same thing: "a fine paste."

If you find the tenses and the mood of these verbs engaging—then you will be alive to the shift that follows the title. The word recipe or receipt derives from the Latin for to take, and the lightly imperative "take" directs what follows.[15] The

---

[14] Thomas Dawson, *The Good Huswife's Jewell* (London, 1597), 17.
[15] Julia Reinhard Lupton makes the same point in her wonderful essay "Thinking with Things: Hannah Woolley to Hannah Arendt," *postmedieval: a journal of medieval cultural studis* 3.1 (Spring 2012):

verb engages you, puts you in your body, directing you to your hands without naming them. It asks you to turn this way and that, to retrieve and assemble the objects and ingredients you need from wherever it is in your kitchen that you keep them. This finite "take" condenses all manner of verbs necessary to assembling and preparing the ingredients: the measuring of the "flour and wheate;" the separating of the egg yolks from their whites; the melting of the butter. It's up to you to actualize the prepositions and to set the list of ingredients-nouns in motion. You are one or become one with the syntax. Then there unfolds an uncertain period of "mixing" marked by the use of a gerund whose duration is decided by the feel of the "past[e]." By this undefined "space" of mixing, your body becomes a little clock, or more properly you and your ingredients become a little clock in series—for by the "feel" of the paste on the skin of your fingers as you work it, and by the heat of the day and your hands as you spread it on the work surface executing what the French name the *fraissage*, you will know the moment when as Julia Child puts it, "an even blending between the fat and the flour" has occurred.[16] There's a *kairos* to this kitchen drama that depends on your fingers, eyes, and nose as they apprehend the quality of the substance in your hands.

Now, on you go to "make your coffins"—the quaintly disturbing sixteenth-century vernacular for the British English "pastry case" and the American English "pastry shell" that intrudes a little graveyard into the kitchen. The graveyard is also, of course, a kitchen, your corpse a veritable buffet for the worms to which your skin offers less and less resistance as it loses integrity in the non-anthropic *fraissage* that John Donne names vermiculation (being eaten by worms).[17] The Polonius-

---

63–79.

[16] Julia Child, Louisette Bertholle, and Simone Beck, *Mastering the Art of French Cooking*, 2 vols. (New York: Alfred A. Knopf, 1990), 139.

[17] John Donne, *The Sermons of John Donne*, eds. Evelyn Simpson and George R. Potter (Berkeley: University of California Press, 1962),

stowing Hamlet plays this same game of inverted anthropo-centrism in Act 4, Scene 3 when King Claudius catches up with him and asks where Polonius is? Hamlet tells him that Polonius is at "supper." "At Supper? Where?" asks the King. "Not where he eats, but where 'a is eaten. A certain convoca-tion of politic worms are e'en at 'em," replies the Prince: "Your worm," he goes on, "is your only emperor for diet. We fat all creatures else to fat us, and we fat ourselves for maggots. Your fat king and your lean beggar is but variable service—two dishes, but one table. That's the end."[18] The world is just one large "dinner" (lunch) or kitchen. "But one table," but "two dishes"—we "fat" ourselves on the world and world eats our fat. Life and death are merely a succession of "service[s]" or courses—tables set for different guests. But this recipe's a comedy or perhaps a history, not a tragedy—no death for the protagonist, though if you're making a meat pie then obvious-ly you will have opted for the broth you have obtained from stewing the cut and roasted bones of a sheep or a cow—otherwise, this "fine paste" attempts to congeal your labor and love without loss.

Typically, when academics read Dawson's recipe for "a fine paste," almost immediately there comes a parting of the ways. Economic historians, social historians and food histori-ans treat such recipes as documents, providing information on key historical questions such as ingredients, diet, social habits, prices, trade, famine, riots, resources, or with an eye to what the kitchen may have been like as a technical space.[19]

Vol. 2., 238 [235–36].

[18] William Shakespeare, *Hamlet*, ed. Edward Hubler (London and New York: Signet Classic, 1987), 4.3.16–25.

[19] Space precludes more than a series of insufficient emblems for this field: Christopher Dyer, *Standards of Living in the Later Middle Ages: Social Change in England c. 1200-1500* (Cambridge: Cambridge Uni-versity Press, 1989); Stephen Mennell, *All Manners of Food: Eating and Taste in England and France from the Middle Ages to the Present* (Carbondale: University of Illinois Press, 1995); and Keith Wright-son, *Earthly Necessities* (New Haven: Yale University Press, 2000).

Allied to this orientation, we might add cultural historians and literary critics who decode the iconographic role of food items or cooking within what they constitute by their labors as a so-called sixteenth-century cultural "imaginary."[20] Less typically, but now more commonly, culinary historians who take their cue from long-standing period enthusiasts, get their hands in some flour and try recipes out to discover what they may learn.[21] For them, Dawson's recipe remains a partially readable routine or set of instructions that might be performed differently but still successfully. In repeating if not replicating the gestures of long dead cooks culinary historians recover the function of recipes as projective texts. They "play," as does Titus, at being cooks. They act "like" cooks, embodying the recipe much as actors embody fictions. In doing so, period enthusiasts and culinary historians stand in the frontline of a practical metaphysics as it has been archived by recipes and cookbooks. Their gesture sequences, improvised, subject to constant monitoring and revision, seek to re-actualize the cascade that the recipe projects, with and by an order of difference that might be understood to constitute the historical as an heuristic merely.

A script for their actions might be found in this passage in Bruno Latour's *Pandora's Hope*:

Whenever we make something *we* are not in command, we are slightly *overtaken* by the action: every builder knows that. Thus the paradox of constructiv-

---

[20] Space (again) precludes more than a series of insufficient emblems for this field: Robert Appelbaum, *Aguecheek's Beef, Belch's Hiccup, and Other Gastronomic Interjections: Literature, Culture, and Food among the early moderns* (Chicago: Chicago University Press, 2006); and Wendy Wall, *Staging Domesticity: Household Work and English Identity in early modern Drama* (Cambridge: Cambridge University Press, 2002).

[21] Ken Albala, "Cooking as Research Methodology," in *Renaissance Food from Rabelais to Shakespeare*, ed. Joan Fitzpatrick (Farnham: Ashgate Publishing Company, 2010), 73–88.

ism is that it uses a vocabulary of *mastery* that no architect, mason, city planner, or carpenter would ever use. Are we fooled by what we do? Are we controlled, possessed, alienated? No, not always, not quite. That which slightly overtakes us is *also*, because of our agency, because of the *clinamen* of our action, slightly overtaken, modified. Am I simply restating the dialectic? No, there is no object, no subject, no contradiction, no *Aufhebung*, no mastery, no recapitulation, no spirit, no alienation. But there are events. I never *act*; I am always slightly surprised by what I do. That which acts through me is also surprised by what I do, by the chance to mutate, to change, and to bifurcate, the chance that I and the circumstances surrounding me offer to that which has been invited, recovered, welcomed.[22]

What the recipe welcomes might be said to be the order of surprise that action elicits. This surprise, which is addressed or nurtured, mid-sequence, mid-routine, and which, if it overwhelms the recipe may result in failure or a different order of success, becomes for the culinary historian a multivalent temporal entity that he or she seeks to know, to experience by and as and through the cascade that the recipe sets in motion. The culinary historian-cum-phenomenologist inhabits this possibility of surprise, of being taken by the recipe, by invention, in order to discover its lineaments, its bounds, all with the expectation of sensing, feeling, registering past kitchen archives as they taste and smell today. Speaking from Marie's script of custom and habit, the culinary historian habituates herself to the recipe as habit archive.

So, why is Irène still worried? Why does the risk-managed shelter of a pre-made pastry case or coffin still beckon? All it takes, so it seems, is practice. While Latour's script for making might capture the essence of the culinary historian's exposure

---

[22] Latour, *Pandora's Hope*, 281.

to kitchen archives, his splicing together the language of inter-secting polities, common becomings, and so the question of a generalized as opposed to anthropic "wellness," with the workings of *poesis* ratchets the rhetoric of responsibility to breaking point. To cook, in Latour's translational sense, be-yond the mutual transformation of cook and ingredients, be-comes a moral philosophical enterprise—one that you could botch quite badly by failing to welcome, failing to host, and then you would be responsible for and subject to interruption by something that you had failed to welcome, for in failing this test you denied something entry to a world in common that you, small as you are, have a hand in constituting, com-posing, or composting. Worse still, Irène tends to find herself alone in the kitchen, facing a series of guests (human and not) for which no Archimedean point or pronoun provides viable menu, portion control, or seating plan. No Marie to help—just a few of her sister's recipes to work, an archive she has to decode and put to work. How then to know whether we will be judged to have been sufficiently welcoming? How to triage our prospects and to see off the un-making that we may have set in motion by our attempts to make *this* or *that*?

At such moments, as the ground spirals away and ontolo-gy flattens (quite properly), Latour tends to make the follow-ing kind of statement that aims to designate a ratio or qualitative difference by which we may judge good acts of making from bad. In *On the Modern Cult of the Factish Gods*, he writes that "it is no longer a matter of abruptly passing from slavery to freedom by shattering idols, but of distin-guishing those attachments that save from those that kill."[23] In "An Attempt at a 'Compositionist Manifesto," he writes that instead "of the old opposition between what is constructed and what is not constructed" what's key is the "slight but cru-cial difference between what is *well* and what is *badly* con-structed (or composed).[24] How may we, in other words, know

---

[23] Latour, *On the Modern Cult of the Factish Gods*, 61.
[24] Latour, "Compositionist Manifesto," 478.

as we do, and thus escape a structure of belatedness?

For Latour, the homology between techniques, mechanisms, protocols, and moral philosophical results plays out in the form of his frequently lyrical renderings of scientific practice and in his increasingly complex model of translation. Belatedness may be seen off the premises by the protocols of scientific practice. The desire for immanence or *kairos* manifests as a concern with the media specificity, tool, or *techne* employed in order to perform a certain operation—working on the assumption, following Stengers that a "tech-nically well-modeled" question is "ethically well-modeled" also.[25] This co-imbrication of ethics and technics has the effect of transforming every technical operation necessarily into an archive of its own procedure.[26] And for Latour the project of crafting a circulating model of reference, the refiguring of fetish and fact as "factish," the rewriting of iconoclasm as iconoclash, the rewriting of "translation" as an issue of chains of mediators that transform, the transformation necessary to effective translation, as opposed to the inferiority of the copy, serve as key supports or enablers in the making possible of immanence. Latour's recipes or compositions never quite end. Instead they deploy and comprehend the moment or advent of critique or interruption in optative mode. The key ends up, if you like, lying not in *poesis* itself but in its archives, in a mode of *poesis* that operates already as a self-conscious and self-aware archiving or auto/zoo/bio/archiving of its opera-

---

[25] Isabelle Stengers, *Power and Invention: Situating Science* (Minneapolis: University of Minnesota Press, 1997), 216.

[26] In essence I am arguing that Latour's model of techniques as always also inquiries into their own propositional content attempts to craft a necessary link between *poesis* and critique between construction and deconstruction conceived, following Niklas Luhmann, as "second order observing." See Niklas Luhmann, "Deconstruction as Second-Order Observing," in *Distinction: Redescribing the Descriptions of Modernity*, trans. Joseph O'Neil, Elliott Schreiber, Kerstin Behnke, and William Whobrey (Stanford: Stanford University Press, 2002), 94–112.

tions, of all it makes and unmakes. What new kinds of "speech impedimenta" must we discover—what kinds of imperfect tools must we fabricate in order to expand the composition are the questions that concern the composition of the collective in *Politics of Nature*—whose parliament of things never ceases to inquire into who and what it composes?[27] "No future, but many prospects" reads a key sub-heading in the "Compositionist Manifesto." But how may we archive our projections before the fact?

Still then the "worry" Irène voices haunts me. For this worry seems indexed to the problem of the ratio by which we will know the 'well' from the 'poorly' made, the ties that will save from those that kill. This difficulty, as Graham Harman describes it in *Prince of Networks* is that "the translation model of truth renders the correspondence theory impossible," but "if there is no correspondence between knowledge and world, it might seem that 'anything goes'." "But this conclusion does not follow," he continues,

> there can still be better or worse translations, just as there can be limitless French versions of Shakespeare of varying ranges of quality. But here the metaphor breaks down: after all, there really is an original text of Shakespeare (though philologists have a hard time establishing it) and by analogy we might hold that there is also an original world that is the subject of all translation by actors. But such a notion makes a poor fit with Latour's relationalism. The analogy with Latour would apparently work only if Shakespeare's text existed only at the moment of being translated and were in fact defined by that very translation.[28]

---

[27] Bruno Latour, *Politics of Nature: How to Bring the Sciences into Nature*, trans. Catherine Porter (Cambridge, MA: Harvard University Press, 2004), 184–228.
[28] Graham Harman, *Prince of Networks: Bruno Latour and Metaphysics* (Melbourne: re-press, 2009), 79–80.

The reference to Shakespeare is fortuitous, merely, but beyond that, what Harman enables me to recognize, via his good faith in philology, disclosing perhaps less a realism than a robust textual idealism, is the way that, for Latour, the flattening of ontology that his metaphysics requires empties out the ability to know this difference. Accordingly, making acquires or needs to acquire a self-archiving awareness, the ability to touch itself as it makes, and by folding onto itself, to stay in contact with its effects. In such a way, *poesis* will never have to surrender its prospects to the wild card phenomenalization of its projects.

From Irène's perspective, then, Latour seems to handle the loneliness of cooking, of making, and its attendant blindness to action, by the willed contracting of an auto-archive fever, all in order to prevent the auto-production of really bad archives. Such an archive aims to see off the failure of hospitality that comes with any act of making. Of course, Titus, whom we met at the beginning of this paper, has been up to something quite similar in *Titus Andronicus*. The desire to craft a link or passage from *poesis* to critique and back (even as they may be logically distinct categories) has a long history in humanist thought. Let's see what Titus has to teach us—what his lesson in pastry making has to offer Irène, Bruno, and me.

§ GESTURE SEQUENCES (2)

"Hark, wretches, I mean to martyr you." Mouths "stopped," ears open, Chiron and Demetrius cannot choose but listen:

I will grind your bones to dust,
And with your blood and it I'll make a paste,
And of the paste a coffin I will rear,
And make two pasties of your shameful
    heads,
And bid that strumpet, your unhallowed
    dam,
Like to the earth, swallow her own increase.

This is the feast that I have bid her to,
And this the banquet she shall surfeit on.
(*Titus Andronicus*, 5.2.187–94)

Reading over the recipe to the ingredients, Titus enumerates a
set of actions that *will* unfold. The simple parataxis of the recipe, as we saw in Dawson's recipe for "a fine paste" does not
decide on outcomes or results but delimits a field of action,
setting in motion what is understood to be a chaotic and un-
stable process, a cascade. In the kitchen, then, Titus redis-
covers the *kairos* that elsewhere has gone missing from the
rituals or "gesture sequences" of a Rome that is no longer his.
Demoting himself from patrician to cook, like today's culinary
historians, Titus plays the cook, dresses "like a cook," and by
his difference from himself, by the deployment of a set of routines attendant upon the banqueting scene, renders himself
effective. Titus bi-locates.

Tamora, as you may recall, "swallow[s] her own increase"
(5.2.191), dies with her sons in her mouth. She is then expelled
from the city for "birds and beasts to prey" on (5.3.197). Aaron is buried up to his neck, and left to famish, even as he
himself becomes food for beasts. Chiron and Demetrius are
butchered, subjected to the procedures and techniques of the
kitchen, served up, and eaten by their mother in what Titus
symbolizes as a reverse pregnancy. Tamora eats her sons as
they lie in their pastry coffins, becoming by her own death a
second coffin, which is consumed by birds. Titus, if we follow
Eugene Thacker, deploys a mechanism which enables an
anonymous, deterritorialized cuisine, a general economy of
cooking/concoction, a "cooking as desolation," that oblite-
rates the possibility of Chiron and Demetrius "living on" as
corpses that indicate, paradoxically, a life beyond life that is
not life but the life of decay.[29] Enlisting Chiron and Demetrius
as ingredients, Tamora, their mother-*cum*-kitchen, as on-

---

[29] Eugene Thacker, "Spiritual Meat: Resurrection and Religious
Horror in Bataille," *Collapse* VII (2011): 437–97.

stage kitchen, as an opening into an anonymous, generalized economy in which kitchen and graveyard co-presence, Titus's banquet re-engineers the uses of the mouth. His killing of Tamora interrupts the act of eating and the possible expression of revulsion that may follow (the mouth as conduit for scream, speech, or vomit). And by this interruption, he stops her anus, even as he stopped Chiron and Demetrius' mouths, postponing their digestion, so as to effect a mode of collective excretion. Enlisting the physiology of Tamora as kitchen-grave, Titus turns back the clock, rewrites the botched *poesis* by which Tamora and all in her household become "incorporate" with Rome, and sloughs off the existence of Chiron and Demetrius. Such is the flavor of his revenge.

The Romans (Titus, Saturninus, and Lavinia), by contrast, will be buried in their family tombs. They are archived. The invasive Goths are an/archived, returned to the food chain—they will leave no historical markings, no trace except the skeletal remains of a headless Aaron, an impression left on soft ground. Thus is Rome purified, rebooted in "safe mode?"

What then does the ending of Titus offer us? Not a "positive" instantiation of a poetics of translation, obviously, even as the text might be said to sponsor a neutral, parasite reading that unmoors the question of the "well" or the "good" from any available ratio or rationality—prompting, perhaps, an order of kitchen *ataraxia*, or lucid freedom from worry—such that seizes Michel Serres at the end of *The Parasite*.[30] The mutual capture of stage and kitchen in the play, by and in their difference from one another produces, offers instead a set of translational opportunities that may be explored, inviting us to consider the impressions different orders of media make on one another, each or several, by the effects they generate for their own audiences, archives of the other.

One of the challenges, for example, to the staging or filming of Act 5, Scene 3 lies in the relative lack of dialogue. Ti-

---

[30] Michel Serres, *The Parasite*, trans. Lawrence R. Schehr (Minneapolis: University of Minnesota Press, 2007), 253.

tus's speech is minimally descriptive. Tamora is given no opportunity to speak. There is also an installed uncertainty as to who else eats the pie. Do Marcus and those Romans at the table of such a completely abstract cuisine live on as cannibals or witnesses to Titus's act? The play does nothing to disambiguate this issue. Instead, there is action merely, followed by a series of minimally monumentalizing speeches. In Act 5, Scene 3, we watch, just as Titus said we should, the unfolding or completion of the recipe read aloud to Chiron and Demetrius in Act 5, Scene 2. The cooking takes place off-stage, black boxed by the technical limits of the stage.

The efficacy of Titus's culinary revenge marks the play-text therefore by the script's reduction. The cooking of Chiron and Demetrius by their re-absorption into, and "cooking" by Tamora is not allied to an anthropocentric, nutritive cuisine, but to a regime of anonymous process. The kitchen appears, then, by and in its translation to a grave, realizing a dramatic figure for the tragic logic of "variable service," "two dishes, but one table," that Hamlet describes in his conversation with Claudius. The metaphysics of the kitchen are rendered by and in its translation and transformation to a theatrical medium.

The stage will never capture the metaphysics of the kitchen, however, no more than the kitchen of a nutritive, anthropocentric cuisine may capture the metaphysics of theater. But they may render one another via a mutual capture or translation that interrupts the other's routines. In Act 5, Scene 3 of *Titus Andronicus*, this capture manifests as the co-incidence between role and actor swells. Tamora becomes simply she who eats, a mouth and no anus. The (boy) actor playing her engages in a mimesis that, like Latour's auto-archiving *poesis*, folds upon itself, disclosing or confirming, perhaps, the stage's own relation to culinary desolation as itself a relay for providing the long dead and decomposed with living "ghosts," "spirits," "walking shadows:" the human actors who agree for a certain time to become living corpses. The theater *qua* kitchen opens the grave, as do our own acts of humanistic inquiry open the archive.

For Latour, Titus's re-engineering of the uses of the mouth and the play's invitation for stage and kitchen to co-presence, suggests something probably already taken for an axiom: the poetic acts of one translational relay may be grasped only by the impression they leave in the media of a differently situated relay. Reference circulates. Such a conclusion, however small, might provide the seeds of a dormant *kairos* allied to what seems so hard still to achieve: an ecology of practices that understands the way moral philosophemes, housed in the humanities, inhabit already the technics of the Sciences. So, like Irène, cooking worries me, "I don't know why?"

A Recipe for Disaster: Practical
Metaphysics
Response to Julian Yates

Liza Blake

There are two ways of approaching the topic of Speculative
Medievalisms. On the one hand, one might consider the role
of the medieval or medievalism within speculation or the
speculative. Allan Mitchell offers a version of this approach in
his piece in this volume, "Cosmic Eggs, or Events Before Everything," when he reflects on how the medieval is already to
be found in the speculative, whether consciously or uncon-
sciously. Another way of approaching the topic would be to
consider how the theses, ideas or propositions found in speculative realism translate to a medieval—or in Yates's case, an
early modern—literary critical practice. This second approach
serves as the focus of Yates's essay, and so it will be the subject
of my response. In this response I will re-compose Yates's
essay, schematically restructuring it so as to draw out the implications for speculative medieval critical practice.

Harman's technique in his book *Prince of Networks* is a
complicated one, but one whose mechanisms are worth studying.[1] Harman takes as his starting point Bruno Latour's criti-

---

[1] Graham Harman, *Prince of Networks: Bruno Latour and
Metaphysics* (Melbourne: re.press, 2009).

cal practice for, and as, sociology, science studies, and actor network theory (among others). From Latour's practice, Harman then extrapolates its underlying, more or less explicit metaphysics. In Part II of the *Prince of Networks,* Harman tweaks this metaphysics slightly to present a new or slightly modified version of Latourian metaphysics, and this tweaked Latourian metaphysics becomes Object Oriented Ontology. The end of the book leaves readers with one critical practice (Latourian practice, as embodied in his work) and two metaphysics (the Latourian metaphysics Harman describes and the metaphysics he himself elaborates). The third section of Harman's book—the section of the book where he works back from Part II's metaphysics to a critical practice—has not been written yet. If Latourian critical practice can produce or imply a metaphysics, then what are the contours of the critical practice that might correspond to the metaphysics of Part II? What is a Harmanian or speculative realist critical practice?

The lack of this imaginary third section, but also the license allowed by this lack, is the key element that serves to create productive intersections between Speculative Realism and Object Oriented Ontology, on the one hand, and medieval and early modern studies on the other. The missing third section allows us to think about the relationship between metaphysics and what we might call critical practice more generally. Is it only Latourian practice that implies or suggests an underlying metaphysics, and if so, what are the distinguishing characteristics of Latourian practice that mark it as capable of deriving a metaphysics? Behind my subtitle, "Practical Metaphysics," lies a genuine question: could the path between metaphysics and practice be a two-way street? Harman shows that it is possible to work backwards from a practice to the metaphysical principles structuring that practice, but whether or how one could work outwards from a metaphysics to a practice (whether that practice be critical or otherwise) is still unresolved. In addition, it is unclear whether there is a necessary or singular relation when moving from metaphysics to practice: Is any given metaphysics capable of deriving only one practice, or many possible practices? It would be interesting to investigate whether the Latourian metaphysics that Harman sketches in Part I might in fact be capable of producing practices other than Latour's. Likewise, it is unclear whether there is only one critical practice corresponding to Part II, the tweaked Latourian metaphysics. Another way to think through these issues that draws on Yates's vocabulary would be to ask the following questions: Could we make a recipe for metaphysics? Could we make a metaphysical recipe for practice?

These are not exactly the questions that Yates's essay asks, but they are questions that his paper enables, and to get to the question his paper asks I would like go first through my questions, even if they are, potentially, a recipe for disaster. If anyone has been concerned with translating Latourian metaphysics into a literary-critical practice, it has, without a doubt, been Julian Yates. Yates names an interest in what he calls the "practical metaphysics" of projective texts. I would like to consider the contours of this "practical" metaphysics, as well as what makes it practical. In order to get at the role that practice plays with respect to metaphysics in Yates's essay, we need to throw into the mix an understanding of cooking as a form of making or *poesis*. If cooking as *poesis* is conceived in the Latourian sense of making or *poesis* then, according to Yates, the "rhetoric of responsibility" is pushed to its absolute limits. This is because, with Latour's understanding of making as composing along with nonhuman actors, the moral philosophical question that Yates addresses early in his essay— "How to live well?"—becomes a generalized question of wellness, no longer centered on human life but on questions of cooking, making, and *poesis*, as well as on human and nonhuman actors who participate in, compose together, and are composed by that act of *poesis*. As Yates describes, a failure to follow a recipe—cooking badly— no longer constitutes merely an individual failure that affects a human individual alone; to quote Yates, "in failing this test you denied something entry to a world."

I paraphrase and bring out this point in Yates's composition in order to stress what I think is key about his approach in this moment, a moment on which much of the essay, and perhaps even the larger project, hinges. Yates, in this moment, is precisely not asking the metaphysical question, the question of the metaphysics underlying Latour's account of making. He is of course aware of the kind of flattening of human hierarchies and the creation of mutual interrelations between objects—as he says, "the ground spirals away and ontology flattens." However, his interest seems to lie not in the exfoliation or elaboration of Latour's flat ontology, but in the question of what kind of *practice* can arise out of this flat ontology. In this particular case, he focuses the question further, on what kind of ethical or moral-philosophical practice develops out of a flat ontology, a practice that might go about, as he puts it early in his essay, "answering the question, 'How to live well?'"[2]

I would argue that Yates's essay suggests two possible answers to this question that he puts to himself. First answer: the recipe. Any "answer" about the nature of a metaphysical practice must not be a prescriptive set of rules, but a recipe in the sense Yates gives: a projective text, designating actants in a cascade, suggesting perhaps gesture sequences, but, crucially, contingent and subject to improvisation. To put it another way, an answer to the question of metaphysical practice will be a recipe, in the sense of the word in the phrase "recipe for disaster." The ingredients may be in place, and their assembly may set something off, but there is no controlling where things might go from there.

Second answer: composing. Yates says early in his essay that *Titus Andronicus* "deploy[s] the metaphysics of the kitchen in order to render the metaphysics of the stage," but he later revises this: "The stage will never capture the metaphysics of the kitchen, however, no more than the kitchen of a nu-

---

[2] Yates's question also resonates with the question Kellie Robertson asks in her essay "Abusing Aristotle": what kind of ethics might arise from this weird Aristotelian ontology?

tritive, anthropocentric cuisine may capture the metaphysics of theater. But they may render one another via a mutual capture or translation that interrupts the other's routines." This revision is crucial, because it shows that, ultimately, it is not a question of what new metaphysics is formed. Rather, it is a question of what is made, what is composed, and how these two practices of kitchen and stage interrupt, compose, and decompose one another, and point to a new practice altogether. If I had to point to one moment in Yates's essay that indicates what it would mean to compose in critical practice, it would be this: "I'll engage in a running conversation with the modeling of agency and making on offer from Bruno Latour, to see what the four of us, Irène, Bruno, Titus, and I can learn."

This response essay began with the question of what makes a practical metaphysics, or how a practice might derive or follow from a metaphysics. Now, following Yates, I might tentatively say: composition may be the recipe for deriving a practice from Object Oriented Ontology or speculative realism, but the disaster is up to us.

○ Sublunary

Jeffrey Jerome Cohen

for Eileen

"Between the moon and the earth there live spirits whom we call incubus-demons."[1] So declares Maugantius, summoned before the king to explain how a boy named Merlin could have been born without a father. *Inter lunam et terram,* between a celestial globe in ceaseless circulation and the dull earth: in this intermedial space dwell creatures at once human and angelic. Incubus-demons can assume mortal forms and descend to visit earthly women. "Many people have been born this way," Maugantius asserts. Among the progeny of such intercourse is Merlin, destined to become our iconic wizard. This genesis narrative marks Merlin's advent into the literary tradition. The story yields no evidence of his future as a bespectacled and senescent figure, cloaked in robes and wielding a wand. Dumbledore is a diminished and modern avatar. The

---

[1] Geoffrey of Monmouth, *The History of the Kings of Britain* [*Historia regum Britanniae*], ed. Michael D. Reeve, trans. Neil Wright (Woodbridge: Boydell Press, 2007), 138–39. All further quotations in Latin and English from this edition, cited parenthetically by page number; translation sometimes silently modified.

primordial Merlin is much more difficult to emplace. Between moon and earth is a gap that opens because the two realms cannot touch. Merlin arrives from a kind of heavenly lacuna, a suspended and disjunctive space created because two bodies that are two worlds endlessly withdrawn from each other. Aerial and moonlit, this middle realm is knowable only at second hand. Maugantius makes clear that his knowledge of what dwells between lunar possibility and the cold earth's heft arrives vicariously, through books of history and philosophy.

Speaking of philosophy books and strange intermediacy, Graham Harman has argued that, "Objects hide from one another endlessly, and inflict their mutual blows ['physical relations'] only through some vicar or intermediary."[2] The Merlin episode suggests a medieval version of this statement that is just as true: "Worlds hide from one another endlessly, and enjoy their mutual embraces ["physical relations"] only through some vicar or intermediary." Merlin's birth is the weird result/enabler of an asymmetrical, humanly inassimilable relation. Merlin's mother is a king's daughter and a cloistered nun who nightly finds a handsome man in the solitude of her cell. The incubus-demon who fathers Merlin is of unknown biography and intentions. He sometimes touches the ordinary world, but just as often withdraws from terrestrial connection. His desires cannot be reduced to the merely sexual. He wants at times to kiss and hold the nun, at times to converse invisibly on unstated subjects. Merlin arrives, that is, through an abstruse relationship that unites for a while two beings from oblique realms. The angel-demon and the solitary princess never fully touch, or do so askew, in a conjoining that is textually enabled only backwards, through the strange progeny who makes possible and embodies their "shared common space" (Graham Harman's term for the third object within which two others meet[3]) or "*thalamus*" (Geoffrey of Mon-

---

[2] Graham Harman, "On Vicarious Causation" *Collapse* II: "Speculative Realism" (Falmouth: Urbanomic, 2007), 189–90.

[3] Harman, "On Vicarious Causation," 190.

mouth's word for the nun's cell, a Greek noun that also means "chamber," "bedroom," "bridal bed" and, metonymically, "marriage": that is, the space of an unequal, complicated, potentially disastrous, possibly transformative caress [*The History of the Kings of* Britain, 139]). The relation between the nun and the incubus engenders a creature who if not wholly unprecedented is nonetheless unpredetermined. Though Maugentius can invoke a history for such an arrival, moreover, he cannot account for Merlin's erratic life to come.

The text that I am speaking about in this language that weds Object Oriented Ontology to Latin historiography is Geoffrey of Monmouth's *History of the Kings of Britain* (c. 1136). Geoffrey's history is most widely known for having bequeathed to the future the King Arthur of enduring legend. Without Geoffrey this provincial British warlord would be an obscure medieval footnote rather than the progenitor of a still vibrant world. At his first appearance in Geoffrey's text Merlin is a precocious and quarrelsome young man. As the story unfolds he will reveal surprising abilities, demonstrating that seemingly inert rocks may contain within them bellicose dragons; foretelling grim futures that include incineration, poison, and flowing blood; enabling through his transformative potions an adultery-minded Uther Pendragon to engender Arthur. Merlin alters completely the timbre of the text in which he appears. The *History of the Kings of Britain* has until the moment of his entrance offered a chronicle of the island's early days. Its sedate Latin prose describes how Britain was founded and who ruled its civil war loving kingdoms. Wonders and supernatural events before his advent are few. A tribe of giants to kill, a sudden rain of blood, a sea monster and some ravenous wolves are scant exceptions to a martial account of settlement, inheritance, dissent, and political intrigue. Merlin appears just after the first mention of magic in the narrative, in the form of incompetent *magi* [sorcerers] whom the perfidious King Vortigern summons to assist him in finding a way to escape the persecutions of the Saxons. Merlin is not himself a magician; *magi* are figures of failure in the story. For Geoffrey of Monmouth Merlin is a prophet, a poet, a schemer, an architect and an author, a figure of singular ingenuity rather than of saintly or demonic inspiration. He cannot be domesticated into mere category.

After his unexpected advent the rules for how the story unfolds change. Earlier in the *History* when an earthbound king dreamt of traveling spaces tenanted by clouds and restless air, his fate was to plummet with his manufactured wings to a shattering death (Bladud, who practices *nigromantium* [necromancy] rather than magic, *History of the Kings of* Britain, 36). That stretch between earth and moon had not yet opened for narrative sojourn. Merlin, however, born of the meeting of nocturnal radiance with mundane constrictedness, conveys the wheel of Stonehenge across the sea "with incredible ease." This transmarinal relocation is not accomplished through supernatural agency. There is nothing divine or occult about the lithic movement. Merlin works with the earth's givenness, its alliance-seeking materiality. The monoliths are swiftly transported via his *operationibus machinandis* ["feats of engineering"] and *machinationes* ["machinery," "engines," "contrivances," *History of the Kings of* Britain, 171]. Merlin is an engineer, a vicar of causation who knows that objects launch into motion only through the intermediary agency of other objects. The stones are disassembled, loaded onto ships and carried to their current home for repurposing as a British monument, thus proving the power of ingenuity (*ingenium,* the Latin word that gives us "engineer"). Significantly, we are never told of what Merlin's *machinationes* consist. A materialist but not a reductionist, Merlin knows well that "inscrutable depths" intractably hold the objectal world.

Merlin is likewise a vicar or engineer of diegesis. He moves the narrative, but cannot be absorbed back into it. He remains an essential mystery, a figure who changes everything and at a certain point simply vanishes, but even after his quiet disappearance his presence permeates what follows. Though he never meets Arthur, that king's ambiguous destiny on Avalon is inconceivable without Merlin's having set into motion the

path of his ambivalent life. The text that Merlin creates is ec-
centric to what precedes: what sought to be history opens into
a possibility-laden new genre, a mode to be christened in the
future, in another tongue, *romance*.

Merlin embodies the strange prospects offered by that
space *inter lunam et terram*, between the earth's banal givenness and the moon's unreachable allure. This suspended geography might be called *sublunary*, but by that term I do not
mean mundane. The sublunary designates a region neither
terrestrial nor empyrean: unregulated by tedious rules about
proper history, untouched by diurnal limitations, immune to
the stasis that holds heaven. Sublunary means unpredestined
by humans and gods, an intermedial sweep where the fixities
of doctrine, custom and theology do not necessarily obtain.
The wandering incubus who traces this space, celestial but not
heavenly, a lover of earthly things but not bound to the small
spaces of earth's human dwellers, imbues in his progeny the
ability to escape constricted textual spaces as well.

"Between the moon and the earth there live spirits whom
we call incubus-demons." The pithy declaration is sudden,
breathtaking. It opens an unforeseen space and populates it
with creatures who are both familiar and utterly strange. The
advent of the sublunary floods the text with alien lumines-
cence, and for me calls to mind another strange phrase about
lunar glow. In his essay "On Vicarious Causation," Graham
Harman describes the solitude of reticent objects, describing
how these cloisters are sometimes breached by oblique, transformative, but carefully mediated relations. He writes that
"*While its strangeness may lead to puzzlement more than resistance, vicarious causation is not some autistic moonbeam
entering the window of an asylum.*"[4] The metaphor does its
Merlin-like work, transforming a philosophy that might have
contemplated the "dull realism of mindless atoms and billiard
balls" into "an archipelago of oracles or bombs that explode
from concealment . . . [the] sacred fruit of writers, thinkers,

---

[4] Harman, "On Vicarious Causation," 187.

politicians, travellers, lovers, and inventors."[5] Harman employs this lunar and lunatic metaphor to convey (and reject) meager, inviolable solitariness. We can see already from Geoffrey of Monmouth, though, that radiance from the sublunary sphere cannot be immured in an asylum or convent. It engenders strange and rules-changing progeny by placing into communication seemingly isolated bodies or objects. An angel-demon enters the window of a nun's cell and enables the advent of Merlin, he who can discern in dead stone the possibilities of dormant dragons and of lithic wheels ready for conveyance across vast waters. No moonbeam is in the end solipsistic, even if some objects in this world attempt withdrawal into utter isolation. Lunar pull is incessant, drawing artists and philosophers to speculative modes, to dreaming of incongruent but at times imbricated worlds where even magic is not weird enough.

Geoffrey of Monmouth is not the only medieval writer to have populated sublunary expanses so vibrantly. Incubus-demons in their inscrutable flights share interlunar space with voyagers who traverse the clouds in ships. Gervase of Tilbury describes a congregation who, upon leaving church, witness an anchor lowered from the clouds (*Otia imperialia*, c. 1214). A mariner shimmies down its rope, hand over hand. He is seized by the onlookers and drowns in the moistness of terrestrial air.[6] Between heaven and earth sail aerial vessels of unknown design, dwell "beings neither angelic, human, nor animal" (as Robert Bartlett entitles a wonderfully miscellaneous section of *England Under the Norman and Angevin Kings*).[7] This sublunary space might also open underwater, as in Ralph of Coggeshall's report of a merman caught in the nets of an English fishing boat, or the belligerent fish-knights of the *Ro-*

---

[5] Harman, "On Vicarious Causation," 212.

[6] I have treated the episode at greater length in *Medieval Identity Machines* (Minneapolis: University of Minnesota Press, 2006), 16.

[7] Robert Bartlett, *England Under the Norman and Angevin Kings 1075-1225* (Oxford: Clarendon Press, 2000), 686.

man de Perceforest.[8] Always radiating at a slanted angle to lived human reality, these intermedial realms also frequently erupt from underground. In the Breton lays that are among the literary progeny of Geoffrey's *History*, the space is most often called 'Fairy.'

The Breton lays are short, romance-themed narratives, often with Arthurian settings. *Sir Orfeo*, a good example of such a work, describes the lays as full of marvels ("ferli thing"), war, woe, joy, trickery, adventures, enjoyment, fairies, and love.[9] The Breton lays are an English genre set within a 'magical' Welsh or Breton past. Composed in French and English, the stories are replete with radiant objects, magic, strange beings, monsters, and music. Their worlds open repeatedly into unexpected geographies, into spaces similar to Geoffrey of Monmouth's sublunary expanse: across the roiling sea traversed by the lovers' ship in Marie de France's *Guigemar*, for example. Or within the rock that the author of *Sir Orfeo* envisions as the entrance to the Fairy Realm, a seemingly underground kingdom where all normal rules for objects, agency, telos and time are suspended. A hunt proceeds without prey, bodies are caught in eternal disaggregation, captivity is a pleasant slumber, being endures without becoming. The Breton lays are a medieval version of speculative fiction, a space to think the possible without recourse to theology, to explore a terrain rich in mysterious objects without predetermined answers or even clear objectives.

---

[8] For the story of the sea-dwelling man who lived on a diet of raw fish, see *Chronicum Anglicanum,* ed. Joseph Stevenson (R.S.: London, 1875), 117–18, and Bartlett, *England Under the Norman and Angevin Kings*, 688–89. For a penetrating examination of the *poissons chevaliers* of *Perceforest*, see Karl Steel and Peggy McCracken, "The Animal Turn: Into the Sea with the Fish-Knights of Pereceforest," *postmedieval: a journal of medieval cultural studies* 2.1 (2011): 88–100.

[9] "Sir Orfeo," in *The Middle English Breton Lays,* eds. Anne Laskaya and Eve Salisbury (Kalamazoo: TEAMS, 1995), ll. 4–12. Further references are given parenthetically by line number.

Sir Orfeo is a queer story, grafting the classical myth of Orpheus and his lost Eurydice to elements of English history and romance. Its setting is Thrace, but the city has been relocated from ancient Greece to not-so-long-ago Winchester. The queen does not die, but is abducted into Fairy by its enigmatic king. His domain is accessed in two ways: at a grafted ("ympe") tree under which Queen Heurodis falls asleep, and "in at a roche" ("through a rock," 347). That Fairy should be a kind of omnipresent underworld resonates uncannily with Graham Harman's description of the objectal world. He writes that we are "moles tunneling through wind, water and ideas no less than through speech-acts, wonder and dirt."[10] A subterranean milieu, "numberless underground cavities," but a place of neither finitude nor negativity. And sparks from that distant satellite do penetrate from time to time, perpetually exploding and renewing a wide sublunary world, "an archipelago of oracles or bombs."[11]

The Fay world obliquely and multiply touches our own. After ten years of wandering, Orfeo discovers his stolen wife in a kind of non-juridical Hades, where bodies are forever arrested in their self-undoing: headless, butchered, burnt, bound, slumbering in a fragmented nondeath, caught in the moment at which they have been taken ("y-nome") by the Fairies. This is a somnolence removed from time, preservation in the agony of capture, a withdrawal into untouchable solitude. Among these grotesque sleepers Heurodis is anomalous: the kidnapped queen slumbers peacefully beneath a grafted tree ("ympe-tree") while the dismembered, the mad, the strangled and the drowned neighbor her dreams. Perhaps the peacefulness of Heurodis arrives because she did not resist the advent of her taking. The Fairy King warned her that should she not appear at the appointed time at the grafted tree in the courtly world, "thou worst y-fet / And totore thine limes al / That nothing help the no schall" (170–72). By surrendering to

---

[10] Harman, "On Vicarious Causation," 210.
[11] Harman, "On Vicarious Causation," 212.

adventure, to the thing that arrives unwilled and sometimes undesired, she is transported. An ambivalent future opens that otherwise could not have arrived. The queen is the only one of these sleepers who is also glimpsed in movement outside of Fairy, where she accompanies on his aimless hunt the King who stole her from her familiar world.

In her surrender to advent Heurodis is like her husband. Once his wife is abducted by the fairies, Orfeo dons a pilgrim's cloak but seeks nothing. He wanders the wilds in a bare existence, a barren space of "snewe and frees" (247). Nothing pleases ("seth he nothing that him liketh," 251). Whereas Henry David Thoreau famously discovered in the sunbathing of a serpent the appearance of "thing-power," the invitation that the world's materiality offers to "be surprised by what we see," Orfeo discerns only "wilde wormes," unsatisfying roots to eat, and "berien but gode lite" ["berries of little worth," 258].[12] No vibrant materiality here. Yet through the music of his harp he allies himself with "weder . . . clere and bright," with a forest yearning for resonance, with birds and wild beasts hungry for "gle" and "melody" (267-80). The ecological conjunction that he creates through his harp seems to call forth the King of Fairy, who wanders the woods with his retinue on a chase in which no animal is pursued. Orfeo, ten years in the forest and transformed now into an arboreal semblance ("He is y-clongen also a tre!" exclaim his subjects upon his return, 508), has given himself over to adventure: a coming or à-venir that like the Fairy King's hunt moves without aim. Adventure is surrender to an overlap of worlds, an embrace of an intermedial cosmos larger than the confines of a single subjectivity.

Orfeo speaks for the first time since his exile began when he beholds the falcons that the fairies bear. These effulgent birds remind him of his abandoned life ("Ich was y-won such werk to se!", 317). Once he conjoins Otherworld and relin-

---

[12] Jane Bennett, *Vibrant Matter: A Political Ecology of Things* (Baltimore: Johns Hopkins University Press, 2010), 5.

quished court he finds his opening. Adventure is an act of worldly intersection, like the arrival of an incubus at a conventual cell: you cannot seek it, it's an object rather than an objective, but you can train yourself to perceive its arrival, to recognize the dangerous invitation to the sublunary that adventure offers, an allure that warps the orbit of ordinary life. Orfeo follows the fairy retinue into a rock and across the flattest of plains. He rescues Heurodis with his music. The Fairy King fears the two are ill-matched, but offers no impediment to their return: no fateful injunction not to look back as they depart the Fairy realm, only an unexpected benediction: "Of hir ichil thatow be blithe" ["I hope that you are happy with her," 471]. Orfeo is.

The Breton lay abandons the grim ethos of the classical myth from which it arises: no fading of Eurydice at the threshold of the underworld, no dismembering of her grieving husband by crazed bacchants. While speculative realism seems to prefer the gloomy and the somber for its image store (black metal, H.P. Lovecraft, dark ecologies), the Breton lays tend to conclude with the equivalent of sunshine and rainbows, suggesting a happier but no less serious register at which objectal relations might be explored. Nor do I wish to turn Geoffrey of Monmouth's *History* or the Breton lay *Sir Orfeo* into allegories or *romans à clef* for the working of Object Oriented Ontology. While it is true that there is an uncanny intersection between Graham Harman's work on vicarious causation and Geoffrey's originary myth of Merlin, you won't find the latter briskly expostulating "five kinds of objects . . . and five different types of relation."[13] Geoffrey's sublunary is too chaotic to be organized into a metaphysics, no matter how fascinated he is by causation and allure. He did not compose in 1136 an uncanny prophecy of the advent of flat ontologies in 2011. Art is tangled, sprawling and untidy compared to philosophy's crisp distinctions. Having explored what is enabled by the conjunction of Geoffrey's "between the

---

[13] Harman, "On Vicarious Causation," 201.

moon and the earth" and Harman's "autistic moonbeam entering the window of an asylum," I would now like to ask what is eclipsed when that moon moves into such momentary terrestrial congruence.

Erratic angels like the incubus-demon, the Fairy King and Merlin are the vicars or intermediaries who make possible the world's vibrancy by enabling contact and relation. They allow the emergence of transformative textualities, even while they themselves are left behind at that luminous advent. These messengers can be dangerous. In the Breton lay *Sir Gowther*, the same incubus who engenders Merlin impregnates another woman with a son who will become a rapist, a murderer, and his family's undoing.[14] *Sir Orfeo* oscillates between a vibrant materialism and a dark vitalism, replete with the messy, melancholic, admixed and unbeautiful stuff of the world that is as just as much an ethical ecology. Such a textual expanse is also an artistic thought experiment conducted through the objects of the everyday world, rendered marvelous through the excitation of objectal and material potency—but it is an experiment in which not every participant is allowed a full story. As the Fairy King, the incubus-demon, the nun, and Merlin learn, a mediator's love is necessary to make the machinery (ingenuity, contrivances, art) of the text spring into action—and a mediator's love is unrequited. Though these figures open new worlds for and bestow unexpected futures to others within their texts, their shared fate is silent abandonment. Speculative awareness comes through the labor of those reduced to mere go-betweens, those who move from one place to another in order to change both. These mediators are literally sublunary angels, messengers who in their erratic flights refuse reduction into narrative or philosophical order. Perpetually conveyed, traveling without necessary destination, these dis-

---

[14] "Sir Gowther" is published in the same volume of the *The Middle English Breton Lays* as "Sir Orfeo" (see note 7 above). Both may be found online at http://www.lib.rochester.edu/camelot/teams/tms menu.htm.

ordered angels remind us that a retreat into tidy heaven leaves too many abandoned on the rubbish heaps of the earth.[15]

Speculative realism requires speculative narrative, along with its troubled and troublesome angels. We need to examine the world as it is, in its catastrophic givenness, but also to consider as well how it might be, not just in the past or in the future but in the now: a place where the inhuman has agency, narrative, the power to withdraw, but also to caress, to create sublunary realms that with or without our consent touch us, take us out of our immurement, create strange new beings of futurity, menace, and promise who will vanish into our stories, our futures that are ever arriving—futures that are narratives of the air and the lofty moon, but unfold just as easily in an asylum, a convent, or "in at a rock."

---

[15] I am thinking here of Michel Serres's work on angels, most notably in *Angels: A Modern Myth*, trans. Francis Cowper (Paris, New York: Flammarion, 1995).

Casting Speculation
Response to Jeffrey Jerome Cohen

Ben Woodard

In Alan Moore's *The Killing Joke*, after the Joker has been apprehended for doing all sorts of awful things to Barbara Gordon, he tells Batman the following joke:

> See, there were these two guys in a lunatic asylum . . . and one night, one night they decide they don't like living in an asylum any more. They decide they're going to escape! So, like, they get up onto the roof, and there, just across this narrow gap, they see the rooftops of the town, stretching away in the moonlight . . . stretching away to freedom. Now, the first guy, he jumps right across with no problem. But his friend, his friend didn't dare make the leap. Y'see . . . Y'see, he's afraid of falling. So then, the first guy has an idea . . . He says 'Hey! I have my flashlight with me! I'll shine it across the gap between the buildings. You can walk along the beam and join me!' B-but the second guy just shakes his head. He suh-says . . . He says 'Wh-what do you think I am? Crazy? You'd turn it off when I was half way across!'[1]

---

[1] Alan Moore and Brian Bolland (illustrator), *Batman: The Killing Joke* (New York: DC Comics, 1995), unpaginated.

I will try and bring this kind of lunacy to Speculative Realism and develop a parallel kind of path to Jeffrey's paper. I will do this through weird fiction. In addition to his massive collection of works the weird author Clark Ashton Smith wrote several synopses of tales he never produced. There are at least two of these tales which are of a lunar nature and which I will read in full.

The first is called "The Lunar Brain": A great brain in the center of the moon, formed of an unknown life-substance allied both to protoplasm and the radioactive minerals. It is growing old, and requires an increasing amount of food—animal food. It has devoured nearly all the underground inhabitants of the moon, and begins sending out waves of thought-attraction to the earth. Scores of rocket ships start for the moon—and none of them return.[2]

The second is called "The Lunar Path": about a man who finds a strange, unknown path at the full moon, and follows it into an ultra-mundane valley of ethereal loveliness. Here he finds a sylph-like being, and dwells with her in a sort of dream-like timeless existence; in which, after a while, he is troubled by a growing sense of unreality. The sylph warns him to depart, since the valley is subject wholly to the moon, and wanes with its waning; so that the sylph—and her lover too, if he stays—must perish. He refuses to go; and feels himself fading like a shadow.[3]

In both instances the moon is a lump of vibrant matter; in the first case it is a nightmarish living planet capable of telepathy (or extreme lines of speculative thought) and in the second it is a strange territorializing and deterritorializing agent that evaporates its earthly colonization as it shifts its appearance due to the complicity between it, the earth, and the sun.

---

[2] Synopsis from Clark Ashton Smith, "The Lunar Brain," *The Eldritch Dark* [website], December 1, 2006, http://www.eldritchdark.com/writings/short-stories/117/the-lunar-brain-(synopsis).

[3] Synopsis from Clark Ashton Smith, "The Lunar Path," *The Eldritch Dark* [website], December 1, 2006: http://www.eldritchdark.com/writings/short-stories/118/the-lunar-path-(synopsis).

Furthermore, both passages assert the inexplicable capacity of matter to think and of thought to matter, or the devastating capacities the distant and ephemeral have on thought and thought on them. The space between the moon and the earth, the sublunary, is thick with weird action, with the alchemical association of silver with the brain and with the moon. Paracelsus, who outlined this triadic relation was one of the first medical thinkers to attach sickness not merely to internal imbalance, but to the external invasion of minerals and other substances, thereby acknowledging the importance of the outside. This outside, or great Outdoors, is the territory of Speculative Realism, and the problem of speculation vis-à-vis thought's traction on the real, whether in Iain Hamilton Grant's non-substantial monism against substantiality,[4] Quentin Meillassoux's hyperchaos in tension with scientific realism,[5] Ray Brassier's concepts versus a non-naive evolutionary naturalism, or Harman's withdrawn objectal cores with vicars of causation.[6]

William Herschel, the great romantic astronomer, discoverer of nebulae, and lifelong examiner of the moon wrote in an essay "On the Construction of the Heavens": "If we indulge a fanciful imagination and build worlds of our own . . . these will vanish like Cartesian vortices," but he then also stated that adding observation to observation was no better.[7] This seems an obvious statement, yet the rhetorical barrage against armchair theorizing, particularly in books of popular science, often forget this necessary tie. An even odder example (and to return to the moon) would be Johannes Kepler's *Somnium*

---

[4] See Iain Hamilton Grant, *Philosophies of Nature After Schelling* (London: Continuum, 2008).

[5] See Ray Brassier, *Nihil Unbound: Enlightenment and Extinction* (London: Palgrave Macmillan, 2007).

[6] See Graham Harman, "On Vicarious Causation," *Collapse* II: "Speculative Realism" (Falmouth: Urbanomic, 2007), 171–205.

[7] Richard Holmes, *The Age of Wonder: How the Romantic Generation Discovered the Beauty and Terror of Science* (New York: Pantheon, 2009), 122.

('Dream') as one of the first works of science fiction (which began as a dissertation) working with the question of how the earth and heavens would appear from the standpoint of the moon and then became a work of theory-fiction that led to Kepler's mother being arrested as a witch (since the protagonist was clearly Kepler and therefore the protagonist's witch mother must be Kepler's mother who contacts a demon to transport him to the moon). It has been argued that Kepler meant the work not merely as a speculative fiction but coded the text as a dream in order to escape the ire of those still locked in Aristotelian cosmology as it was for a time after Tycho Brahe but long before Isaac Newton.

This cloud of observation and speculation starts to become a kind of third space. The question of a third space, or the moment between the vital material and the speculative thought, or the thing and the emission, or ground and cause, seems to be something navigable but only accidentally. Magic or sorcery do not seem to fill in the third space in any sense but to announce its malleability, yet the capacity for magic (or thought's self-relation that escapes its own limits and burrows into the real) is bracketed off from any sense of the real or the material (as unthinkable)—the cause of that which fills the space of strange causation becomes a cause (thought) that is divine, or some other immaterial irruption. In other words, the cause of non-material cause is the idea dematerialized. It needs to be realistically resurrected.

The relationship then between speculation and observation or between thought and its material base becomes a self-propelling thought, a speculative narrative that has buried its own non-speculative advent as non-thought, and it floats over much of speculative realism like a specter, particularly in the form of causality. The Humean line of a psychologized causality is radicalized by Meillassoux, yet what form of real causality takes its place is uncertain in his work as well as in Brassier's, where thought seems to be protected, in the last instance, from being purely understandable (while caused by) evolutionary naturalism. The issue becomes that of how to parse the traction of thought on the real with thought's limitation, with the utility of speculation and the need for a formal distinction between the metaphysical and the non-metaphysical. Or, in other terms, how do we explain the ingenuity of Merlin, where his seemingly ungrounded thinking leads to feats of engineering, without over-selling the power of thought or degalvanizing the effect of materiality?

This I think can be addressed through Leibniz's approaches to causality. His critique of Occasionalism (the closest relative to Harman's vicarious causation) was in part because it denied basic physics, since, on the mechanical level, only bodies could affect other bodies. But, in another instance, Leibniz critiqued Occasionalism in an anti-Spinozist vein, arguing that Occasionalism would be too undermining, reducing objects to an expression of God as substance. What makes Leibniz interesting, in placing him between the earth and the moon, is that his approach seems to support withdrawal and yet also interconnectedness, a flatness and a stratified philosophy. Leibniz maintains the importance of what is commonly derided as folk physics, but that also distinguishes it from more metaphysically rigorous pre-established harmony, a monism but a disjointed monism. In Leibniz we have a philosophy where there is a distinction between the metaphysical and the non-metaphysical, but again, how those realms interact are both pre-established ontologically, yet, in their own strata, dependent upon the strata of the actual.

In this sense, Leibniz is a great thinker of the third or the ontological, or between affective and ontological intermezzo, because he acts as if it is not there. While Deleuze and Guattari invoke sorcery in their discussion of becoming, the actualizability of thought vis-à-vis non-thought remains obscured in their privileged ontological category.[8] Yet Leibniz's own onto-

---

[8] See Gilles Deleuze and Félix Guattari, "Becoming-Intense, Becoming-Animal, Becoming-Imperceptible . . .," in *A Thousand Plateaus: Capitalism and Schizophrenia*, trans. Brian Massumi (Minneapolis: University of Minnesota Press, 1989), 232–309.

logical crutch is the divine, and if this crutch is removed his universe becomes far more interesting and there rises a nature which emanates flows of substance that nevertheless harden soon after and express in a multitude of forms. By obliterating the tidy heaven, what becomes important is the forces and powers which create and how those creations then collect on the earth.

Leibniz famously said: "Although the whole of this life were said to be nothing but a dream and the physical world nothing but a phantasm, I should call this dream or phantasm real enough, if, using reason well, we were never deceived by it."[9] Leibniz is one of the last great universalists to understand the importance of the metaphysical and the reality which brewed atop of it, and he tried, perhaps not successfully in the end, to maintain those separate worlds. The unintended side effect is two poles that the speculative lands upon productively, the place where Orfeo wanders impossibly into the Fairy King's monad, into a world apart. While the monads are often cast aside as rationalist baubles, there is still something to be said of Leibniz's radical attempt to synthesize the dynamic and the static, to work out the monads as fermentations of becoming, of actuality with history. It may be that, metaphysically, we have only made the transition from wizardry to alchemy, with chemistry still far off.

The devolution of Merlin, of the wizard, into the less ingenious and the more simply magical may be indicative of a double-edged sword, of an inability or fear to abandon what we see as the human grasp on the world (at least as it is guaranteed to always, in the last instance, reform the world), while seeking to improve the means of operating on the world as a seemingly impossible craft, however utopian it may be. In Clark Ashton Smith's odd lunar synopses the lunar brain is seen as the power of speculation but wedded to materiality

---

[9] Quoted in Hermann Weyl "The Mathematical Way of Thinking," in J.R. Newman, *The World of Mathematics* (London: George Allen and Unwin LTD, 1960), 1832.

and the necessity of that materiality (the actual work of stratification), and the lunar path (the moon beam) is pushing speculation into dematerialization, disintegrating like a shadow.

To make this an even more confused mess, and to risk violating my contractually obligated gloominess, I will end on a steampunkishly optimistic note. Neal Stephenson's *The System of the World* (a mix of fantasy and historical fiction, where Leibniz takes a large role) has the following sentiments at its end:

> This journey began with a wizard walking into his door. Now it ends with a new kind of wizard standing on an Engine. Gazing down on this boiler from above, the wizard has the sense of being an angel or demon regarding Earth from Polaris. . . . in this, his masterwork, the seams and rivet-lines joining one curved plate to the next radiate from top center just like meridians of Longitude spreading from the North Pole. Below is a raging fire, and within is steam at a pressure that would blow Daniel to Kingdom Come (just like Drake) if a rivet were to give way. But that does not come to pass. . . . At some point the whole System will fail, because of the flaws that have been wrought into it . . . . Perhaps new sorts of Wizards will be required then. . . . he has to admit that having some kind of a System, even a flawed and doomed one, is better than to live forever in the poisonous storm-tide of quicksilver that gave birth to all of this.[10]

Perhaps then the sublunary, as the way-point between the lunar madness of speculation and the coruscating solar death of the real, stands as an emphatically weird universalism in

---

[10] Neal Stephenson, *The System of the World (The Baroque Cycle,* Vol. 3) (New York: William Marrow Paperbacks, 2005), 886.

which, and of which, a properly metaphysical system can be cast.

Aristotle with a Twist

Graham Harman

§ INTRODUCTION

In several publications, I have made the case for *objects* as the central theme of philosophy.[1] It might seem paradoxical that Heidegger is cited as a key inspiration for this proposal, since "object" is almost never a positive term in Heidegger's philosophy, where it refers to the one-sided *objectification* of things, reduced to presence-at-hand for consciousness or manipulable stockpiles of material for the enframing work of technology. In the later Heidegger we find the word "thing," a more positive term for the individual entity as it mirrors the fourfold play of earth, sky, gods, and mortals.[2] Additional alternate terms might be considered: Bruno Latour prefers to

---

[1] See, for example, Graham Harman, *Tool-Being: Heidegger and the Metaphysics of Objects* (Chicago: Open Court, 2002); *The Quadruple Object* (Winchester: Zero Books, 2011); and "On the Undermining of Objects: Grant, Bruno, and Radical Philosophy," in *The Speculative Turn: Continental Materialism and Realism*, eds. Levi Bryant, Nick Srnicek, and Graham Harman (Melbourne: re.press, 2011).
[2] Martin Heidegger, "Einblick in das was ist," in *Bremer und Freiburger Vorträge* (Frankfurt: Vittorio Klostermann, 1994).

speak of "actors" or "actants."[3] Ian Bogost employs the term "units,"[4] with a Latin etymology whose Greek equivalent "monads" in Leibniz is another candidate term.[5] There is also the more traditional word "substance," which I have sometimes used myself, less for shock value than to show the classical roots of the theme of object-oriented philosophy. Though all terminology is somewhat arbitrary, it should not be chosen carelessly. While it is tempting to coin neologisms in order to avoid being confused for someone else, it is often possible to retain traditional terms while cleanly removing their now irrelevant connotations. The reason I prefer the term "object" is simply because of its roots in the tradition of phenomenology. Husserl tells us openly in the *Logical Investigations* that experience is made of "object-giving acts," and Heidegger's "thing" is an attempt to modify and amplify the famous Husserlian battle cry "to the things themselves."[6] When speaking of "objects" in what follows I refer *not only* to objects as something objectified in consciousness (though these certainly exist, and must be accounted for), but also to objects as described in Heidegger's tool-analysis, incommensurable with any form of presence before the mind.

However, I do not mean objects as opposed to *subjects*. Much recent philosophy wants to safeguard the special status of human beings, and worries that speaking of objects means risking human freedom and dignity by reducing everyone to

---

[3] Bruno Latour, "Irreductions," in *The Pasteurization of France*, trans. Alan Sheridan and John Law (Cambridge, Mass.: Harvard University Press, 1988).

[4] Ian Bogost, *Unit Operations: An Approach to Videogame Criticism* (Cambridge, Mass.: MIT Press, 2006).

[5] G.W. Leibniz, "Monadology," in *Philosophical Essays*, trans. Roger Ariew and Daniel Garber (Indianapolis: Hackett, 2000).

[6] Edmund Husserl, *Logical Investigations*, 2 vols., trans. J.N. Findlay (London: Routledge and Kegan Paul, 1970); Martin Heidegger, *Bremen and Freiburg Lectures: Insight Into That Which Is and Basic Principles of Thinking*, trans. Andrew J. Mitchell (Bloomington: Indiana University Press, 2012).

slabs of objective physical matter of the same order as plastic, silicon, and wood. At the same time, such reduction is precisely what many other philosophers *want* to achieve, by their wish to demonstrate that the purportedly special kingdom of the mind is governed by laws no different from those of physical nature. Ultimately, I sympathize with neither of these groups. The concept of objects as *physical* objects is too reductive in spirit, and succeeds only by asserting that non-physical or large-scale objects such as armies, cities, and mythical archetypes are mere "folk" concepts fit to be eliminated in favor of some deeper stratum of the real. On the other hand, the concept of human subjects as a special rift in the fabric of the cosmos is equally unsatisfying, since the obvious fact that human thought seems to be more fascinating and complicated than the movement of rocks and electrons does not entail the unjustified claim that this difference is so important that it must be built into the very foundation of philosophy, in the form of a radical dualism between human and world. The situation is not improved if we add that human and world always come as a pair, such that we cannot think world with human or human without world, but only a primordial correlation or rapport between the two. This view, which still feels dominant in the continental philosophy of our time, was named "correlationism" by Quentin Meillassoux in his 2006 book *After Finitude*.[7] The critique of correlationism became the sole common program of the authors grouped under the name of "speculative realism," who disagreed about almost everything else.[8]

To summarize, objects are not just images or phenomena present-at-hand in human consciousness, although these are objects too, and must form part of the theory. Objects are also not to be identified with traditional substances or monads, or

---

[7] Quentin Meillassoux, *After Finitude: Essay on the Necessity of Contingency*, trans. Ray Brassier (London: Continuum, 2008).

[8] See especially Graham Harman, *Quentin Meillassoux: Philosophy in the Making* (Edinburgh: Edinburgh University Press, 2011), 77–80.

with Latour's actors. Nor are objects part of a permanent correlation or marriage between objects and the human *subject*; what is normally called the subject is just a special form of object. And here we must add that "object" is not restricted to physical, material objects moving through time and space, as the root to which all else must be reduced. Object-oriented philosophy is not a materialism, since materialism ignores the partially mysterious character of objects, replaces them with an easily masterable theory about what they are, and then uses this theory to debunk everything in sight. In some circles this is called "Enlightenment": using a very narrow theory of objects as material particles to demolish the gullible beliefs of less enlightened alchemists and astrologers. And finally, objects are not simply the trailing anti-valet of the human subject, doing nothing more than resist our wishes. Objects are not part of a human-world correlate, since human beings are also objects in the sense I mean, and what people call "world" is not a single resistant lump, but is made up of trillions of dueling objects. And furthermore, all these human and inhuman objects interact according to one set of laws.

So much for negative remarks about what objects are not. What they positively *are* will be sketched briefly during this talk, even though the only proper name in the title is "Aristotle." The present moment is one where no philosopher seems less futuristic than Aristotle. Everyone knows he was important once, and to some extent even now, but it seems inconceivable that he might eventually return as a figure of the cutting edge. Instead, Aristotle seems like the grandfather of a decrepit tradition of Medieval Scholasticism blown sky-high by the moderns, and even the tone of his writing strikes many as dull, middle-aged, and oppressive. I will try to make a better case for Aristotle than this, showing that he is well-positioned to address a key fault-line in present-day continental thought.

Two important roots for the philosophy of objects can be found in Husserl and Heidegger, and while these familiar figures have begun to seem like respectable but aged uncles for our discipline, my view is that they have not yet been fully digested and assimilated by more recent developments. In Husserl's case the role of objects is clear, since he uses the term himself when speaking of "intentional objects."[9] Against the empiricist model of bundles of qualities, which treats "horse" and "apple" as code words for bundles of palpable impressions in no need of an underlying object, Husserl is a staunch defender of objects that precede all their qualities, and he is surely the first idealist to do so. When we rotate pears and wine glasses, we encounter different profiles or adumbrations of them at different moments. When we circle city walls and construction sites, we view them from ever-different angles. The intentional object is not attained by adding up all the different profiles, but is already there from the start, imbuing each of the profiles with its characteristic style. As Husserl sees it, we encounter our friend Hans as a unit, not as a set of loosely related Hans-images linked together by family resemblance. Intentional objects do not "hide"; they are never withdrawn or concealed; they are simply encrusted with extraneous sensual data that it takes much work to strip away in order to reach their more austere underlying essence. Any hiding and concealing of objects is found not in Husserl, but in Heidegger. Against the view that "to the things themselves" means "to the things themselves as they appear in consciousness," Heidegger famously argued that what is characteristic of objects or things is precisely that they *do not* appear as present in consciousness, which occurs only in such infrequent cases as malfunctioning equipment, theoretical comportment, or perception.[10] Unlike Husserl's intentional objects, Heidegger's tool-beings *are* hidden and concealed. Generally we do not realize they are there until something unusual happens that *makes* us aware. They are withdrawn into subterranean darkness, deeper than any possible presence to us. They

[9] Husserl, *Logical Investigations*.
[10] Martin Heidegger, *Being and Time*, trans. John Macquarandie & Edward Robinson (New York: HarperPerennial, 2008).

cannot be accessed directly, but only through gradual and imperfect unveiling– or as I prefer, through indirect *allusion*. Husserl's objects cannot withdraw from the sphere of consciousness, because there isn't anywhere else for them to go. By contrast, Heidegger's objects can *only* withdraw from consciousness into subterranean depths, because by definition they are the surplus that resists all possible presence, guaranteeing some residue or reserve behind any possible configuration before the mind.

These two concepts of objects are very different, yet what they share in common is that both intentional and real objects are units irreducible to any sum total of qualities, and equally irreducible to their constituent pieces. While only Heidegger allows objects to be hidden, withdrawn, or concealed, Husserl would also agree that objects cannot be replaced by a specific set of qualities present to the mind right now, since the object is always a unit deeper than any of its transient incarnations in any given moment. And though only Husserl forbids us to undercut phenomena by grounding them in a sub-phenomenal sphere, both would agree that we get nowhere by breaking up genuine units into tinier material or other pieces. Even for Heidegger, what withdraws from view during efficient construction work is a hammer, not quarks and electrons of which the phenomenal hammer is made.

In short, both Husserl and Heidegger give us philosophies basically devoted to the integrity of individual things, despite their two very different concepts of the object. And this is what links them most closely with the tradition of Aristotelian philosophy, despite their numerous other differences from it. Against all pre-Socratic attempts to pulverize everyday things and turn them into deeper underlying elements, and against the efforts of Plato to replace individual things by universal forms, it was Aristotle who defended the role of primary substances or individuals in the world. And here we must consider a distinction between the undermining of objects and what I have called by analogy the "overmining" of objects.

§ UNDERMINING AND OVERMINING

If individual objects are rejected as the first principle of philosophy, this will be for one of two basic reasons: objects will be treated either as too shallow or as too deep. There is also a third case in which objects are treated as too shallow *and* too deep simultaneously. Each of these three kinds has numerous sub-variants, but all are united in attacking the supposed naiveté of a philosophy of individuals and all score most of their points by whipping, slapping, and beating objects to a pulp.

Let's begin as Western philosophy began, by treating objects as too shallow to be the truth. In this way objects are *undermined*, subverted from beneath by a supposedly more fundamental layer of the cosmos. This is the dominant theme of pre-Socratic philosophy. Whereas common sense lives in a world of horses, donkeys, vegetables, and trees, the pre-Socratics undercut these objects in two different basic ways. One is to find a most primitive physical element to which all objects can be reduced. Whether it be air, water, fire, atoms, or air/earth/fire/water mixed by love and hate, the everyday objects of the world are shown to be too large and bulky to be fundamental; instead, they are made of some finer root stuff. The other way is to treat the cosmos as a single underlying lump from which all differentiation emerges. This is the famous *apeiron*, and the main disagreement is over whether it exists right now without our realizing it (that's "Being" in Parmenides), will exist in the future after the work of justice is done (that's Anaximander), or existed in the past before it was shattered to pieces whether through spinning very rapidly (as for Anaxagoras) or through inhaling void and breaking the *apeiron* into pieces (that's Pythagoras).

While it is tempting to view the pre-Socratics as quaint or romantic figures belonging to a long-dead era of simplistic theories, we should note that these theories are alive and well today. Mainstream materialism still thinks that everyday objects are fully reducible either to quarks and electrons, to something even more basic than these, or at least to some underlying mathematical structure. And the theory of the *apeiron* is alive and well in the recent philosophies of the pre-individual which cannot succeed, since the pre-individual is either one or more than one. If one only, then it is a lump; and if more than one, we already have a theory of individual objects.

The problem with these undermining theories is their tendency to treat all layers higher than the most basic as nullities existing only for the senses, or only for some observer in terms of some outward effect, not as anything in their own right. Real horses and trees are supposed to be replaced by appearances or by horse-effects and tree-events. But this badly understates the autonomy of things from their own pieces. Even if we are radical materialists who scoff at any notion of a human soul, the human *body* has numerous aspects that do not belong to the individual tiny elements of which it is composed. Various atoms of someone's body could be replaced without it becoming a different body. An object can also have retroactive effects on its own pieces, as is especially easy to see in the case of humans: I can decide to remove a tooth or some other inessential organ for medical reasons, and the body in that case only changes accidentally. Finally, we can choose to add new parts to our body through various piercings or physical implants—and the range of options here is likely to increase beyond belief by century's end. It is purely arbitrary to say that all these descriptions of higher layers of the cosmos might be eliminated in favor of a description of tiny physical movements or hypotheses about mathematical structure.

If we look at Plato's philosophy we find the opposite movement, which can be designated with the new term *overmining*, by analogy with the existing English word "undermining." According to overminers, the reason reality is not made up instead of individual things is because it is made up of forms or universals capable of inhering in many different things, and graspable in principle by the mind. But there are even more obvious examples of overmining that have nothing to do with Plato. The more obvious examples are cases such as idealism, where the object is *nothing more than* its appearance to some human or divine mind; or relationism, where the object is *nothing more than* its sum total of effects on all other things here and now; or social constructionism, where the object is *nothing more than* the way it is coded by a given social structure; or even correlationism, that weaker form of idealism where there is always a world to accompany the mind, but where that world does *nothing more than* resist humans, without having any internal life or structure of its own; or empiricism, for which there are no objects, just bundles of qualities, with objects being nothing more than arbitrarily posited and useless chunks in which all these directly encounterable qualities are supposed to inhere. According to all these overmining philosophies, the object is a gratuitous fiction, a meaningless X posited beneath a world of human access that is the only thing to which we have direct access. The problem with overmining philosophies is that they cannot explain why anything would ever change. If things are nothing more than what they are right now—if they are entirely expressed in their current state in the world—and if this holds for absolutely everything, then there is no reason why anything would ever shift from one state to another. For change to occur, there must be something held in reserve, an excess to the things behind their current interactions with all other things, beyond their current state of being shaped by society, language, or the mind. If undermining philosophies tend to be *realist* in spirit due to their commitment to some deeper layer of the world, overmining philosophies tend to be *anti-realist* in tone, since they hate the notion of any cryptic or hidden layer beneath what is purely accessible to the mind or at least immanent in the world. The only way overmining philosophies can escape this difficulty while still resisting the philosophy of objects, I believe, is to take a radically overmining stance like that of Meillassoux. What he tells us is that things are able to change, despite the *lack* of any hidden depths, due to the principle of absolute contingency that anything can happen at any moment without any reason at all. In this way the principle of sufficient reason is abolished, a terribly high price for a philosophy to pay, whatever its fascinating results. Against this theory it would be necessary to defend the principle of sufficient reason against Meillassoux's fascinating critique, but that is a subject for another time.

There are also philosophies that overmine and undermine simultaneously. In fact, the two are inherently parasitic on one another, and this is simply more explicit in some cases than in others. One of the explicit cases is materialism. For on the one hand, materialism seems to be a textbook example of a philosophy that views everyday objects as not deep enough to be the truth. If you actually believe in the existence of bananas, cities, and minds (or so the story goes) then you are a fool, for each of these supposed things is a mere surface-effect of tinier motions. But notice that when we finally arrive at the ultimate basis of the cosmos according to these theories, we end up instead with an *overmining* theory. For whether our final layer of the universe is water, an atom, a quark, a string, or a mathematical structure—in all these cases, this miniature little alpha factor turns out to be something no different from a bundle of tangible properties. It will be said that an atom is nothing over and above all the true facts about atoms; that there is no cryptic withdrawal of the being of the atom behind all positive facts, since this belief would be typical of an unscientific attitude. In short, materialism turns inevitably into a form of *idealism*, replacing the permanent mystery of things with some dogmatic set of traits. That's one example of a philosophy that overmines and undermines at the same time. Another would be when process philosophies are placed in a single package with philosophies of relation. For on the one hand, the appeal to "process" suggests that individual objects are petrified constructions of the mind, compared with the dynamic flux and flow of the cosmos: an infinitely creative lava lamp or kaleidoscope, compared with which all individual objects are nothing but rigid, middle-aged bores. "It's not a horse—it's a dynamic process from which horse-images sometimes emerge for certain observers, or horse-events occur like lightning-flashes," and so forth. This is the undermining side of such theories. But on the other hand, the simultaneous appeal to *relation* treats objects not as too shallow, but as too deep. "Things are nothing more than their sum total of current impacts on other things; there is nothing 'hidden' in a thing, since it is fully deployed in the world, and things mutually define one another," and so forth. And this is the overmining side of such theories. Incidentally, it should be said in passing that Latour and even Whitehead are not really "process" philosophers, despite Whitehead's constant use of that term. After all, both philosophers are pure overminers, thinkers of extreme concreteness, so concrete that things cannot endure even the least change in their relations. In fact, both are radical philosophers of *cinematic* instants that simply happen to pass away very quickly, and this makes them highly inappropriate partners for Bergson and Deleuze, who are pure underminers when it comes to the notion of individual instants or individual things.

Materialism and combined process-relational philosophy are just two of the more glaring examples of simultaneous overmining and undermining. But in nearly every case, a philosophy dominated by one of these attitudes needs to call on the other as a supplement. The simplest example can be found in Parmenides, who after denying all motion and all plurality at least needs to admit that it *seems* like there are many things in motion, and thus he has to make room for *doxa* or opinion, which deals only with surfaces. Individual things are skipped over, lying midway between Being and Opinion, and thereby lack autonomous existence. Another example would be all those philosophies of language or the subject which, as if horrified by the prospect of slipping into outright idealism, posit some sort of formless matter as a reservoir beneath formatted actuality, but without allowing this matter to do much of anything but resist *humans*, and without letting it have any internal duels among its own pieces.

The most difficult thing to do is think *between* these two extremes. It is necessary to conceive of objects as not fully reducible downward to their constituent pieces, and also as not fully reducible *upward* to their relations with the mind or with other things. Objects must be conceived as autonomous individuals not entirely disconnected from their components, or from the other things against which they bitterly or happily strike. Yet it must also be seen that they are sealed off from one another. The first figure in Western philosophy to avoid the downward spiral into raw physical elements or lumps *and* the upward spiral into intelligible ideas higher than individual things was Aristotle. There was much in his theory of substance that we can no longer accept today, but wherever the individual thing reasserts itself in philosophy across the centuries, there are generally Aristotelian roots to this tendency. When choosing the title of this article, that is what I meant: our future path cannot run through some new variant of undermining or overmining philosophies, but only with a subtler and more unusual approach to objects.

§ OBJECTS AND RELATIONS

Early in his controversial book on Deleuze, Alain Badiou says that, "our epoch can be said to have been stamped and signed, in philosophy, by the return of the question of Being. This is why it is dominated by Heidegger."[11] Assuming that we agree with this statement (and I do, though for reasons different from Badiou's own) it follows that the way out of "our epoch" is to digest Heidegger fully, so as to ensure that any apparent steps forward are not just lateral steps that fail to assimilate what Heidegger added to philosophy. It seems perfectly true to say that "the return of the question of being" is what Heidegger gave us, since this theme obviously dominates *Being and Time*, his major book. But this return is not just a "return," however rooted it may be in Ancient Greek thinking, since the question of being is asked in a new way. And neither

---

[11] Alain Badiou, *Deleuze: The Clamour of Being*, trans. Louise Burchill (Minneapolis: University of Minnesota Press, 2000), 18.

does Heidegger just pose the question and leave it open. Instead, he gives us a perfectly good provisional *answer* to the meaning of being. This is a point that Hans-Georg Gadamer seems to grasp better than anyone else, when midway through *Truth and Method* he gives us the following outstanding summary of Heidegger's philosophy:

> What being is was to be determined from within the horizon of time. Thus the structure of temporality appeared as ontologically definitive of subjectivity. But it was more than that. Heidegger's thesis was that *being itself is time.* Thus burst asunder the whole subjectivism of modern philosophy—and, in fact, as was soon to appear, the whole horizon of questions asked by metaphysics, which tended to define being as *what is present.*[12]

Gadamer's *realist* conception of Heidegger, as reflected in this passage, is basically correct. The widespread notion that Heidegger in *Being and Time* is asking about the transcendental conditions of any possible posing of the question of being is misleading. Time in the Heideggerian sense is less a structure of *Dasein* than of being itself, and what we can say about being itself is that it is never reducible to any form of presence. Being *withdraws* from presence; it is the excess that makes all overmining philosophies impossible. There is a strong nucleus of reality in Heidegger, despite his apparent obsession with the correlate of *Dasein* and *Sein*, or human and being, and Heidegger cannot be assimilated (let alone surpassed) by any new philosophy that downplays this deeply realist core of *Being and Time*.

We first need to clear our minds of the usual connotations of time as related to change or movement, since that is not

---

[12] Hans-Georg Gadamer, *Truth and Method*, 2nd rev. edn., trans. Joel Weinsheimer and Donald G. Marshall (New York: Continuum, 1993), 248; emphasis added.

how Heidegger uses the term. Whereas for Bergson it is simply impossible to treat time as made up of cinematic frames or instants, Heidegger's point is completely different. For Heidegger *even within* any cinematic frame or instant, there would be an ambiguous threefold structure undercutting any sheer presence. We could say that for Bergson, the static instant is impossible for "lateral" reasons, since there is a movement that cannot be recomposed of isolated instants in the first place. For Heidegger, by contrast, the static instant is impossible for "vertical" reasons, insofar as an instant is always more than what it seems to be, even if it were frozen and never passed away at all. Time for Heidegger is the ambiguous interplay of withdrawal and clearing, along with the presencing composed of these two extremes. This is due not to categories of *Dasein*'s existence, but to the structure of being itself.

The point is best grasped in the famous tool-analysis of 1919, first published eight years later in *Being and Time*.[13] Since I have often made the case elsewhere, we can pass briefly in review through the topic of tool-being in Heidegger. He makes an effort to radicalize phenomenology, which holds that "to the things themselves" means to the *phenomena* themselves since only the phenomena are directly given, and any notion of a sub-phenomenal world is at best a mediated *theory* that must first be grounded in the phenomena present to consciousness. Heidegger's famous counter-claim is that only rarely are things present to consciousness. For the most part, they withdraw into subterranean effectiveness, appearing to view only when they malfunction or go awry in some fashion. This is often read as saying that all explicit theory emerges from tacit background practices. Given this interpretation, it is no wonder that some people claim that John Dewey already gave us Heidegger's philosophy thirty years ahead of

---

[13] The 1919 course is available in English as Martin Heidegger, *Towards the Definition of Philosophy*, trans. Ted Sadler (London: Continuum, 2008).

time. Richard Rorty, for instance, claims that the main thing Heidegger added to Dewey's vision was thousands of pages of history of philosophy writing that we never find in Dewey.[14]

Yet Heidegger goes quite a bit further than this. For one thing, the difference in question cannot be a difference between theory and praxis, because if theory falsely objectifies the things by turning them into caricatures of their deeper, withdrawn realities, the same is equally true of praxis. Antoine Lavoisier in his chemical laboratory objectifies hydrogen and oxygen in his theory, reducing them to a series of distinct properties. But Lavoisier's practical relation to his beakers, alembics, desk, and chair is no more direct than his relation with hydrogen and oxygen themselves; his practical relations with these latter things distorts them no less than his theory distorts the chemicals. In other words, reducing things to present-at-hand properties is not a unique fault belonging only to the brain and the eye, but is also performed by Lavoisier's hands as they move the equipment, and his hindquarters as he drops into the chair. *Any* human contact with things is doomed never to drain them to the dregs, never to exhaust the subterranean darkness and plenitude of their full reality. This is what temporality in Heidegger *means*, after all: that we cannot gain direct access to the things themselves, as Husserl aspired to do, because the things themselves simply cannot be made present, cannot be accessed outside any context of interpretation and use. This holds for practical activity just as it does for the most heroic theoretical comportment.

But now we need to take an additional step that Heidegger's deeply Kantian presuppositions never allowed him, though Whitehead took the step for him. It is not *humans* whose limitations cause reality to withdraw, as though being were there for the taking if only *Dasein* were not cursed by a joint theoretical and practical original sin that forbade us from returning to the Eden of being ever again. Nor can we

---

[14] Richard Rorty, *Philosophy and the Mirror of Nature* (Princeton: Princeton University Press, 1981),12.

merely share the blame with other species by adding smart dolphins, monkeys, and crows to a longer list of conscious entities cursed by the withdrawal of being. The withdrawal of reality from presence is not a special privilege or curse belonging to a limited class of entities with full-blown consciousness. Instead, it is *relationality per se* that is responsible for the falsity of presence. No entity *ever* makes full contact with another, whether conscious or not. Here I have often used the favorite example of medieval Islamic philosophy: fire burning cotton. While human *Dasein* cannot fully grasp the depths of withdrawn cotton-being, and while untheoretical cotton planters also fail to exhaust it through the mere act of harvest, it cannot even be said that the *fire* makes contact with all aspects of the cotton. The fact that the fire has the power to destroy the cotton is irrelevant; humans have a similar power to shred and disperse it. Destructive power is not enough to give humans full contact with this entity, and neither does it give fire that sort of power. The key difference in Heideggerian philosophy turns out not to be *Sein* and *Dasein*, but *being and relation*. Being is that which exists in excess of all relational effects, or of all contact with anything else. These relations do occur, but they simply do not exhaust the being of things.

One last point about Heidegger: it is clear that his *Sein*, by acting as a dark subterranean residue eluding all access, is a challenge to overmining philosophies which hold that what you see is what you get, or that the world is nothing but a plane of self-affecting immanent reality. But the claim could still be made that Heidegger is an underminer of objects. There is plenty of textual evidence that Heidegger's being is not only withdrawn, but also that it is meant as singular rather than plural. In this way it becomes something like a pre-Socratic *apeiron* or unified molten plasma devoid of any contact or conflict between specific beings, so that individual entities would be no less illusory than presence itself. And true enough, Heidegger does have this side. Even in his later meditations on the thing, one aspect of the fourfold is a unified "earth."[15] Meanwhile, the case for a unified being is made quite explicitly by one of the most talented and original of his admirers in the 1940's, Emmanuel Levinas, who speaks of a unified *il y a* broken into pieces only by human consciousness.[16] Without going into too much detail, I would make the counter-claim that Heidegger shows several flashes of awareness that the realm deeper than presence is made of things (though admittedly it is only in the later work that we hear many explicit statements about the relations between jugs and wine, bridges and shores, and other pairs of entities that should be able to interact despite the lack of a human witness). The point remains ambiguous in Heidegger, though in the end we need not follow Heidegger's interpretation of Heidegger any more than scientists follow Einstein's interpretation of Einstein.

There is a very different conception of individual objects in Husserl, as mentioned earlier, but since it will be less relevant to the present discussion than Heidegger's objects, it can be summarized briefly once more. Husserl's world is absolutely riddled with objects, even if they are not real objects withdrawn from all presence. On the contrary, these so-called "intentional objects" are nothing if not present. For phenomenology we exist at each moment in a world of triangles, blackbirds, citrus fruit, chairs, mailboxes, and even centaurs and unicorns. These objects present themselves to the senses or the mind, yielding constantly different facets, surfaces, and adumbrations. Yet these objects are not *hidden* from us behind all these shifting and flickering qualities. If Heidegger's blackbird is always *more* than our relations with it, Husserl's blackbird is always *less*. The bird is there for us (even if hallucinated), fully present from the very first moment we expend our energy in taking account of it. But for us it is never simply an austere bird-object capable of various stances, actions, and

---

[15] Heidegger, *Bremen and Freiburg Lectures.*
[16] Emmanuel Levinas, *From Existence to Existents*, trans. Alphonso Lingis (The Hague: Martinus Nijhoff, 1988).

appearances at different moments. Rather, we always encounter the bird overdetermined as sitting at a *specific* difference from us in a *certain* direction, either silent or chirping or tweeting, either flying or sitting or falling from the sky. But all of this is simply *bonus experience* of the object. It does not hide or conceal the bird from us, since the bird is already there in our experience from the start. It is accidental and superfluous, and can be stripped away by analysis to help us clarify things, but does not obstruct our experience of the bird itself. How different this is from Heidegger, for whom bird-being forever withdraws into a dusky underworld inaccessible to all direct access.

Returning now to Heidegger, once it is seen that objects withdraw from all relation, there is a genuine problem with knowing how objects can affect one another at all. That they do so seems clear enough, but the fact that reality somehow solves the problem for us does not mean that philosophers have the right to call it a pseudo-problem. Quite the contrary: our primary task is to explain how things happen that seem to have no obvious reason for happening. Given that objects withdraw from all relation (and this cannot only be "partial," for since objects are unified rather than glued together out of parts, contact is all or nothing) how is that objects relate anyway? As I have written elsewhere, this problem was raised above all by Islamic theology, which first gave the answer that objects *do not* affect one another, since only God affects them.[17] "Occasionalism" is the famous name by which this theory is known.[18] The problem later flared up in Europe for philosophical rather than theological reasons and initially concerned only the apparent difficulty of *different kinds* of substances interacting with one another (extension and

---

[17] Graham Harman, *Prince of Networks: Bruno Latour and Metaphysics* (Melbourne: re.press, 2009).

[18] Dominik Perler and Ulrich Rudolph, *Occasionalismus: Theorien der Kausalität im arabisch-islamischen und im europäischen Denken* (Göttingen: Vandenhoeck & Ruprecht, 2000).

mind).[19] But it was quickly re-broadened by Descartes's successors into a more general theory in which body-body interactions became problematic again, just as they had been among the Ash'arites of Basra and those influenced by their tradition, such as al-Ghazali.

Occasionalism is often mocked today, but only for the reason that almost all discussion of God is now mocked by philosophers. Yet the real problem with occasionalism is not that *God* is involved, but that any *particular* entity is involved at all. No one being or kind of being should be given the special power to engage in direct causal interaction when others cannot. In fact, I have made the same complaint about the upside-down occasionalism of Hume and Kant, in which human habit or mind is treated as the only locus of interaction, and would make exactly the same complaint about any theory of a unified world-lump or quasi-lump whose unity is said to allow for mutual influence between things unable to do it to each other directly, insofar as the lump is viewed as both heterogeneous and continuous. As I have written elsewhere one of the best things about Bruno Latour's philosophy is his "secular occasionalism," in which all entities are forced to do the causal work themselves despite great difficulty, without easy recourse to the monopolistic God of the Ash'arites, Malebranche, or even Whitehead.[20]

In the Islamic tradition the occasionalism of the Ash'arites was generally opposed by the rationalist neo-Platonic and Aristotelian tradition of such familiar names as al-Kindi, al-Farabi, Avicenna, and Averroës. But in some ways it is remarkable that Aristotle never found his way to the occasionalist problem. Devoted as he was to the autonomy of individual substance, he never seems to have found any difficulty with one entity exerting influence directly on another. He is right to have avoided any notion of a central mighty causal agent.

---

[19] Steven Nadler, *Occasionalism: Causation Among the Cartesians* (Oxford: Oxford University Press, 2011).

[20] See Harman, *Prince of Networks*, 115 and 159.

There is a Prime Mover in Aristotle's metaphysics, of course, but this Prime Mover is simply a first and most powerful mover, not one who intervenes in the burning of cotton balls or the falling of every hair from our heads. Nonetheless, Aristotle does brush against the interesting question of how absolutely withdrawn objects could ever exert influence on one another, and it is worth taking a brief look at how he does so.

§ ARISTOTLE

Let's turn to the *Metaphysics*. It is safe to say that Aristotle is not one of the most fashionable classic philosophers in present-day continental thought, no matter how many passing mentions he may receive. A good dispute could be had as to how Aristotelian Heidegger really is; in my view the relation has been tackled incorrectly, but the point can certainly be disputed. What is much clearer is that Aristotle plays no especially important role in the Deleuzian counter-history of philosophy, nor do Badiou or Žižek make any especial use of Aristotle, to say nothing of his rude handling in Derrida's "White Mythology" essay.[21] But once we start to look at individual things as the central topic of philosophy, Aristotle's dominant position is hard to overlook.

It is safe to say that in the *Metaphysics*, Aristotle's first concern is to protect primary substances or individual things from what I have called "undermining" and "overmining" attacks. In the former case the primary danger is the pre-Socratics, for as we have seen, they reduce things downward either to a "One," or else to some multiple of physical elements. Unlike Heidegger's reverential treatment of these earliest Western thinkers, Aristotle is often quite harsh in his witticisms, comparing the pre-Socratics to lisping youngsters who are just learning how to speak and to amateur boxers

---

[21] Jacques Derrida, "White Mythology: Metaphor in the Text of Philosophy," in *Margins of Philosophy*, trans. Alan Bass (Chicago: University of Chicago Press, 1982).

who land nothing but lucky punches (*Metaphysics*, 9) and even to household slaves and livestock who act at random without foresight (*Metaphysics*, 249).[22] The problem with all these philosophers, Aristotle holds, is their obsession with the material cause (*Metaphysics*, 6). They cannot explain *why* matter changes, (*Metaphysics*, 8) and forget that a statue is stony, not just stone; and that a house is wooden, but not just wood (*Metaphysics*, 130). It is true that Anaxagoras also introduces *nous* or "mind" as a cause, but Aristotle follows the imprisoned Socrates of the *Phaedo* in complaining that Anaxagoras makes use of this mind only as a last resort whenever recourse to material causes fails (*Metaphysics*, 10). He also notes that those who make one or more physical elements the first principle have difficulty in accounting for the existence of non-physical things (*Metaphysics*, 18) As for philosophies of Being or the One, Aristotle does not see how the many could ever arise from such a principle, since according to Parmenides, all that is other than Being *is not* (*Metaphysics*, 48). In short, individual things cannot be undermined either with a monolithic Being or with some physical element, and though I might give different reasons for why this is so, Aristotle's rejection of it is perfectly sound.

But there is another sort of claim rejected by Aristotle as undermining, and this is a point where we must eventually disagree with him. An individual thing for Aristotle turns out to be an individual form (as opposed to a common universal), and since the form must be one, it cannot be made of active independent parts, but only of potential ones (*Metaphysics*, 146). For instance, the bones, joints, and flesh of a human are only material components, not formal parts (*Metaphysics*, 136). What divides into parts is the composite whole made of form and matter, not the substance or thinghood of the thing (*Metaphysics*, 137). As Aristotle puts it, in relatively rare

---

[22] Aristotle, *Metaphysics,* trans. Joe Sachs (Santa Fe: Green Lion Press, 1999), 28. All in-text citations of the *Metaphysics* refer to the Sachs translation.

agreement with a pre-Platonic thinker: "if an independent thing is one, it will not be made of independent things present in it in that way, which Democritus says correctly; for he says it is impossible for one to come to be out of two, or two out of one" (*Metaphysics*, 146). Aristotle admits that this leads to an *aporia*, one that is later noticed by Leibniz: if the form is purely one, then how can a thing have parts? We will return to this problem shortly.

But Aristotle is equally critical of the "overmining" approaches to individual thinghood. His chief opponent here is obviously his own teacher Plato, whose theory of forms is criticized as a rival doctrine throughout the *Metaphysics*, despite Aristotle's occasional expressions of regret for having to criticize a friend. Among other difficulties, Plato never really explains how the individual things would "participate" in the forms (*Metaphysics*, 15). Furthermore, each individual would have to be made up of a wild menagerie of often partially redundant forms: Socrates, for example, would have to participate simultaneously in the forms of animal, human being, and two-footed, among many others (*Metaphysics*, 24). If the forms are separate from the things, it seems difficult to see how they can make up the substance or thinghood of things (*Metaphysics*, 24). Instead, Aristotle holds that the form must be *in* the substance of the individual thing, and in fact must constitute it (*Metaphysics*, 126). In short, *there are* no forms in Plato's sense (*Metaphysics*, 206). This leads to a surprisingly Heideggerian moment in Aristotle, though he does not press the point. Namely, universals such as Plato's forms cannot be the substance of things, since this is always individual, while the universal is shared by many things, and thus an individual thing cannot be built out of universals (*Metaphysics*, 145). And moreover, universals are indestructible, whereas individual things are in most cases utterly destructible (*Metaphysics*, 148) (in fact, Aristotle was the first Western philosopher to believe in a destructible primary substance, a bold venture for which he receives too little credit). These incommensurabilities between things and universals, coupled with the fact that knowledge is always knowledge of universals rather than of particulars, leads Aristotle to the rather astonishing claim that *no form can be defined* (*Metaphysics*, 148). As he puts it, with his underrated but odd sense of humor: "For example, if someone were to define you, he would say 'a skinny, pale animal,' or something else that would also belong to some other thing" (*Metaphysics*, 148). There is a radical gap between the individual things that are the primary substance of philosophy, and any attempt to grasp them with the *logos*. Individuals are deeper than anything we can see or say about them.

But there is another important form of overmining that Aristotle rejects, and that comes in his well-known attack on the Megarians in Chapter 3 of *Metaphysics*, Book Theta. The Megarians hold that a thing is nothing more than it is right now, with nothing held in reserve: a house-builder is only a house-builder while actually building a house. Aristotle counter-attacks with his theory of the potency in things, which gives individual substances an unexpressed excess or residue not found in their actuality here and now. And finally, there is another passage in which Aristotle anticipates a critique of overmining found in Husserl and Saul Kripke as well.[23] This happens when Aristotle rejects those who define the sun by such phrases as "going around the earth" or "hidden at night" (*Metaphysics*, 149). For if these features change or turn out to be false (and "going around the earth" has turned out to be a false trait of the sun) we would not conclude "if it does not go around the earth, then it cannot be the sun," but rather: "we have discovered that we were wrong: the sun does not really go around the earth." In this way, the individual thing is deeper than its apparent attributes, even if not deeper than its real ones. And certainly the thing is deeper than its accidents. We cannot define a dog, for example, by the exact position of its legs and ears at a given moment, since these are accidental and

---

[23] Saul Kripke, *Naming and Necessity* (Cambridge, Mass.: Harvard University Press, 1980).

can change rapidly without the underlying dog having changed.

Most of these objections work as well now as they ever did, as do some others that Aristotle never needed to dream up. But there is one that we need not accept, and really ought to reject: namely, his assumption that the individual forms must be final layers of reality that can have parts only as parts of a material composite, and cannot be made up of other forms. Here we see Aristotle's distrust, later found in magnified form in Leibniz, of the idea that composites or machines or aggregates could ever be individual things. According to this view a human can be a thing, but a family, team, conference, or army cannot; a tree can be a substance, but a forest cannot. This unduly restricts the range of what might be called an object, substance, or thing, and is thus a variant of the reductionist maneuver, reducing things to so-called "natural kinds" rather than to the pre-Socratic water, air, fire, or atoms. If we allow for emergent entities to exist, such that the city of Chicago has qualities not possessed by its parts, is robust to constant changes in the residents and buildings within it, has retroactive effects on its parts, and is able to generate new parts (this is DeLanda's list of criteria, and I happen to like it), then Chicago is no less an individual thing than the individual police officers, cottonwood trees, and Asian longhorn beetles found within the city limits.[24] Nor is there any good reason to exclude elevated trains or the city's five major sports teams from the list of individual things. The Chicago Cubs baseball franchise, no less than its players or the blades of grass on its playing field, is an autonomous reality not exhausted by its current effects on or relations with other entities in the vicinity. It is neither reducible downward to its human components nor reducible upward to its functional effects on the environment.

[24] For a summary of DeLanda's list, see Graham Harman, "DeLanda's Ontology: Assemblage and Realism," *Continental Philosophy Review* 41.3 (2008): 371[367–83].

The Cubs cannot be undermined or overmined, not that it helps them much.

Aristotle's main worry with such a model seems to be the idea of an infinite regress. Those who defend an infinite regress, in his own words, "abolish knowing, since it is not possible to know until one has come to what is indivisible" (*Metaphysics*, 32). This is why he also takes care to state that none of the four causes can have an infinite regress, (*Metaphysics*, 30) and he also links the infinite regress with the trollish sophistry of relativists who *pretend* to want reasons for absolutely everything, even though they act on the same ultimate assumptions that the rest of us do. After all, they like us do not walk off cliffs, while they do walk to Megara whenever they wish to go there rather than sitting motionless in place. But Aristotle himself recognizes that there are many different kinds of infinity, of which it is important here to distinguish two in particular. One is the infinity of intermediate points between any two places, exploited so nicely in the paradoxes of Zeno, though also attacked by Aristotle in the *Physics*. In order to move from Point A to Point B, it is first necessary to go to Point C midway between the two, then Point D midway between Points B and C, and so on *ad infinitum*. This is certainly "contrary to reason," since we know that the motion does occur. But an infinite regress of substances is merely counter to common sense, not counter to reason. Once we recognize that some individual things are aggregates made up of smaller components, it is a small step to realize that *all* things must be such aggregates (though the converse does not hold: not all aggregates are things). Aristotle recognized this himself when he admitted that it leads to an *aporia* if we hold that individuals cannot be made of other individuals, since this would mean that individuals have no parts and hence no distinct individual features. Kant is slightly more open on this question, holding in the Antinomies merely that we *cannot know* whether there are simples or only an infinitely descending chain of composites. But if we follow the insight contained in Aristotle's *aporia* while ignoring his needless fear of this infinite regress, we find that individual things *must* be divisible into sub-components if they are to have distinct individuality at all, and this requires an infinite regress into the depths of things. But here again the reverse does not hold: there need not be an infinite progress upwards into larger and larger entities and finally into some "world as a whole," since there is nothing forcing substances to enter into combination with other substances.

Aristotle gives us a quantized world made up of individual chunks. He is aware that since none of these objects are made of universals, none of them can be defined, and this means that in a way they must withdraw from the power of language and thought, although he does not pursue this point at length in the way that Heidegger does. But I would claim that not only the human *logos* encounters things in terms of universals; instead, inanimate objects must do this to each other as well. Fire encounters *the flammable*, not the individual concreteness of this cotton and this paper, and in that respect cotton and fire withdraw from each other no less than they do from us. The first occasionalists in Iraq, more than a millennium after Aristotle, were forced to this insight for theological reasons, and it later found fertile soil in seventeenth century philosophy. It has never really left us, bewitched as we still are in philosophy by gaps in the world of various kinds, or by all the various attempts to deny or bridge those gaps. The problem with Aristotle's model of a quantized world of individual, autonomous things is that they ought to be closed off from all causal interaction entirely. In order to affect one another, they would have to meet in a continuum of some sort. The continuum, of course, is the great theme not of Aristotle's *Metaphysics* but of the *Physics*. There we learn that time, magnitude, and motion are not atomistic, but continuous. But this solution cannot immediately work for the relation between substances in Aristotle, since substance is what is *not* continuous, but made of discrete individuals. This room has the potential to be divided into a thousand or a million spatial sectors, and the elapsed time of this lecture can be split arbitrarily into three, fifteen, or seventy-five thousand parts. But the same does not hold for the number of people present in the room, who are individuals of a certain determinate number, not a lump-like human continuum ready to be arbitrarily carved into whatever number we please. For things to have mutual influence, they must not only reside in private vacuums as individual chunks. They must also be partially transformed into portions of a continuum, but *without* their individuality being treated as a mere surface-product. How this might happen is a problem that Aristotle never solves, but one that he raises for us more urgently than expected.

Three Notes, Three Questions
Response to Graham Harman

Patricia Ticineto Clough

1.

When I was invited to respond to a talk to be given by Graham Harman at a conference on Speculative Medievalisms, my first thoughts were not about Aristotle. My first thoughts were about Harman's work on Bruno Latour, who has famously claimed that *we have never been modern*. So perhaps we are becoming medieval, I thought: circuiting back through the Enlightenment and the Renaissance to a future age where darkness is to be revalued, with speculative realism, the measure.

Although I first read Latour in the late 1980s when some few sociologists studying science and technology were doing so, Harman's reading of Latour was pleasantly surprising on two counts. His positioning of Latour as a philosophical thinker who is essential to the current ontological turn was resonant with my own early situating of Latour not only in science and technology studies but also as part of the philosophical debates of the late 1980s and 1990s around post-structuralism. However, Harman's Latour offered another pleasant surprise in that it re-oriented my thoughts about philosophy and sociality, giving them a new direction beyond social construction, discursive construction, psychic or unconscious construction, and finally deconstruction. Harman's Latour instead points to a rethinking of sociality that necessitates an ontological re-booting that aims to restore the wonder of objects, conceive of a causality of allure, and offer a take on aesthetics. In all this a refreshing aporia is inserted between ontology and epistemology, such that objects are allowed to be regardless of our consciousness of them.

While the necessity of turning to ontology already had made me a fan of Gilles Deleuze over many other philosophers of the 1980s and 1990s, Harman's Latour introduced me to a critique of 'correlationism,' or a critique of the presumed impossibility of world without human knowing or of a philosophy without the assumption of a primordial rapport between human and world. Harman's critique of correlationism was different than Deleuze's critique of humanism and even stronger than the critique offered by Quentin Meillassoux who had coined the term correlationism. Harman's stronger critique involved his read of Latour as a relationist. Against Latour's view that objects are constituted through relations with other objects, Harman emphasizes that objects are not reducible to their relations. No relation exhausts an object; it endures beyond its relations. This was an ontology different than that suggested by Deleuze or even Whitehead whose philosophy was often made compatible with Deleuze's in critical theory, especially theories of affect to which my work has been deeply indebted.

While for Deleuze and Whitehead relations are external to objects, that is, objects are not reduced to their relationships, nonetheless objects do not exist outside all relations, as Harman argues they should be thought to be. Here Deleuze's thought of *virtuality* and Whitehead's of *eternal objects* come under criticism as correlationist in that in these philosophies a world pre-existing us nonetheless pre-exists for us as a world of potential or virtuality. After all, virtuality and eternal objects are thought to subsist in pre-individuality or prehension, *overmining* and *undermining* objects, as Harman would put it. And so at last one can think of Aristotle who on Harman's read of him, conceived the individuality of the object with a form that is not universal and therefore is withdrawn from the power of language and thought. But we might also wonder about Aristotle's potentiality and how it differs from Deleuze's virtuality or Whitehead's prehension of eternal objects. Or, to put it more plainly, what specifically is different about the dynamic of the fourfold object? This is my first question.

2.

When first asked to respond to Harman's talk, after first thoughts about Latour, I thought about Max Weber who, before he wrote *The Protestant Ethic and the Spirit of Capitalism*, had produced studies of the development of Roman land tenure and of medieval trading and law, presaging his later works, including *The Protestant Ethic,* all of which would examine economic life within the context of a geographically and historically specific culture that was to be taken as a whole. I thought of Max Weber because when I teach him just before I teach Karl Marx in a course on classical sociological theory, I give students a brief treatment of the *Catholicism of Feudalism*, preparing them for those elliptical expressions in Weber that they cannot easily fill in about Saint Paul, Thomas Aquinas, or even Martin Luther or John Calvin. I ask them to think of feudalism as the background that supports the analyses that would be the foundation of modern western sociology. And just as students come to think feudalism as background to that great protestant loneliness, that private endless self-judging that as Weber sees it, motivates capitalist productivity, they are shocked by a sudden turn to book one of *Das Capital*, for there, as part of its invitation to a secular materialism, appearing at the very start of the text, are *things things things*, or as Marx puts it, "an immense accumulation of commodities that holds the secret of the wealth of those societies in which the capitalist mode of production prevails." Thus, there is a warning at the very start of the text, a warning that the commodity is only the phenomenal form of something contained in it but distinguishable from it. As Marx would have it, it is the potential or capacity of labor power that has been abstracted from use or utility and as an abstraction becomes a matter of perverse desire and pleasure as relations between things become fetish, displacing relations between humans. In the capitalist mode of production, Marx suggests sardonically, commodities therefore abound "in metaphysical subtleties and theological niceties." And if today in what Steven Shaviro has tagged as "aesthetic capitalism," the commodity is said to be designed to sensually transmit a creative juice that will be transformative for its user such that the aura and value of the commodity is its transmission of affective capacity, when the exchange seems to be a direct one of energy-matter, or a transmission of affect to what is awkwardly called the prosumer, the question would seem to be: does an object-oriented ontology, with its protection of the essence of the object, provide a solid ground for a political economic critique of what has been described as the immeasurable value of affective labor-power or the affective transmission through the commodities of an aesthetic capitalism?

This is my second question: Is the critique of materialism, attendant upon Harman's object-oriented ontology, an unhealthy symptom of these times or does it offer a radicalization of the object's ontology that assists us in rethinking a Marxist treatment of the commodity? After all, Graham's critique of materialism as not realist but idealist in its presumption of underlying objective states of physical substance would seem to refuse much of what is implied in Marx's separation of the mere phenomenal form of the commodity from the hidden inner thermodynamic workings of labor power, yet to be revealed or uncovered so that truth will be found, a truth that is meant to restore consciousness in the human mastery of nature and the object world. This has led to the idealization of human laboring in Marxism no less than in Protestantism. In an aesthetic capitalism this may not only be mistaken, since the political economic issue is not simply the human laborer who is exploited in producing surplus value but also a generalized affect that produces and distributes wealth in a wildly unequal manner. It is therefore also mistaken to idealize human laboring in that the necessity to understand the so-called immateriality of affective labor is missed as is the necessity for a thorough deconstruction of material and immaterial. If we have never been modern, it is perhaps the case that we have never been secular, or better, realist about materiality.

3.

And would not an object-oriented ontology thus require rethinking fetish or perversion and their link, at least since Sigmund Freud, to repetitious enactment of unconscious fantasy as opposed to reality? Without correlationism, Harman might be said to suggest, that fantasy is as real as pencils, paper, angels, horses, cows and chairs. While Freud may well have contributed to decentering consciousness with his pointing to the insistent intrusion in body and mind of unconscious fantasy, psychoanalysis has not yet let us return to what before it might be called the medieval or what Eugene Thacker has recently called *the horror of philosophy*, that is, a return to a whole bestiary of impossible life forms, but also demonology, occult philosophy and theology, mysticism and apothecaries for drugs and charms. Psychoanalysis has not yet been able to level the ontological ground for all objects or to stay far enough away from cure through *words words words*, or an insistent return to consciousness, the reality principle or normality that are not actually realist or speculative enough for an aesthetic capitalism.

With an insistent return to reality, consciousness and normality, there is a failure to respond to the way in which speculative realism and object-oriented ontologies are refurbishing aesthetics as a first philosophy and with that recognizing a causality of allure. Or as Harman puts it, causality is alluring in that it is through sensuality or by proxy of the sensual, a real object touches a real object in the interior of some other entity and from which all else is derived: time, space, extension and intension, quality and quantity. This *vicarious causality*, where the sensual is vicar of the real, calls forth a rethinking of methods or practices of presentation or measure in the sciences, the humanities and the arts that necessarily will have to be speculative realist, that is, practices for encountering the realities of entities that are constituted through other-than-human perception, cognition or consciousness, against a horizon of a world that is without us. Such practices, where there necessarily would be a musicality of expression, a poetics of performance and an ethics or even a politics of measure, would be thought as a continuation of touching the real through sensual allusion: an aesthetic measuring that creatively makes new relations. This is my third question: Does, or in what ways does, object-oriented ontology motivate a deep transformation of the disciplines and all authored styles of presentation of being, doing and knowing?

Obiectum
Closing Remarks

Nicola Masciandaro

I see an elision or lacuna in these proceedings, possibly significant: the lack of discussion, in a conference rather inspired to
speculate objects in the mirror of medieval works, of the medieval origins of the concept and word *object*. Is this an over-
sight, a structural failure of vision to bump into what it ought
to see? Or is it a purer kind of non-event, the causeless not-
happening of something? Sometimes I get the feeling that
what does *not* happen is inexplicably powerful, an abyssically
negative spontaneity ruling and seducing all existent things
from its universal invisible domain. The issue might provide
an interesting playground for thinking the objecthood of the
inexistent, of what is not *there*. This is a good limit-problem
for any philosophy wanting to relate to reality as constituted
by how things are. It is also a question that the medieval, as a
zone where a saint recommends preaching to non-existent
creatures, philosophers theorize divine alteration of the past,
and mystics see nonbeing as an excess of being, is already answering.

But I prefer not to go there, wishing that I could instead
move (or realize that I am only ever moving) like the guild
navigator in David Lynch's *Dune*: "I did not say this. I am not
here." Instead I will close the event by trying to open it into
some avenues of understanding along which the medieval

origination of *object* might lead the way. To find the start of these avenues, imagine a generic medieval intellectual, that is, someone infused with 'the love of learning and the desire for God,' encountering contemporary object-orientedness. First the bad news: there is no absolute knowledge, no arriving at the omnipresent center. Then the good news: we really have figured out what everything is: objects. Bad news: objects incommensurably withdraw, remain irreducible to relation, are never knowable in themselves, so no theosis, henosis, subject-object union, incarnation, soul-body suppositum, eternal individuals, or anything like that. Good news: it is because of the above that anything is happening at all . . . and so forth. Maybe the fellow would find relief, like a good bloodletting, in the demotion of his desire from the desire to be everything to a desire to be with things. Perhaps he would despair. Perhaps he would think he was in paradise, intoxicated with the idea that these objects are God. Or perhaps he would object, discovering new truth through his own understanding of the word *object*.[1]

§ OBIECTUM

Obiectum is a substantive meaning the object of a power. From *ob-jacere* [to throw something before, to make it appear, present], the word has a verbal meaning:[2] a casting before, a putting before, a lying before, a being interposed and thus what presents itself to movement or perception, what gets in the way.

Importantly, the sense of objection (argument, accusation, charges) is developed *in advance* of the philosophical sense of

---

[1] The essential study, on which I rely on and freely borrow from throughout these remarks, is Lawrence Dewan's "'Obiectum': Note on the Invention of a Word," in *Wisdom, Law, and Virtue: Essays in Thomistic Ethics* (New York: Fordham University Press, 2007), 403–43.

[2] The verb-noun relation was also addressed earlier in this symposium.

object: *obiectum* (objection): 1125-1343; *obiectum* (object): 1286-1444.

Obiectum is both what we go after and what *strikes* us. Compare this with the problem of distinguishing facts and judgments. Likewise, *obiectum* indicates objects of both apprehensive and motive powers (passive or active).

"Objects are things/appearances thrown over against (*objecta*) subjects who are thrown under (*sub-jecta*) the field of manifestness."[3]

The primary philosophical sense of *obiectum* is the object of a power, typically a human power. In that sense it is a term of human-world correlation and would fall under the same Heideggerian critique of *object* that Graham Harman mentioned in his lecture "Aristole with a Twist." The medieval *obiectum* in this sense is exactly not the sense of object pursued by object-oriented philosophy, which seeks to redefine things or entities as objects. However, the semantic firstness of *obiectum* as dialectial objection or argument should alert us to suspicion of such a 'purified' notion of object, precisely because it suggests an occluded or unspeakable relation between the philosophical concept of *object* and the intellectuo-appetitive practice of raising arguments and throwing down objections. Is object-oriented philosophy's 'hypostasizing' of the object a correlate of its will for real philosophical argument, for objective jousting over reality itself?

Harman's call for "universal philosophical dialogue" on the model of premodern intellectual smack-downs, "a more wild and fruitful form of intellectual combat of a kind that no longer exists," does seem to confirm this medieval semantic diagnosis. He writes, "The Middle Ages are widely remembered as a period of rampant intolerance in intellectual history. Minute subtleties of theological dogma served as ground for harassment and excommunication . . . . Although intellectual persecution is usually the result of stupid authoritarian

---

[3] Rober E. Wood, *Placing Aesthetics: Reflections on the Philosophic Tradition* (Athens: Ohio University Press, 1999), 3.

behavior, it nonetheless suggests an atmosphere in which the consequences of ideas are taken seriously . . . . I would like to describe a sense in which all of these persecutors are closer to the ideal model of universal dialogue than we in the tolerant and apathetic West."[4] That a fantasy and/or event of contiguity between objection and object is at work in object-oriented philosophy is suggested more specifically in Harman's recommendation for the production of such an atmosphere of serious consequences, in which different philosophical positions would be encouraged to hit each other like free objects via the mysterious occasionalist mediation of "a powerful blind-reviewing committee":

> . . . the dominance of insular specialists would come to an end, and universal philosophical dialogue would prosper at the hands of those willing to risk a staged combat between ideas of different philosophers or altogether different traditions. The measuring stick in such combat can only be reality itself . . . Although I have no wish to be burned at the stake, I would also prefer not to work in a profession in which there is was never any real combat over fundamental principles.[5]

The desire here is for a testing and proving of thought on the universal battlefield of objectal relation, not because that would constitute real discourse in the sense of authentic communication, but precisely because real communication is impossible, because the only way things ever 'talk' is by touching and hitting each other: "When a meteorite strikes the moon, it hardly matters that these objects are not 'conscious' of one another. They have to appear to one another in the sense that they affect one another. And they never appear to one another in the totality of their being, but only in a limited,

---

[4] Graham Harman, "Some Preconditions of Universal Philosophical Dialogue," *Dialogue and Universalism* 1-2 (2005): 165–66.
[5] Harman, "Some Preconditions," 179.

perspectival way."[6] Combat is in this sense an object-oriented criterion of philosophical truth, precisely because it can *never* effect the cores of things, because violence does not alter their autonomous essences. In other words, the prospect of being burned at the stake is for GH a fit, flirted-with image of a world of real intellectual stakes because, like cotton, he is an object that would not be exhausted by burning: "When fire burns cotton, it does not matter whether the fire is 'conscious' of the cotton in some primitive panpsychist manner; all that matters is that the fire never makes contact with the cotton as a whole, but only with its flammability. The rich reality of cotton-being is never drained dry by the fire, any more than by human theories of cotton or human practical use of it. There is a certain unreachable autonomy and dignity in the things."[7] Among the first question this legible correlation between the two senses of object—"Some might object that inanimate objects . . ."[8]—raises is the question of the appetite or motive for combat, the question of the originary semantic element that is elided in object(ion)-oriented thinking. What is the power that seizes object-oriented philosophy as its object?

Rather than pursuing that question, I will simply try to furnish some relevant facts and thoughts, materials through which we might converse with OOO's imaginary medieval interlocutor, through which the medieval genesis of *object* may be meaningful in a philosophical 'third zone' or 'great outdoors' beyond the subject-object correlate.[9] On this note it is significant that Harman's atheistic or secular occasionalism does not and perhaps cannot dispense with negatively deploying the name of God, that it seems to fall under discursive necessity for a kind of apophasis, of defining the absolute oc-

---

[6] Harman, "Some Preconditions," 172.

[7] Graham Harman, "Asymmetrical Causation," *Parallax* 16.1 (2010): 100 [96–101].

[8] Harman, "Some Preconditions," 171.

[9] The logic of 'the third' was a de facto theme of the symposium.

casional power as a not-God or immanent infinite absence. Contrarily, thinking the speculative medieval *object*, the object as both autonomously real *and* the correlate of human powers, may lead toward the (always) new great indoors, a third universal conditioned neither by God nor not-God, an outdoors that one not only points to from inside, but actually lives *in*.

§ OBJECT IS APPETITIVE

The relation between object and appetite is clear from the Latin-to-Greek context where *obiectum* translates as, 'that on which power depends,' 'for which there is desire,' 'to which a power is related,' Aristotle's *to antikeimenon/ta antikeimena* ['that which lies over against']. *Object* is soul food, as represented by Aristotle's discussion of nutritive powers in the *De Anima*. It is what keeps a body going and is thus intimate to life as animation, movement. Here *object* represents a kind of close/distant opposite, as the stomach is alterative of food. Dewan shows that *obiectum* is not the product of simple translation, that the commentary tradition creates the concept out of Aristotle and does not take it from him as such.

The appetitive sense of *object* may be compared to OOO's predilection for models of burrowing and tunneling, the worm being the perfect and traditional figure for appetitive animation. "We do not step beyond anything, but are more like moles tunneling through wind, water, and ideas . . . . We do not transcend the world, but only descend or burrow towards its numberless underground cavities."[10]

---

[10] Graham Harman, "Vicarious Causation," *Collapse* II: "Speculative Realism" (2007): 210 [187–221]. For a critique of such subjective enclosure, see Nicola Masciandaro, "Mysticism or Mysticification?: Against Subject-Creationism," *English Language Notes* 50 (2012): 255–60.

§ OBJECT IS OBSTACULAR

Dewan analyzes the word in the context of the *De Anima* of Robert Grosseteste, which concerns how the soul, like the eye, is *affected where it is not*. Similarly, the obstacular nature of *object* is central to Augustine's discussion of the extromissive theory of vision in *De quantitate animae*. Boethius's *Consolation of Philosophy* (5.5) similarly concerns the indeterminate substantiveness of *obiecta* as things being thrown up against powers. Chaucer's translation makes this especially clear, where he uses the verbal "thinges objecte from withoute-forth" to translate *obiecta extrinsecus*. Boethius is a possible source for the application of the word *obiectum* to the Aristotelian context.

But Augustine also uses *corpus obiectum* as corporeal object of sense, not in sense of object of a power but more purely in the sense of *obstaculum*, what stands in the way. Here we should consider the fascinating paradox of how the objects of powers/appetites also stand in the way in a more essential sense, how precisely what satisfies or fulfills a desire is also what thwarts and hinders its fulfillment. *Obstaculum* is what rays of light issuing from the eye hit up against. The sensed is the impassible, which also means that what is seen is exactly what is not. For Thierry of Chartres, only earth and water are truly visible, not fire or air. This was applied to the question of the invisibility of God: God cannot be seen because he lacks obstacularity. What is everywhere hinders nothing. The model is applied to the operation of intellectual powers and also concerns the effect or lack of effect of a power on its object when it 'offends' or strikes it (*offendere*)—another space of conceivable correlation between attack and understanding. Cf. deconstruction and Harman's interest in understanding something as intellectually 'ruining' it. Boethius, for example, address how the freedom of a being is not disturbed by its being an object of divine knowledge. God's invisibility and omniscience are two sides of the same reality.

The obstacularity of *object* reveals the interplay between the movement of the soul to things and the movement of things into the soul. Here we must consider the equation or identity of what strikes you and what you hit up against. Note how humans ignorantly love to strike back at what they have, under their own power, first bumped into.

§ Object is Argumentative

As noted above, the use of *obiectum* to mean object (of a power) develops after the sense of objection and remains contemporary with it. Is there a substantive connection? Perhaps a connection is visible in the use of *object* in Middle English to mean objection, in that there is a logical continuity between tangibility and objection, the sense is which things are objections, arguments. Nothing is simply there but is also pressing itself into the world, talking to it and continually imposing itself on other things in one way or another. Things *are* objects, arguments. An entity is something that says, *what about me?* Biosemiotics investigates this domain.

Continuity between the nominal and verbal senses of *obiectum*, and thus indeterminacy regarding the substantiality of objects, is communicated by *object* as adjective in Middle English, as in the phrase 'object thing'. Here we should consider the question in relation to the good as the will's object and truth as the intellect's. That is, how shall we go about sorting out the interplay between telos and obstacle with respect to argumentation? Is not argumentation, as a practice of raising objections, often a form of *futile telos* or confusion of end and obstacle? Argumentation at once aims toward the good, the true and prevents passage to them. Argument is an art of laying down an object in both senses before your interlocutor, both something they should stumble upon, hit up against, and thus be prevented from arriving at their own object, and something that should become their object in the sense of telos or aim, their new truth.[11]

Dewan considers the double meaning of *obiectum* (objection and object) to be insignificant, a point of possible linguistic confusion, but not an inherently significant polysemy. He writes: "we might ask what attraction was to be found in the word '*obiectum*.' There was one obvious drawback. Its equivocal double was already in use to mean an objection. Still, this is a much less grave difficulty than with the other words mentioned above [*oppositum, finis, motivum*]. The reason is that in the case of '*obiectum*,' the double or equivocal pertains to the discussion of discourse itself, rather than '*obiectum*' being a word to signify an aspect of things in their own intrinsic entity. In fact, one is rarely in doubt as to which of two 'obiectum' equivocals one is dealing with."[12]

On the other hand, one can see that this is precisely the blindly constitutive doubt of philosophy itself, which determines its objects on all levels via the *decision to philosophize*, to treat the world as there for philosophy in the first place. My suspicion is that the philosophical word-concept of *object* is the product of a climate of intellectual objection and appetitive love of argument traced in the temporal gap between the senses of the word (1125-1286), which is precisely the period marked by reception and scholastic institutionalization of Aristotle, roughly, from Abelard's *Sic et Non* (1120) to the Condemnation of 1277 at the University of Paris. In other words, *object* is essentially a medieval document of philosophy's fundamental aberration, as recognized by Nietzsche: "The aberration of philosophy is that, instead of seeing in logic and the categories of reason means toward the adjustment of the world for utilitarian ends (basically, toward an expedient falsification), one believed one possessed in them the criterion of truth and reality. . . . This is the greatest error that has ever been committed, the essential fatality of error on

---

[11] The symposium discussion about telos vs. becoming is relevant here.

[12] Dewan, "Obiectum," 442.

earth: one believed one possessed a criterion of reality in the forms of reason—while in fact one possessed them in order to become master of reality, in order to misunderstand reality in a shrewd manner."[13]

§ CONCLUSION

"All of the Bilateria are worms, including men (and in this, medieval theology is not mistaken). That is, they have a longitudinal axis, a 'monumental axis', a right side and a left side. This differentiates them from the Radiata, in which several rays radiate from a centre. For us Bilateria the world is bilaterally symmetrical: there either 'is' or 'is not, and *the third* is excluded. The dialectic of the worm."[14]

"Things are not outside us, in measurable external space, like neutral objects (*ob-jecta*) of use and exchange; rather, they open to us [*sono esse stesse che ci aprono*] the original place solely from which the experience of measurable external space becomes possible. They are therefore [the very beings, *esse stesse*] held and comprehended from the outset in the *topos outopos* [placeless place, no-place place] in which our experience of being-in-the-world is situated. The question 'where is the thing?' is inseparable from the question 'where is the human?' Like the fetish, like the toy, things are not properly anywhere, because their place is found on this side of objects and beyond the human in a zone that is no longer objective or subjective, neither personal nor impersonal, neither material nor immaterial, but where we find ourselves suddenly [*improvvisamente*] facing these apparently so simple unknowns: the human, the thing."[15]

---

[13] Friedrich Nietzsche, *The Will to Power*, trans. Walter Kaufman and R.J. Hollingdale (New York: Vintage, 1968), 315.

[14] Vilém Flusser, *Vampyroteuthis Infernalis*, trans. Rodrigo Maltez Novaes (New York: Atropos Press, 2011), 25.

[15] Giorgio Agamben, *Stanzas: Word and Phantasm in Western Culture*, trans. Ronald L. Martinez (Minneapolis: University of Minnesota Press, 1993), 59.

Made in the USA
Charleston, SC
18 January 2013